1960 *Philadelphia Eagles*

The Team That *They Said* Had Nothing but a Championship

Robert Gordon

Sports Publishing, L.L.C.
www.SportsPublishingLLC.com

About the Author . . .

ROBERT GORDON lives outside Philadelphia with his wife, kids, cats, and dog. When he's not writing on subjects ranging from sports to fine dining, he consults and provides executive placement services for clients in energy-related industries. Bob has been covering the Philadelphia sports scene for over 13 years, including five years as the sports editor of *Delaware Valley* magazine. Bob speaks three languages; unfortunately, as an Eagles fan, he hasn't been able to say: "We're number one" in any of them for 40 years. That's a long time for a lifelong Pennsylvania resident who colors his world in Eagles green and Phillies red.

©2001 Robert Gordon
All rights reserved

Layout and design: Erin J. Sands
Cover design: Kenny J. O'Brien

Photos courtesy of Philadelphia Eagles and Jimmy Gallagher, Chuck Weber, Tom Brookshier, Pete Retzlaff, Tommy McDonald, John Wilcox, Vic Sears, Gerald Huth, Lynn Van Brocklin, and Dick Bielski.

ISBN: 1-58261-248-x

Printed in the United States

Sports Publishing L.L.C.
www.SportsPublishingLLC.com

~ To Dad ~
The best title of all

At their 25th reunion in 1985, the Five "B's"—Brookshier, Baughan, Burroughs, Bednarik and Barnes—laugh about 1960's "glory days."

Contents

Acknowledgments vi

Introduction vii

Chapter One: *Yellow Jackets and Steagles and Eagles, Oh My* *1*

Chapter Two: *The Slippery Slope: The Fifties* *14*

Chapter Three: *Number 60* *24*

Chapter Four: *Chocolatetown and Getting Ready* *34*

Chapter Five: *The Baron* *65*

Chapter Six: *Humiliation* *77*

Chapter Seven: *Slow Start: Face Breakers, Game Breakers, and Game Faces* *90*

Chapter Eight: *Touchdown Maker* *106*

Chapter Nine: *Double Dutch and Red Dogs* *115*

Chapter Ten: *Dutch* *130*

Chapter Eleven: *Toppling Giants* *141*

Chapter Twelve: *Clinching and Cloud Eight* *166*

Chapter Thirteen: *The Opposition* *182*

Chapter Fourteen: *December 26, 1960* *194*

Chapter Fifteen: *Aftermath* *212*

Chapter Sixteen: *Where Are They Now?* *222*

Acknowledgments

To my mother, for love and long-suffering, my father, for the tickets, for everything, for being a dad. To Susan, for her belief, optimism, patience, support, understanding, love, ideas, and editing. To Ryan, for his computer work, his interest in a time when his parents lived in a galaxy long ago and far away, and for taking dad at his word that Number 60 was Philly's greatest-ever football player.

To Aubrey for giving us a someday.

To every player on the 1960 Eagles who gave of their time, wit, and hearts, to talk about the first football champion of the New Frontier.

To Dutch, Joe Robb, Bobby Walston, Jesse Richardson, Howard Keyes, John Nocera, Gene Johnson, Buck Shaw, Jerry Williams, and Charley Gauer, the deceased members of the 1960 Eagles, sorely missed by all.

To Jimmy Gallagher, a Philly institution in kelly green, who hunted down phone numbers, addresses, and contacts like Concrete Charley hunted down ball carriers.

To Gentleman Ed Khayat, for his help, enthusiasm, effort and his genuine love of his teammates and his old town of Philly.

To Paul Rogers, author of *The Whiz Kids,* for all the help and support.

To Pat Summerall, for his outside-in slant on the Eagles. Despite being a 1960 Giant, Philly fans should know he is a nice guy. Honest.

To the Van Brocklins—Karen, Lynne, and Judy—wonderful ladies, and alumnae that Friends Central should be proud of.

To John Rogers, keeper of the Eagle rolls, who helped me start my search.

To the Frankford Historical Society, especially Marge Labman, Ed Moore, and Max Rowland for teaching a Holmesburg/Father Judge alumnus about the history of a great Philly neighborhood. Thanks also for the great information on the Frankford Yellow Jackets.

To John Furlow, former football coach at West Chester, and 70-something boxing coach at Salisbury State University. That's right, 70-something boxing coach. He can still tag you with a left hook.

To Bob Ream, for all his statistics on Pete Retzlaff, and for his tireless quest for truth, justice, and getting Pete Retzlaff a spot in Canton.

To the Philadelphia Public Library for putting up with my near-residence there, and for their help with my endless requests for microfiche.

To Mike Hackenbruch, John Frantz, Eric Gerstel, Harry Sheneman, and Jan Shalom for friendship.

Introduction

There had to be more. In listening to endless opinions about how the Philadelphia Eagles managed to shock the football world and win the NFL championship in 1960, I kept hearing the same answer. And, the answer seemed too simplistic, too lightweight, too unsophisticated—after all, in this millennium, even a phone bill is complicated.

"We got along, and we had great leadership."

That was basically the answer. Everyone's answer. One after another, the 31 living members of the Eagles' last championship team fingered the same two culprits: harmony and leadership. And, the players weren't the only ones. Others came up with the same reasons. Their announcer, their coach, their rivals, and their front-office people echoed the players' sentiments. Yet, somehow, the two words, harmony and leadership, blended into one force, at least for that one year, at least for that one team. The two concepts intertwined and fed off each other. On the 1960 Eagles, the group's harmony seemed to strengthen the leaders every bit as much as the leaders seemed to strengthen the group's harmony. It was hard to separate the dynamics. In fact, the secret of the 1960 Eagles seems to be a rare amalgam of both. The Eagles found a formula that molded team harmony and leadership into one tight ball. Then, once the '60 Eagles set that ball in motion, they rolled it all the way to an NFL championship. Along the way, they rolled over some pretty good football teams. When the ball finally stopped rolling, the 1960 Philadelphia Eagles had accomplished what no other team has ever done. They beat Vince Lombardi's Green Bay Packers in a postseason game.

Quarterback Norm Van Brocklin, or Dutch, as he was known to all, was the nucleus in every sense of the 1960 Eagles. He was smack dab at the center of the team's psyche, the force that held everything together. Every level of the team's energy revolved around him. He kept the team, and everyone on the team, in proper orbit.

Make no mistake about it, the 1960 Eagles were Van Brocklin's team. He was the leader and the guy who used the team's harmony as its major weapon. Harmony as a weapon is an incongruous notion, but Van Brocklin and his teammates were an unconventional bunch. Besides, Van Brocklin was a driven man that year, driven by a race against time.

Dutch was 34 years old in 1960. He approached the 1960 season, which he declared early on to be his last, like a man on a mission. He craved one final championship before he retired. He knew it wouldn't be easy. The team that surrounded him as the season began that year was still a work in progress. Philadelphia, over the previous two years, had assembled a rag-tag collection of veterans and rookies and journeymen and stars and unknowns. The Philadelphia squad that emerged in 1960 after a bunch of roster tinkering, was lightly regarded. They were far better than they were given credit for, and far better than history records, but they were not considered viable contenders in their day. Dutch's team was unsung and underrated, and was certainly not, on paper, among football's elite.

Van Brocklin quickly assessed that, if this team was going to succeed, it would require contributions up and down the roster. The Eagles could not muster the firepower needed to win a championship on sheer star power. Baltimore, New York, and Cleveland had the biggest stars. Van Brocklin chose not to compete at that level. He found other ways to compete. Just as he did in the huddle, Dutch improvised. He consciously brought the team together, made them interact, and encouraged them to bond in off-field, informal meetings that became team rituals. He infused a disparate group of athletes with self-confidence and faith in each other. It was a bold approach for Van Brocklin, inasmuch as he, himself, tended to be acerbic and curt at times. But, Dutch was not in this crusade alone. Whenever Dutch needed the other team leaders, they were there. The team's powerful sense of harmony started with the leadership. It started there and thrived there.

The 1960 Eagles had extraordinary team intelligence. Their roster was stuffed with leaders endowed with strong personalities. Chuck Bednarik was an icon—a strong, experienced, colossal figure in the NFL. Marion Campbell and Ed Khayat later became head coaches themselves. Tom Brookshier was garrulous, glib, and charismatic—as well as an analytical student of the game. Many other members of the squad became head coaches in college, or assistant coaches in the NFL—Maxie Baughan, John Wilcox, Billy Ray Barnes, Jimmy Carr, Bobby Jackson, and Chuck Weber, to name a few. But the Eagles' leaders sublimated their egos to the good of the group. As star lineman Ed Khayat puts it: "We had a bunch of guys on that team who were strong leaders themselves, but they had the gift of knowing when to lead and when to follow. That Philly bunch knew how to listen as well as how to lead, and they knew how to do what was good for the team."

At every level of the organization, the leaders went out of their way not to step on each other's toes. That respect started with the coaching staff. Popular lore has it that every Sunday morning, when the club arrived in the locker room, coach Buck Shaw flipped the football to Van Brocklin, and said: "Here, Dutch, go win it." Shaw's act, whether fact or fiction, was symbolic. It was not an act of abdication. It was a shrewd and effective act of empowerment. His attitude affirmed Van Brocklin's role as leader. In taking that approach, Shaw tapped into one of the team's bountiful resources: its football savvy. The coaches let their leaders lead. They let their players play. They let their Eagles soar.

"We got along."

Getting along is tough stuff—whether it's in a kindergarten school yard, a UN General Council meeting, a corporate board meeting, or an NFL locker room. When the makers of football teams jumble up a mix of strangers from all parts of the country, from all sorts of backgrounds, with all sizes of egos and all varieties of insecurities and all shades of personalities, they're never sure what's going to emerge. There were teams with better personnel than the Eagles. The Eagles will admit that. But there wasn't a better *team*. By hook and by crook, the Eagles assembled the right ingredients on that '60 team—the right ingredients in the right proportions.

Of course, harmony is a big concept. It encompasses a host of more conventional reasons for success, like strength at the skill positions, versatility, and remaining injury-free. But stock justifications are moot. None are accepted unanimously by the guys who were actually there. What is universally acknowledged is that the athletes who suited up in Eagle green that year were a team, in every sense of the word. And the behaviors associated with being a team made for winning football. Each player gave his own particular spin, of course. "We had great camaraderie." "We liked each other." "We had great team chemistry." "We had tremendous esprit de corps." "We had no cliques." "We partied together." "We hung around together." "We never pointed fingers." "Everyone was supportive of everyone else." "No one ever got down on anyone." "We tried to pump people up, not tear them down." "We had respect for each other." "Each guy tried to pick up for everyone else." The words vary, but the common thread smacks you in the head after a while. Since that championship season, these men have worked in many different kinds of environments with many different groups, on and off the gridiron. Yet, 40 years down life's road from that championship, they still marvel at how well that group interacted. They've never experienced its equal.

Their comments have a familiar ring to anyone who frequents the corridors of our big corporations. In describing teamwork, the Eagles speak the same platitudes that clog those corporate employee-value proclamations currently strewn in workplaces all around the nation. Corporations annually spend millions—billions — trying to squeeze good team behaviors into their work cultures. Too often, their desires are unfulfilled.

Maybe some things are just natural. Somehow, the guys in the green in 1960 practiced those teamwork principles naturally, on their own. They had a commanding, charismatic leader in Van Brocklin who had the wherewithal to lead the Eagle horses to the well. Once there, the Eagle team had the collective intelligence and instinct to drink. In any event, for a variety of reasons, a team personality, at once powerful, singular, and fleeting, jelled in a flicker of time in Philadelphia at the start of JFK's New Frontier. When it did, the whole exceeded the sum of its parts. That type of math was foreign to football experts of the time. Of course, to the experts, nothing about the 1960 Eagles really added up. The team still leaves them scratching their heads.

The 1960 Eagles confound standard analysis, because, aside from harmony and leadership, there is no overwhelming 1960 Eagle strength. They were inconsistent, and, therefore, as unpredictable and dangerous as could be. They were full of surprises. Pragmatic and opportunistic, they could rise to any occasion. They had the second-worst defense against the run in all of football that year. Yet, when the chips were down and they had to stop the Packers, one of the NFL's most powerful running teams, they did it. They themselves averaged fewer yards per rush that season than any other NFL champion before or since. Yet, in the title game, they marched down the field totally on the ground for the winning score and the championship.

The 1960 Eagles teetered on the cusp between two distinctly different eras. Behind them was an era of financial struggle that marked and marred much of football's first three decades. Before them was the bonanza that television, the media, and a sport-crazed society brought. The 1960 Eagle team was a throwback to a more straightforward era. On football's timeline, they are nearer Jim Thorpe and Ernie Nevers than Curt Warner and Randy Moss. They looked a part of the old era. Two of the '60 Eagles, Tommy McDonald and Jesse Richardson, refused to wear facemasks. They were the last NFL players to do so.

Football spent the '60s reinventing itself. Age-old paradigms were tested, challenged, and shattered. Don't forget, it was the '60s. Jimmy Brown, a 232-pounder with sprinter's speed, devastating power, iron will, and uncanny instinct, redefined the position of running back. Tom Landry, Vince Lombardi, and a cast of AFL innovators rethought practically every aspect of the game, on and off the field. Franchises developed new systems for everything. Football became big business. The complexities of the game escalated. Players became media figures. Coaches became teachers. Coaching staffs and the number of front office brass inflated. Football's popularity soared. So did salaries. So did the stakes for winning and losing.

And that decade, when football started its frenzied dash to modernity, was ushered in by the Philadelphia Eagles' victory over the Packers. Yet, history has shoved the '60 Eagles aside. At best, they are regarded as a minor aftershock to the Colts' stampede of the late '50s. At worst, they are dismissed as inconsequential, or anomalies, or lightweights. In reality, they are one of the more interesting champions in history. They were, in many senses, inscrutable—a team straddling two eras. They were a walking contradiction. Their personality was a throwback, but their pass attack was ahead of its time, a precursor to the pass-crazy attacks of today. But, their aerial game by itself wasn't enough to win them a championship. They did that by harnessing the power of those hokey, old-fashioned virtues of teamwork, unselfishness, and sacrifice—the same virtues American business is now trying to reclaim.

The Eagles' short-lived reign began and ended when transistor radios were a novelty. Slightly more than a decade before their '60 triumph, Philadelphia had won back-to-back world championships, playing to gates of 22,245 and 29,751 spectators. A year after their reign, football boasted its first million-dollar gate.

Seven years later, the first Super Bowl was played. The event has grown into a global extravaganza. In this swirl of history, the 1960 Eagles somehow got lost.

It's been over 40 years since Philadelphia has cheered an NFL champ. That band of Eagle champions is still near and dear to the hearts of Philadelphians. Four of their biggest stars—Tom Brookshier, Chuck Bednarik, Pete Retzlaff, and Tommy McDonald—still live in the Philadelphia area. In a city that has loved football for a century, the 1960 Philadelphia Eagles are a homespun success story. They were put down as the "Team that had nothing but a championship"—a tag as cynical as it is untrue, as superficial as it is unfair. Unlike the celebrated football dynasties who have authored the gaudiest chapters in the game's history, the glory of the 1960 Eagles does not leap from a line-up card. Their glory was in enriching the nature of a team sport and the spirit of a great game.

The team with "chemistry" celebrated one more time with a cooler of champagne at Dick Bielski's home before heading off to training camp. (Seated: Billy Barnes, Bobby Walston; standing: Dick Bielski, Lee Riley, Bob Pellegrini.)

One

Yellow Jackets and Steagles and Eagles, Oh My
Pro Football Strikes Out in First At-Bat

A history of pro football in Philly

In order to understand the 1960 Eagles, it's enlightening to take a long look at the history of football in Philadelphia.

As the nineteenth century gave way to the twentieth, the Industrial Revolution stoked up the American sport scene. Baseball had already burrowed into the national consciousness. Town populations soared. Mass transportation shrank a nation whose borders now pushed their way out to another ocean It seemed an auspicious time for football to tap into the new-found prosperity of the city dweller. At least, Cornelius Alexander McGillicuddy, popularly known as Connie Mack, thought so. Later tagged the "Grand Old Man of Baseball," Mack took a swing at starting a professional football league, which would be headquartered in Philadelphia. He swung and missed.

Mack's Philadelphia Athletics (the A's) were the reigning American League baseball champs in 1902. Mack, along with Philadelphia Athletics owner, Ben Shibe, and John I. Rogers, who owned the Philadelphia Phillies, recruited a guy named Dave Berry, who had managed a football team in Latrobe, Pennsylvania (home of golf legend, Arnold Palmer), to help set up a professional league comprised of three teams. The league didn't catch on. Each of the three teams played only four league games that year. Each of the three finished with a 2-2 record, and each claimed the championship. A "World Series" was held, supposedly to settle the matter. The World Series was the brain child of Madison Square Garden manager Tom O'Rourke. The world would little note nor long remember that first World Series, which flopped, inasmuch as none of the three teams in Mack's league bothered to participate. Thus, football, not baseball, staged the nation's first World Series. And it's a great beer bet. If you want to up the ante to beer and a pizza, the Syracuse Athletics won that first World Series.

Mack scrapped the pro football experiment after one try. Pro football moved to the Midwest, out to Ohio and beyond. For the next few decades, the pro game resided in small-town America, in marked contrast to baseball, which boomed in the eastern urban centers. Due in great part to this disparity, for three-quarters of the century, pro football was baseball's weak little sister. Even as late as 1960, the Philadelphia Eagles' championship victory didn't rate a front-page headline in the Philadelphia *Bulletin*, one of the city's major newspapers. Yet, the 1960 World Series, which pitted two out-of-town clubs, the Pittsburgh Pirates and the New York Yankees, hogged every front-page headline in the city daily.

THE FRANKFORD YELLOW JACKETS

In colonial times, Frankford was a small farming community northeast of the city of Philadelphia. It was later incorporated into the city of Philadelphia. In 1899, a neighborhood group, the Frankford Athletic Association, sponsored an independent amateur football club, which they called the Frankford Yellow Jackets. By 1922, the Yellow Jackets had grown into a gridiron power. Their president, Shep Royle, and another club official, Howard Bowker, convinced local merchants and businessmen to shoot higher. The Frankford Club wanted to go big-time and field a big-time professional team. To fund the enterprise, the Association sold 15,000 bonds at $50 apiece to raise the necessary cash. The profits generated by the team were to go to local charities, like the Frankford Hospital, Frankford Day Nursery, Frankford Legion Post, and the Boy Scouts.

The Frankford Yellow Jackets debuted in 1922. They were a smashing success, outscoring their opponents 300-25 while crafting a glittery 13-0-1 record. They

Due to front office wheeling and dealing, the 1941 Pittsburgh Steelers became the 1942 Philadelphia Eagles (shown here).

encored with a 9-2-2 mark in 1923—good enough to merit admission into the fledgling National Football League on September 23, 1924. The NFL, at that point, was entering its fifth year of actual operation, although it was only its third year as the NFL. The NFL had been called the American Professional Football Association in its first two years, 1920 and 1921. The Jackets wowed their new league, finishing with an 11-2-1 record in 1924, which remains today the third highest winning percentage in the annals of major professional sports in Philadelphia.

Two years later, in 1926, Philadelphia professional football set its all-time highwater mark. The city boasted not one, but two, professional football champs. Frankford, with a sterling 14-1-2 mark, took the NFL title, while the Philadelphia Quakers wore the mantel of the rival American Football League (AFL). The American Football League of 1926 was completely unrelated to the AFL of the Sixties. In fact, there have been four different American Football Leagues. The 1926 version was hastily contrived by Red Grange in order to capitalize on his own larger-than-life image. Grange had finished his collegiate season at Illinois in 1925, and joined the professional Chicago Bears after Thanksgiving. He played several games with the Bears late in 1925, and, everywhere he played, the Bears packed them in. Grange, the Galloping Ghost, became more like a Galloping Gatsby. Reckoning he could make more money on his own, he struck out on his own.

Unfortunately for Grange, that's exactly what he did. Like Mack, he struck out. His league flopped. The AFL's brand of football was dull. Attendance was poor. However, the AFL did play an entire season, and the Philadelphia Quakers shocked Grange and everyone else by compiling an 8-2 record and locking up the title. In ten games, the Quakers scored a measly 93 points. Almost one-third of their points resulted from field goals. After the season, in December of 1926, the AFL-champion Quakers were trounced, 31-0, by the NFL's New York Giants in an exhibition game at the Polo Grounds. The death knell had sounded for Grange's league. In 1927, the NFL once more became the only professional football show in town.

~ Back-to-back over New York ~

There's a quirky common thread that ties practically every Philadelphia pro football championship together. Every pro football champ from Philadelphia has beaten New York in back-to-back games. Not just two wins in the same season, but back-to-back, consecutive-game wins. There are two exceptions, but only two: the 1948 Philadelphia Eagles and the 1984 Philadelphia Stars. Aside from these two exceptions, the road to glory passes through the Big Apple. All the rest of the Quaker City's pro gridiron champs: the 1926 Eagles, the 1926 Quakers, the 1949 Eagles, and the 1960 Eagles squashed New York in two consecutive face-offs.

In 1926, the Yellow Jackets beat the New York Giants 6-0, 6-0, on consecutive *days*. Frankford beat New York on October 16th in Frankford. That night, the squad, as well as 900 fans and the Yellow Jacket Band and Bugle Corps, hopped aboard a special train to New York. The next day, which was the Giants' home opener at the Polo Grounds, a crowd of 20,000 witnessed a 6-0 rerun of the previous day. The Big Apple's Mayor Walker marched around at half-time with the Frankford band, which paraded from 42nd and Broadway to the Pennsylvania Hotel after the game. According to contemporary newspaper accounts, overzealous Yellow Jackets fans did $10,000 worth of damage to the hotel.

Also in 1926, the Philadelphia Quakers beat the American Football League's New York Yankees on Thanksgiving Day, and followed it up two days later with another victory. The Yankees boasted the big names (some things never change), like future Hall of Famers Red Grange, and Penn State's Mike Michalske, but the Quakers prevailed with "who-dey?" home-towners like Johnny Scott from Lafayette, and Downingtown High's Charlie "Pie" Way. Philly's victories were even sweeter, since the Yankees had dumped the Quakers, 23-0, earlier in the season. When the two squads squared off on Thanksgiving Day, the Quakers' record stood at 6-2; the Yanks, at 8-3. By Saturday evening, the AFL championship had been decided. With the two wins over the Yankees, Philadelphia closed with an 8-2 log. The Yankees finished second, winning two meaningless subsequent games for a 10-5 mark.

The 1949 NFL champion Eagles beat the Giants in the final two games of the regular season. Philadelphia had clinched the East Division before entering this two-game series, so the games were not critical to the campaign. Nonetheless, the Birds cranked up two masterpieces, holding the Giants to a two-game total of six points while scoring 41 themselves. Philadelphia's defense also contributed six points when defensive back Joe Muha scored on a 28-yard interception runback. The Giant games jump-started the Eagles' defense, which had surrendered 17 points to the Steelers the week before the first game against the Giants. A week after the second Giants' game, the Birds shut out Los Angeles in the championship game. As for the Giants, the two losses to the Eagles knocked New York out of second-place money. Pittsburgh, who had trailed New York prior to the Philadelphia-New York series, sneaked into second place by a half-game.

The 1960 Eagles also posted back-to-back victories over New York, but more on that later.

The 14 wins that Frankford registered in 1926 set an NFL single-season record for most wins that lasted till 1984, when the San Francisco 49ers won 15. The Bears matched the number the following year to share the record with the 49ers. The '26 Yellow Jackets' only loss was a 7-6 heartbreaker to the Providence Steamrollers. A missed Frankford extra point cost them a tie, as well as an undefeated season. More importantly, that missed PAT cost them a piece of history; namely, the record for most wins in a single season that San Francisco and Chicago wrested away almost 60 years later.

The Frankford Yellow Jackets pledged their allegiance to the little neighborhood of Frankford, not to the big city of Philadelphia. Frankford's football operation, in its day, was anything but small time. Their football players were housed in their own living quarters four blocks from Yellow Jackets' stadium at Frankford Avenue and Devereaux Street. Their pay was a hefty $250-$300 a game, which was big money in the Roaring Twenties. Each guy pocketed an additional $10 every time he showed up for afternoon practice. The Frankford Athletic Association owned its own stadium, which was funded by the club, not the city. They owned a mule for a mascot. They fielded their own marching band and had their own world-class announcer, Bobby Calhoun. Calhoun was a precursor to Michael Buffer, another Philly-area local who was raised in Warminster, a suburb of Philadelphia. Like Buffer, Calhoun gained national prominence. He announced the Miss America Pageant, as well as numerous marquee boxing events, including Johnson-Jeffries, Willard-Dempsey, Willard-Firpo, and Dempsey-Firpo.

In 1927, Frankford's record dropped off to 6-9-3. This time, consecutive losses to the New York Giants knocked the Jackets out of the chase, a gloomy portent of 1961 when double losses to New York separated Philly from a repeat championship. The Jackets had a winning record and contended every year through 1930, except for 1927. They finished second in 1928 and third in 1929. The Yellow Jackets were a feared powerhouse in the '20s. The Green Bay Packers, another major NFL force in the '20s, selected Frankford as their traditional Thanksgiving Day rival. The series lasted from 1926 till 1930, and ended up even at 2-2-1.

By 1931, the Depression had rocked Frankford, a textile center in the Twenties. A fire damaged Yellow Jacket Stadium, forcing the team to play home games in Phillies Stadium, remembered today as Baker Bowl. Many Frankford rooters, rather than travel cross-town, simply stayed home, and supported neighborhood semi-professional teams, like Saint Leo's and Tacony. They deserted their former heroes, referring to them now as the *Philadelphia* Yellow Jackets.

The Frankford Yellow Jackets faded into history with an awesome 92-46-14 NFL record. Discounting their final two years when their athletic association was decaying, their record was 87-27-12. To put their achievements in perspective, the Eagles have surpassed Frankford's *lifetime* winning percentage of .763 in only *four* of their 68 seasons.

Frankford led the NFL in games played every year between 1924 and 1929. Though the Yellow Jackets were mostly a group of no-name scrappers from local Pennsylvania colleges, they bested the era's glamour teams studded with future Hall of Famers like Grange, Ernie Nevers, Benny Friedman, Curly Lambeau, and Jim Thorpe, all of whom churned the turf up at one time or another in Frankford.

The Frankford Yellow Jackets, led by 142-pound quarterback, "Two Bits" Homan, a Swarthmore College product, roared through the '20s as Philadelphia's most formidable professional team.

~ Doubleheader Weekends ~

In the NFL's early years, each individual team set its own schedule. The number of games played varied from team to team. Pennsylvania's Blue Laws, which forbade football on Sunday, forced the Yellow Jackets to schedule their home games on Saturdays. Even way back then, in the '20s, game day in the NFL was on Sunday. Consequently, the Jackets usually scheduled a Saturday home game, followed by a Sunday away game the *next day*. Granted, since Frankford scheduled the same opponent for each of these Saturday-Sunday series, the Yellow Jackets seemed at no disadvantage. However, cumulatively, over the course of a season, they were at a huge disadvantage. The Yellow Jackets endured those weekend doubleheader marathons virtually every week of the season. Their opponents were only subjected to it once—against Frankford.

Frankford took more than a physical pounding from those doubleheaders. Opponents occasionally reneged on scheduled Sunday games. In Frankford's 1926 championship season, they blew out Buffalo, 30-0, at Frankford on Saturday. That evening, both teams shuffled off to Buffalo for Sunday's return engagement, only to have Buffalo cancel. On Sunday morning, Buffalo management, citing "wet grounds," called the game off. Contemporary newspaper accounts insisted the sidewalks outside the Yellow Jackets' hotel weren't even wet. The likely reasons for cancellation were pretty transparent: poor attendance, a near-certain loss on the field, and a near-certain loss at the gate. The Frankford papers reported:

"They (Buffalo) don't seem to realize that the Yellow Jackets play rain or shine. Under the bylaws of the League, the home club has the privilege of calling off a game due to bad weather. It is not right for a club to cancel a game to save its own hide after the visiting team has traveled a long distance to play the game. By calling the game off, the home club has only the traveling expenses to pay and does not have to pay the guarantee (the visiting team, by league rules, was guaranteed a certain sum for each game). This means the visiting team is in the bucket for their payroll. Frankford has had this trick played on them twice—once last year in Cleveland and last Sunday in Buffalo. After the beating Buffalo received here a great many are of the opinion that Buffalo canceled the game to save another beating and then again it was rumored that the Buffalo team attended the World Series."

The Buffalo football players who opted to attend the World Series game at Yankee Stadium on October 10, 1926, witnessed two of baseball's legendary moments. One of the incidents in this game, the seventh game of the 1926 World Series, was immortalized in the film, "That Winning Season." Ronald Reagan played the role of Hall of Fame pitcher Grover Cleveland Alexander. Alexander, who was 39 years old at the time, was in the bullpen, sleeping off a late night of celebration. The day before, Alexander had pitched his second complete-game victory of the Series. Not expecting to pitch, he had to answer the call in the seventh inning. He struck out Tony Lazzeri with the bases loaded to end a Yankee threat. In a bizarre ending, the St. Louis Cardinals won the Series when Babe Ruth was thrown out trying to steal in the ninth inning. Ruth had walked with two outs. The hard-hitting Bob Meusel was at bat, with Lou Gehrig on deck, when Ruth, inexplicably, took off for second base.

Looking back, maybe the Buffalo guys made the better choice. In any event, Babe Ruth and the Yankees cost Frankford a record. Had the Buffalo players stayed in Buffalo to play football, the Yellow Jackets probably would have clubbed them, and shared the record for most wins in a season with the 49ers and Bears.

THE EAGLE LANDS IN PHILADELPHIA

The Great Depression was sacking professional football. Between 1926 and 1935, the number of NFL teams dwindled from 22 to nine. One '30s-era poll averred that baseball, college football, golf, wrestling, hockey, tennis, basketball, and horse racing all had more fans than professional football. Pro football needed more spectators and more cash, or it would die. Economics dictated that the game move east to the nation's fertile crescent where the big cities and the big gates reside. By 1934, every NFL team was located in a big city with a major league baseball team. The small towns, where pro football had incubated, dropped off the NFL registers. Teams like the Canton Bulldogs, the Rock Island Independents, the Duluth Kelleys, and the Hartford Blues went the way of zoot suits, spats, and spittoons.

The Blue Laws discouraged the NFL from colonizing the Quaker City. Then, in 1933, that obstacle was lifted. On July 8, 1933, the NFL granted Philadelphian Bert Bell a professional football franchise for the city of Philadelphia. Pittsburgh and Cincinnati entered the league at the same time. Each paid a $2500 franchise fee. In Bert Bell's case, the Philadelphia franchise also had to assume the debts that the Frankford Yellow Jackets still owed to other NFL franchises. Philadelphia's new franchise adopted the eagle as its symbol. Time has muddled the reason. One story traces the name to a boat named "The Eagle," that was owned by one of the new franchise's principles. Another story links the Philadelphia Eagle to the eagle that symbolized the National Recovery Act, one of FDR's New Deal programs.

One fact is known. The Philadelphia Eagles were neither a rebirth nor a continuation of the Frankford Yellow Jackets. Not a single ex-Yellow Jacket played for the 1933 Eagles, although Lud Wray, the Eagle coach, was a Yellow Jacket alumnus. Furthermore, the Eagles annihilated the winning tradition of the Yellow Jackets. On October 16, 1933, in their NFL debut, the New York Giants crushed the Eagles, 56-0, to continue New York's roll against Philadelphia teams. Those same

Giants had whitewashed the Yellow Jackets, 13-0, in the latter's final NFL game in 1931. In the Eagles' first three games, they were outscored 116-9. Their first win, 6-0, came against the Cincinnati Reds on November 5, 1933.

The Birds ended their inaugural NFL season with a 3-5-1 log, which, though bad, turned out to be their third best of the decade. When the '30s ended, the Eagle ledger stood at an abysmal 18-55-3.

~ The Eagles and the Draft ~

Long-suffering Eagle fans have forever complained about their club's foibles at the draft table. The Birds have picked too many guys who didn't pan out or didn't put out. The trend traces way back to their first draft choice, the first player ever drafted in the NFL. It's not that he didn't pan out or put out. He didn't show up.

It happened back in 1936. Bert Bell, Eagle founder and owner, pitched the idea of a college draft to the rest of the owners. They liked it. In Bell's scheme, the draft would enhance team parity because last-place teams drafted first. Of course, his idea was more than slightly self-serving. The Eagles were in the cellar at the time, and in desperate need of talent. So, Bell's proposal gave his own team the first choice in the draft. Charity begins at home.

Bell even benefited from the site chosen to hold the draft. On February 8, 1936, the owners sat at a table at the Philadelphia Ritz-Carlton, which Bell's family partly owned at the time. The Eagles, by virtue of their 1935, last-place finish, drafted first, and chose the University of Chicago's Jay Berwanger, winner of the first Heisman Trophy Award. Berwanger rejected the offer, opting instead for a sales career with a sponge rubber manufacturer.

When all was said and done, Bell's idea of a college draft took hold, but failed to help his own club. Berwanger was not alone in spurning the Eagles. The Eagles didn't land a single draft choice in their first draft. Not one of the Eagles' nine 1936 draft choices played in the NFL for any length of time. Thus, the year after the first draft, which was an Eagles' idea conceived to strengthen their club, the Eagles sank deeper into the basement, slumping to a pitiful 1-11-0 log.

~ Eagles Change Owners ~

A few patches of light shined through the dark clouds of the '30s. The 1934 Eagles set an NFL scoring record (which has since been broken), with a 64-0 shellacking of the Cincinnati Reds. After the loss, Cincinnati dropped out of the NFL. You can make your own punchline. The Eagles' premier player of the decade was Davey O'Brien. The 1938 Heisman winner out of Texas Christian, O'Brien had sight in only one eye and played but three seasons. The former TCU star started on both offense and defense, and also returned punts and kickoffs. In 1939, he set the NFL record for most yards passing in a season. His greatest heroics came in his final season, 1940. In the opener that year against Green Bay, O'Brien played the full 60 minutes of the game, something Chuck Bednarik did not do (Concrete Charley was not on the field for kick-offs. O'Brien was). In the final game that year, the final game of his career, O'Brien played 59 minutes and 43 seconds, connected on a record 33 of 60 pass attempts, and intercepted a Sammy Baugh pass. O'Brien retired from football immediately after the game to become an F.B.I. agent.

THE FORTIES

In 1941, Philadelphia and Pittsburgh introduced razzle dazzle into the front office. First, Alexis Thompson, a multi-million-dollar heir to a steel fortune, purchased the Pittsburgh Steelers from Art Rooney. Next, Rooney bought a half-interest in the Philadelphia Eagles from Eagle owner Bert Bell. Finally, the two clubs, the Pittsburgh Steelers and the Philadelphia Eagles, exchanged franchises and locations. The 1941 Philadelphia Eagles became the 1942 Pittsburgh Steelers, and vice versa.

Jimmy Gallagher, who worked in the Eagle front office for over four decades, says the Eagles came out ahead in the long run, because the move brought Greasy Neale to town.

JM GALLAGHER: "Bert Bell graduated from Penn, and picked Lud Wray to coach the Eagles because Lud was a Penn guy, too. But, Lex was a Yale man, and Greasy Neale was coaching at Yale at the time. That's how Greasy wound up in Philadelphia—the Yale connection. Greasy brought the "T" formation with him, which he got from Clark Shaughnessy and the Bears. The Bears and the Eagles were the only teams in pro ball that ran the "T" formation at that time. In those days, colleges came up with most of the innovations in football. Anyway, Greasy got Tommy Thompson, the quarterback, to run the "T" formation here. Tommy was a great leader, just like Van Brocklin."

The new Eagles, unfortunately, looked a lot like the old ones, posting records of 2-8-1 and 2-9-0 in 1941 and 1942. When the curtain dropped on the '42 season, the Eagles had concluded their first decade in the NFL. Their record was a horrid 23-82-4. They had run off 10 straight losing seasons, finishing last in six of them. They had a losing record against every active franchise in the NFL. But, things were about to change.

GO STEAGLES AND THE GREASY ENGINE

No, the Steagles were not a Philly string band, although they were a combo. Confused? Probably not as much as Pittsburgh and Philadelphia players were in 1943.

By 1943, NFL rosters had been decimated by World War II, as players were drafted into active military duty. NFL Commissioner Elmer Layden, one of Notre

Dame's Four Horsemen in the '20s, championed several measures to keep the league afloat. The minimum number of players per team was lowered from 33 to 28. The Cleveland Rams (who later became the Los Angeles Rams and are now the St. Louis Rams) were placed on inactive status for a year, because their owner, Dan Reeves, was in the Navy, and couldn't manage his football business effectively. The league's most drastic move, however, was merging the Eagles and Steelers into a single team (Eagle fans, I know what you're thinking … Where was that Steagle idea when we really needed it — in the heyday of the Steel Curtain?). The decreed merger left the league with eight teams, rather than nine, allowing for a balanced schedule. Thus, Philadelphia and Pittsburgh, the same two cities that swapped personnel and locations in 1941, now joined arms successfully, albeit reluctantly. The Steelers-Eagles combo, officially called Philadelphia-Pittsburgh or Pittsburgh-Philadelphia, was popularly dubbed the "Steagles." The combined club, coached jointly by the Eagles' Greasy Neale and the Steelers' Walt Kiesler, brought Philadelphia its first winning season since the Frankford Yellow Jackets lost their sting in 1929.

The Steagles lasted one year, before splitting up again in 1944. Philadelphia resumed its "single" status. But Pittsburgh merged once again, this time disastrously, with the Chicago Cardinals. The new entity, Chicago-Pittsburgh, lost ten straight games in a winless season. Frustrated owner Art Rooney called them "the worst team in history." The reborn Eagles, in contrast, finished second, with the franchise's best-ever mark of 7-1-2.

The Steagles introduced something new to Eagle football. A win streak. The Eagles chalked up winning records every year from 1943 (as the Steagles) through 1949. To this day, that's the longest unblemished winning skein in franchise history. Philadelphia finished second in both 1945 and 1946. And then the magic really happened.

~ "Black Jack" Ferrante ~

"Black Jack" Ferrante, an Eagle end who played from 1941 to 1950, remembers football in the Depression era.

JACK FERRANTED: "There were mostly semipro teams back then, and they had some pretty good ball players. That's where I got my start. That's how I wound up with the Eagles. See, I never went to college. I quit high school as a freshman. I had to go to work to take care of my brother and two sisters. You know how much money I made? I made $9.09 a week working for a printing company at G and Erie Streets. I was a pretty good ball player, so I had the opportunity to play sandlot football for money in Philadelphia, at Passyunk Field. That was at 48th and Spruce, near the old West Philadelphia High School. I think Eddie Gottlieb, who owned the old Philadelphia Warriors basketball team at the time, ran the league. They paid me pretty good money for those times: $15 a night for Wednesday night games, and $25 for Sunday games. You know why the difference? The lights! They had to pay me less so they could pay for the lights! But playing football sure beat working at the printing company. They tried to get me a scholarship to Georgetown or La Salle, but, it didn't work out, 'cause I had never graduated from high school. I wound up playing for an Eagle farm club, the Wilmington Clippers. Pro football teams had farm clubs back then. They gave me $50 a game, and $25 for expenses, which was good pay in those times."

Ferrante started on all the Eagle championship teams in the late '40s. He quit football in 1951, which, statistically, was the best season of his eight-year career.

"People today don't understand how I could quit. That's 'cause it was so different back then. We didn't have pensions, and we didn't make the money they make nowadays. Fact is, I was doing as well in my other job as I was with the Eagles. You see, what happened was, I got traded to Detroit in 1952. I was 34 years old when that happened, and things had really changed at Philadelphia. After Lex Thompson sold the club to the Hundred Brothers, Greasy was fired. I didn't like what was happening here in Philadelphia, anyway. Greasy was a great coach, the greatest. With him gone, football just wasn't the same for me. I didn't want to go someplace new. Besides, Philadelphia was my home. I had a good job selling Ortlieb beer in town, and—to tell you the truth — I would have lost money going to Detroit, if it meant losing that beer job. I stayed here in Philadelphia and coached Monsignor Bonner High School, one of the Catholic high schools in the city. I coached there from '52 to '61. I have no regrets. Football was a great game back then, better than it is now. It was good to me."

Behind the running of Steve Van Buren and the leadership of Tommy Thompson, the Birds dominated the NFL from 1947 to 1949. In 1948, Van Buren became the second back in NFL history to rush for 1,000 yards in a season. In 1949, he became the first NFL back to rush for 1,000 yards in consecutive seasons. He also sprinted by Clarke Hinkle, that year, to become the NFL's All-Time leading rusher. Van Buren's teammate, Vic Sears, an All-Pro tackle recalls the championship teams, and his own coming of age.

VIC SEARS: "We had fun in those days. Football was such a different game. Greasy always told us, 'We really have a collection of fine boys on this team. We don't make much money, but we sure have fun.' Not that the Eagles weren't good to us. I got married ten days before our second championship game against Los Angeles (in 1949). When it came time for training camp next year in Two Rivers, Wisconsin—I think that's where it was—the Eagles sent tickets for my wife and me to come to camp. We had honeymooned some with my folks on their farm in Oregon before we went to camp. That turned out to be the last year they let us bring our wives to camp. They believed in that 'wilderness thing' in those days.

You know, the team had to be in some remote place in order to concentrate properly. Then, in 1951, we switched to Hershey, which was much better.

"Everything was so different in those days. I grew up in Eugene, Oregon in the '20s and '30s. I went to school in a one-room schoolhouse with fifteen other kids who were all different ages. To tell you the truth, I never even saw football played till I was a sophomore in high school. I had older brothers who played football. I wanted to play too, so I joined the high school football team that year. There weren't any uniforms left, so you know what I did? I made my own. All us farm kids knew how to use that Singer sewing machine back then, so I made my own uniform. Next day at practice, the coach told me to tackle this boy. I was tall and shy, so everyone was chuckling, thinking I wouldn't know what to do. But, I whacked him real good. Next day, they gave me new shoes, pants, everything. I ended up getting a scholarship to Oregon State for football, and majoring in Health Education. I played well in college. You know, I even played against Jackie Robinson at UCLA. What a great runner he was! So fast! But I figured him out. I'll tell you how, too. He gave away where he was going by the way he placed his feet.

In 1951, when the Eagles switched their training camp to Hershey, Vic Sears was a seasoned veteran.

"I was the fourth man picked in the draft in 1941. The Steelers picked me up. Some guy who worked for the newspaper, the Portland *Oregonian*, knew Greasy, and recommended me to him. That's how they found out about me way out there in Oregon. You know, that playboy, Lex Thompson, had just bought the Steelers. I don't think I fit his image of a tackle. I didn't fit Greasy's image, either. Greasy played with Jim Thorpe, you know! To those guys, a tackle had to be a mean-looking guy. I was baby-faced and rangy.

"I came here to Philadelphia at a wonderful time (1941). We had fine players on those Eagle teams, although, to tell you the truth, I think that Sammy Baugh on Washington has to be the greatest player that ever lived. He could punt, and, boy, could he pass! He was a great defensive back, too, you know. But, as a quarterback, he was the greatest. Of course, we didn't try to hurt the quarterback back then. Today, they do, and that's wrong, 'cause, you can't win a championship without a great quarterback. You just can't do it. We had a great one, that Tommy Thompson. What a player he was! Took us to three division titles, and he didn't have any radio in his helmet (so the coaches could send plays into him). He could out-think the other team all by himself. With him and Van Buren, we beat everybody. We had such a wonderful time, and a lot of spirit, too."

Vic Sears and the 1947 Eagles copped their first division title in 1947. They lost, 28-21, to the Cardinals in the championship game, however, and had to settle for the loser's share of $766 per player. In 1948, Philly avenged the loss, besting the Redbirds, 7-0, in a blizzard at Shibe Park (soon to be renamed Connie Mack Stadium). Each Eagle pocketed $1,540, the winner's share. Soon after the Eagles won the 1948 championship, Alexis Thompson sold his franchise to the "Hundred Brothers," a consortium of independent investors, headed by James P. Clark and Frank McNamee.

The football team continued its march toward the championship, unaffected by the change in ownership. They repeated as champs in 1949, shutting out the Los Angeles Rams, 14-0, in a driving rain storm. Van Buren set a standard in that game that would last for years, sloshing 196 muddy yards on 31 carries to spearhead the victory.

Vic Sears and Bucko Kilroy stroll through Duluth, Minnesota in 1949.

The win at LA closed out the '40s, which remains the club's most successful decade (58-47-5). Unlike the NFL champs who preceded them, however, the Eagles were not the unquestioned "world champions." The Cleveland Browns, champions of the All-American Football Conference were claiming that title for themselves.

In 1949, the All-American Football Conference (AAFC) folded after four years of operation. At the dawn of the '50s, four former AAFC teams were absorbed into the NFL: the Baltimore Colts, the New York Yankees (a different franchise than the one Red Grange started in 1926 in the American Football League), the San Francisco 49ers, and the Cleveland Browns. The Browns had won four straight AAFC titles. Their unbroken string of championships, in fact, contributed to the demise of the league. The Browns had no competition. To football experts, that meant that the competition was weak, not that the Browns were strong. Paul Brown, Cleveland's cocky coach, heralded his Browns as the greatest professional football team on earth. In a matchmaker's delight, the Philadelphia Eagles were scheduled to open the new decade against the Browns in Philadelphia. The question of who was the true world champion would be settled conclusively.

TwoTwoTwo **Two** TwoTwoTwo

The Slippery Slope: The Fifties

The promise of the new decade

In the world of sport, Philadelphia sport fans were really fired up as the '50s started to rock 'n roll. The Eagles applied the kindling with back-to-back NFL championships in '48 and '49. They were odds-on favorites for a third consecutive title in 1950. However, Philly had another favorite that summer. Along came the 1950 Philadelphia Phillies, the Whiz Kids. The Phils were the perennial National League doormats. They hadn't won a National League pennant since 1915, when Grover Cleveland Alexander hurled 31 victories and twelve shutouts. In fact, before the '48 Eagle title, the last sports flag of any kind to fly over Philly waved way back in 1931—a Depression and a World War ago. The Philadelphia A's won their final American League pennant that year, before losing the World Series to the St. Louis Cardinals.

Suddenly, in September of 1950, the Whiz Kids, the Quaker City's newest heroes, were battling Brooklyn's Boys of Summer for a National League pennant. And the Philadelphia Eagles were anxious to give the AAFC's Cleveland Browns a very unbrotherly-love type of welcome into the NFL. At the hub of the baseball's National League pennant race, Philly was hosting the most momentous football spectacle in years. The four-time, AAFC-champion Browns were to take on the two-time NFL champion Eagles on September 16.

Cleveland's four straight AAFC flags were viewed as a mere curiosity by football's old guard. The contest in Philly provided the ultimate platform for self-validation, with the same stakes and emotions that would fuel the first four Super Bowls. Each team played not only for itself, but for the pride of the league it represented. The game was so ballyhooed it had to be moved out of the Eagles' normal digs at Shibe Park and into cavernous Municipal Stadium to accommodate the crowd. An overflow crowd of 71,237 awaited the slaughter of the underdog Browns. They saw a slaughter, but it was David who slew Goliath.

The Browns overwhelmed the Birds, 35-10. Ace Eagle back Steve Van Buren missed the game, but his absence wasn't the reason for the loss. Cleveland was simply superior. They whipped Philadelphia in every aspect of the game.

After the crushing opening-day loss to Cleveland, Philadelphia did manage to regroup. They won five of their next six, blowing the opposition out, 217-63. Then the bubble burst. They dropped their final four games in succession. Their record crashed from its peak in 1949, when they were 11-1-0 to a mediocre 6 - 6.

The early '50s belonged to the Browns. Cleveland owned their conference, which was called the American Conference from 1950 through 1953, and the Eastern Conference thereafter. No matter what it was called, the Browns took their conference crown every year from 1950 through 1955. If their years in the AAFC are counted, the Browns played in *ten* consecutive championship games from 1946 to 1955.

In 1951, Philadelphia's '40s dynasty started disintegrating. Coach Greasy Neale was fired. Bo McMillan replaced him, only to be replaced himself by Wayne Milner because of health problems. Tommy Thompson, the team leader throughout the good years of the '40s, called it quits, as did Van Buren, who bowed out as the game's all-time leading rusher. All these hits caused the Birds to slump to a 4-8 record in '51, their first losing season since 1942. In '52, they bounced back. James Clark, chief of the "Hundred Brothers," the group that owned the Eagles, enlisted Jim Trimble as head coach. Trimble, the league's youngest coach, surrounded himself with a cadre of '48-'49 alumni, like Van Buren, Vic Lindskog, and Frank Reagan, to assist him. The Eagles prospered for a few years under Trimble, battling back to 7-5-0 in 1952, and the first of three consecutive second-place finishes. The Eagles reached their pinnacle for the '50s on November 7, 1954, when they beat the Cardinals, 30 -14, to gain a first-place tie with the Giants. Unfortunately, they lost to the Giants and Browns the next two weeks and tumbled out of the race. Philadelphia had started down the slippery slope, a slide that wouldn't be halted till 1959.

~ The 60 Minutes Dress Rehearsal ~

In 1954, Chuck Bednarik previewed his 1960 heroics. In the Eagles' season opener at Philadelphia's Connie Mack Stadium, Bednarik was pressed into full-time duty, playing both offense and defense in the Birds' 28-10 victory. Bednarik started the game at linebacker. When starting center Ken Farragut went out of the contest with an injury on the first play from scrimmage, Chuck replaced him. It took six years, but Bednarik reprised his iron-man routine against the same team, in virtually the same way, in 1960.

Bednarik wound up playing four "60-minute" games in 1960 (technically, he didn't play 60 minutes in any of those games because Chuck did not play on the special teams, but that doesn't undermine his achievement). His '60, 60-minute debut came against Cleveland in the fifth game of the season. In that game, Bednarik started at center on offense. However, on the very first play from scrimmage, starting linebacker Bob Pellegrini was carried off the field. Bednarik was pressed into emergency service at linebacker, and continued to play center. Pellegrini was himself a replacement for the injured regular linebacker, John Nocera. Just as in 1954, Bednarik was brilliant on both sides of the scrimmage line. Just as in 1954, the Eagles won—a victory that many members of the 1960 Eagles felt was the turning point of that championship season.

THE SLIDE

In 1955, the Eagles collapsed. Their tumble down into fifth—next-to-last—place that year would prove to be their best finish until 1959. Dick Bielski, a collegiate star at the University of Maryland, joined the Eagles in 1955. The bruising fullback and kicker describes the unsettled scene that greeted him.

DICK BIELSKI: " When I got to the Eagles, things were really deteriorating. There was a lot of politics and turmoil in the front-office. Vince McNally (General Manager) was the only one in the organization who knew what was going on. The whole atmosphere here was foreign to me. I wasn't used to losing. My high school team won 29 straight. Then, at Maryland, we were undefeated in my senior year. The teams I had played for in high school and college were serious about football. But, when I got to the Eagles, things didn't seem too serious. I'll never forget the time I showed up for practice in one of those early years at Hershey, and the head coach wasn't around. I didn't know where he was. The other coaches were running the practice, and everything just seemed too loose. Then, I found out the head coach was home in New Jersey putting storm windows in for his wife! That's how unprofessional and unorganized everything was. I wasn't used to that kind of stuff. My whole life, practice meant practice, but it didn't mean anything around here."

Trimble left after the '55 season, compiling a 25-20-3 record, good for the third-best winning percentage in Eagle history. Pete Pihos and Bucko Kilroy, two vets from the championship years, retired along with him. Pihos' final year was his second-best receiving year, statistically, in a Hall of Fame career. His 62 catches led the league, as did his 864 yards gained on receptions. When Pihos left the game, he ranked third on the all-time list for most catches. Kilroy, another frequent All-Pro, became an Eagle coach. Their departure left Chuck Bednarik as the sole survivor from the 1949 championship team.

In 1956, the once-mighty Birds dropped into the basement for the first time in over a decade. Bielski laments: "The sad part is we had good personnel. Our defense was as good as any in football. We had Bednarik, Wayne Robinson, Jesse Richardson, Marion Campbell, Jerry Norton, Wild Man Willey, Tom Scott, and Tom Brookshier. Everyone of those guys was a hitter. It's just that everything was so disorganized. With good coaching, we could have been a winner."

~ Kilroy's Scouting Operation ~

"I think a big reason for our success in 1960 was what happened in 1956," Bucko Kilroy crows. Kilroy is referring to the Eagles' brand new 1956 scouting operation. Bucko and Jimmy Gallagher set it up. Kilroy, who still works for the New England Patriots' front office, as he has for decades, chuckles at the state of scouting in the mid-'50s.

"Before 1956, the Eagles didn't even have a scout. You know how teams scouted in those days? The coaching staff would get together and go to a college game on Saturday, in whatever city the game was being played, or some place nearby. That was scouting. The clubs, in those days, went into the draft meetings with names written on match covers. Literally. They'd base their selections on tips from friends around the country. Everybody walked into the draft meeting with a Street and Smith under their arms. They'd draft guys they never saw! I remember one player was drafted because the owner's wife thought he was 'cute!' Things sure changed in the '50s. The L.A. Rams were the first team to hire a scout. So, the Eagles decided it was time to jump in. I think there were only five scouts in the league when we started. Nowadays some *teams* have ten. And the way we scouted back then is nowhere near the way it's done now. Basically, we watched films—just single reels of game films, shot by one camera. Today, they use end zone cameras, sideline cameras— there's much better coverage. And, the offense and defense are on separate cassettes. Back then, we picked our films up from an outfit called TelRA, and another company around 15th and Walnut, who also had highlight films. Jimmy (Gallagher) and I didn't get to see many games live. Still, it paid off. The guys we drafted from that '56 college crop formed the nucleus of the '60 championship team. The '57 draft was probably the greatest draft in Eagle history. We signed up two Hall of Famers in Jurgensen and McDonald. And, we got Barnes, Peaks, and Nocera, too. All those guys started in '60. They all had the right stuff."

Asst. Coach Frank "Bucko" Kilroy helped to set up the Eagles' scouting operations.

ROCK BOTTOM AND BUCK SHAW'S THREE TEAMS

Rookies Sonny Jurgensen, Tommy McDonald, Clarence Peaks, and Billy Ray Barnes all reported for training camp in 1957. The Eagles, under coach Hugh

Devore, lost all six preseason games. The futility extended into the regular season. After losing their first three, the Eagles ended their losing streak with a win against Cleveland, as Sonny Jurgensen was given his first start.

The Eagles won only four of 12 games in '57, with Sonny Jurgensen starting three of the four. In the ninth game that year, Tommy McDonald started at end for the first time. He caught two passes for 97 yards, one of them for his first Eagle touchdown. The Birds didn't know it at the time, but a star was born that day. The former Oklahoma Sooner had found the position that would take him to the Hall of Fame.

Otherwise, the year was uneventful. By 1957, the Eagles' slide had exacted its toll in lack of respect. No Eagles were selected for the first team, All-Pro; however, Bednarik, Jerry Norton, and rookie Billy Ray Barnes started for the East squad in the Pro Bowl game.

In 1958, head coach Hugh Devore was sent packing and replaced by Buck Shaw, who had coached the San Francisco 49ers from 1946 to 1954. Shaw, dubbed the Silver Fox because of his silvery hair, immediately dealt Buck Lansford, Jimmy Harris, and a first-round draft choice to the Los Angeles Rams for quarterback Norm Van Brocklin. Van Brocklin, a 32-year old, nine-year veteran, was unhappy with the Rams' organization, and had asked to be traded. His daughter, Kirby, recalls those days when her dad and her family were ticketed for Philadelphia.

"My dad was dissatisfied with the management in Los Angeles. He told them he wanted to go anywhere but Pittsburgh or Philadelphia. He didn't think the teams there were good enough to win a championship. He wanted to play with a contender. Anyway, I think he was actually happy about coming here after he talked to Buck Shaw."

Shaw reinstated a lost sense of pride in the organization. He brought in guys like Van Brocklin, who instilled a fierce desire to win in the younger players. Bielski, who was on the Eagles before Shaw's arrival explains what the Silver Fox accomplished:

DICK BIELSKI: "Buck brought professionalism to the Eagles. Somehow, the organization had lost it. When Shaw came to town, he said: 'What's going on here? Why don't people care about winning or losing

Vince McNally, general manager, hands the ceremonial whistle to new Eagles head coach, Buck Shaw.

around here?' Buck organized the staff, and he made people perform. Van Brocklin was the icing on the cake. When he came, I knew something good was going to happen in Philadelphia."

Bucko Kilroy, too, praises Shaw's management skills. He remembers how swift and assertive the low-key Shaw was in making changes he believed necessary.

BUCKO KILROY: "Buck was like a corporate officer. He seldom talked directly to the players. He got his messages across through the coaching staff. The players respected him, though. He was quiet, but very demanding in his own way. He knew what he wanted and he insisted on getting it. He wouldn't tolerate anything he didn't like, and he wouldn't tolerate a lack of effort. If he saw someone wasn't performing or trying, that guy would be gone. The same thing went for coaches. Once Buck caught an assistant involved in an impropriety. I'll just let it go at that. That didn't sit well with Buck. He didn't say a word to anyone, but next year, the guy was gone."

Pete Retzlaff remembers Buck's dynamic approach to building a winner.

PETE RETZLAFF: "You'll probably hear this from several other guys on the team, but once Buck saw what was going on in Philly, he told the whole team: 'Till we get the right team here, there's going to be one team coming, one team going, and one team on the field.' He wasn't fooling. He made lots of personnel changes, and most of them worked out."

The Eagles traded or released 20 players in 1958. Others, like Walt Kowalczyk, Lee Riley, and Don Owens survived 1959, but not 1960.

~ Franklin Field ~

The Eagles and Shaw seemed to change everything in 1958, including their home field. The Birds moved from Connie Mack Stadium, where they had played for the previous 17 years, to Franklin Field, home field of the University of Pennsylvania Quakers for the previous 53 years.

Franklin Field was one of football's storied temples. It opened on April 20, 1895, for the Penn Relay Track meet, a huge annual event that has been held there ever since. The facility was built initially to capitalize on the prowess of the University of Pennsylvania's football team. Penn was a national football power at the turn of the last century. The Quakers won four national championships in the ten seasons between 1895 and 1904, which prompted the construction of a new facility.

Originally Franklin Field was constructed as a single-deck facility to seat 20,000 people. By 1922, modifications had upped the capacity to 60,000. Thanks to its huge sport theater, Penn regularly led the nation's colleges in attendance at football games for several decades. The historic stadium was the site of the first radio broadcast (by WIP radio) of a collegiate football game in 1922, and the first televised broadcast of a collegiate football game in 1940. Penn crippled Maryland in TV's collegiate debut, 51-0.

Once the Ivy League was formed in 1954, attendance at Penn football games dropped off drastically. Jerry Ford, Penn's Athletic Director, sought out the Eagles as tenants. Since the stadium offered more capacity, and was, exclusively, a football facility, the offer was attractive to the Birds. The Eagles called Franklin Field their home from '58 till '70, when they moved to Veterans Stadium. At the time of the move, several Philadelphians, led by John Kelly, Sr. (Princess Grace's father) wanted to raze Franklin Field and build a 100,000-seater in Fairmount Park. The idea was eventually scrapped.

The Eagles lost their 1958 opener at Franklin Field to the Redskins, who topped them in front of 36,853 fans. The game marked a first—it was the first NFL game ever played on a college campus. All in all, the Eagles were happy about their move. Of course, you can't make everyone happy, as Billy Barnes recollects:

BILLY RAY BARNES: "I worked for the Eagles in the off-season. I guess you could call my job sort of public relations. One of the things I did was to call the season ticket-holders and talk to them. That wasn't as easy as it sounds. You can't believe how many people complained about those seats! They didn't have any chair backs on them. They were just benches at Franklin Field. At Connie Mack, there were individual seats. I got my earful that year about our move to Franklin Field."

The Eagles hit rock bottom in '58 with a 2-9-1 record, a chilling flashback to their pre-Steagle days. Yet, in many ways, the season was positive. Van Brocklin was skillfully developing his receivers into an outstanding corps, one that rivaled the Fears-Hirsch crew of his L.A glory days. Bobby Walston, a gritty, cagey veteran was reliable, sure-handed, and a sneaky-fast, big-play receiver. Tommy McDonald, his conversion to receiver a complete success, already rivaled any other deep threat in football. And, Pete Retzlaff had blossomed into a potent offensive force, snagging 56 passes to tie the Colts' Raymond Berry for league honors in that department. Van Brocklin rolled up some impressive personal statistics as well. Dutch came within 12 passes of tying Sammy Baugh's all-time mark of 210 completions in one season.

When the season had concluded, Van Brocklin and Retzlaff were among the Eagles selected to the All-Pro game. The Dutchman led the East squad on a fourth-period TD drive that notched a 28-21, come-from-behind win. The winning pass went to Pete Retzlaff. The rest of league didn't realize it, but in Philadelphia, the Eagles were prepping for another flight to glory.

I'LL TRADE THE WHOLE TEAM IF I HAVE TO

Many stalwarts of the '60 squad landed in training camp in 1959. Stan Campbell arrived from the Lions, Gerry Huth from the Giants, Chuck Weber from the Cards, Jim Carr from the Colts, and Joe Robb from the Bears. Shaw's Philadelphia team was still a work-in-progress when they opened against his former team, the 49ers. The Birds were trounced 24-14. Shaw called the performance the "lousiest game the Eagles played since I got here." He reaffirmed his resolve to assemble the squad he needed: "I'll trade the whole team if I have to." The following week, his charges responded, cleaning up on the Giants, 49-21, at Franklin Field. McDonald caught a couple of touchdown passes, and returned a punt 81yards for another six-pointer.

Quarterback Norm Van Brocklin (#11) helped to inspire the Eagles' amazing turnaround in 1959.

~ The Big Bang ~

Game 5 of the 1959 season, October 25, 1959: Eagles 28, Chicago Cardinals 24.

Many Eagles today are convinced that the Eagles comeback that day was the Big Bang that set the Eagles into their championship orbit. Pete Retzlaff reflects on a remarkable game and stunning turnaround:

PETE RETZLAFF: "Looking back, I think that Cardinal game gave us the belief in ourselves and the character we needed to excel. We were down, 17-0 when Dutch gathered the defense together on the sideline. He told everybody, 'You guys have to hold these guys right here. If you don't give up any more points, we'll come back and win this game.' First thing Dutch does is throw an interception to Night Train Lane. The Cards score, and, boom, it's 24-0! So Dutch gets the defense together again, like nothing happened, and tells them the same thing. No apologies, no embarrassment, just matter of fact. Well, the defense did hold, and we came back and won. I think Tommy (McDonald) caught a couple of TD's, and Billy Ray (Barnes) added another couple. After that game, we grew. We believed in ourselves. We believed we could win every game, no matter what the score was. We never thought a game was lost or out of reach. If you look at that

1960 season, how many games did we come from behind to win? Seven, eight, nine? There was never a sense of panic, never any despair, never any finger pointing, never any desperation—just faith, faith that we'd turn the game around and win. We drew a lot of strength and inspiration from Van Brocklin. You felt the confidence on the sideline and in the huddle. I never had that kind of feeling with any other team. The score never phased us. It was powerful, and it grew stronger every week. So, when I look back to how, and when, we started performing and acting like a championship team, I land on that Cardinal game as the start."

The Eagles finished the '59 season at 7-5-0, an amazing about-face from 1958. The Eagles were still a few players shy of being legitimate contenders. But the main ingredients were in place. Their passing attack ranked with football's elite. Their running game, though unspectacular, was solid. Fired by their clever, charismatic leader, Norm Van Brocklin, their team character and toughness was annealing into a steely amalgam. Van Brocklin's hold on the team cannot be overplayed. Jim McCusker, 1960 offensive lineman, recalls how Van Brocklin's inspiration served the team. It was more than an intangible. It led to points on the board.

JIM McCUSKER: "People talk a lot about 'going the extra mile.' They're just words in a lot of instances. Dutch could make those words come to life. He just had that knack. They call it leadership. I'll give you an example. People were always criticizing our line play, whether it be our run blocking, our pass blocking, or whatever. We might not have been the best offensive line on a play-in and play-out basis, but there weren't any better when we really needed it. Dutch could get the entire squad to rise to the occasion when the game was on the line. Dutch's leadership was our secret for all those comebacks we were known for. If we really needed a big play, Dutch would call a certain play where he might need more time in a crucial situation. Like, we had this play where Tommy (McDonald) and Pete (Retzlaff) would cross deep downfield. Dutch needed extra time for that play to develop. He'd tell the linemen in the huddle, 'You guys do what you've got to do to hold everybody out. If you guys give me the time, this play's going to win this game for us.' I'll tell you. It worked! Everyone would reach down and do what they had to do. We believed Van Brocklin would pick the right play in the right situation, and we believed he'd make it happen. It seemed like every time he called that play, it worked. The whole team would rise to the occasion. The linemen would bust their butts to give him all the time he needed. We'd keep everyone out somehow. It wasn't always pretty, but we did it. I still remember those defensive guys cussing and getting up after the play was over and Dutch completed the pass. Van Brocklin could do that. He could inspire a team, and make everyone contribute when it counted. You can't believe how far that can take you. So, we may not have looked good statistically, but we came through when we had to."

Statistically the '59 Eagles weren't impressive. McDonald was the lone Eagle to start in the Pro Bowl. Van Brocklin was supposed to start as well, but sat the game out with the flu. Jesse Richardson and Tommy Brookshier made the East squad, too. Conspicuous by his absence, however, was the Birds' perennial All-Pro, Chuck Bednarik. Chuck had decided to call it quits after the 1959 campaign. In the season finale against Cleveland at Franklin Field, 45,952 faithful bade farewell to Philly's sure-fire Hall of Famer on "Chuck Bednarik Day." The Birds lost, although they managed to give their old nemesis, Cleveland, a scare. Trailing at half-time, 14-0, they took a 21-14 advantage, before promptly losing it again. The Eagles blew a victory at the end, failing to score on six consecutive plays inside the Browns' 4-yard line.

As for Chuck Bednarik, the Eagles had been his team for the last decade. Van Brocklin was the architect of the Eagles' new house, but Bednarik was the bedrock, the foundation. He didn't get the name Concrete Charley for nothing.

Three Three **Three** Three Three

Number 60

Number 60. Could there be a more appropriate jersey number in all of sport?

Chuck Bednarik, *Number 60*, football's last 60-minute man. To teammates, coaches, opponents, broadcasters, and fans, the jersey number and the name are interchangeable. There is only one Number 60 in Philadelphia. His jersey hangs with honor in Veteran's Stadium.

Like Billy Penn atop Philadelphia's City Hall, like the strings of white lights that outline Boat House Row, Number 60 is a chunk of Quaker City landscape. And pride. The last 60-minute man, football's most famous 60-minute man, played for Philadelphia.

Bednarik's story during that championship season reads like implausible fiction. The story line goes like this: the hero is an aging NFL gladiator lured back to the battle, the oldest man on a lightly regarded squad making an unlikely run for a championship. In the season's first crucial contest, a key defender goes down on the first play from scrimmage. The hero, to save the team, is forced to remain on the field of play for the game's full 60 minutes.

The plot's OK, so far. But now it starts to get hokey. Let's make the year 1960. Let's clad the 60-minute hero in jersey number *60*. Let's make him a guy who retired the year before, but came back on the hunch that his team might win a world championship, something they hadn't done for 11 years. Let's make him the only guy left from that championship team 11 years ago. Let's make him the biggest collegiate star who ever played in the same city where he spent his entire pro career. Let's make him ice the victory that leads to the 1960 championship by jarring the ball loose from one of the country's premier players in the biggest game of the year. Let's stage the championship game in the very same stadium where he played in college. And, of course, let's end the implausible little football fantasy on the final play of the championship game—136 grueling scrimmages after the opening kickoff—with Number 60 making the game-ending, victory-saving tackle, as he pins a snarling, swearing, squirming ballcarrier to the ground as the time ticks away to zero. Let's end the novel with Number 60, blood stained and mud spattered, popping to his feet to the roar of the home town crowd.

Chuck's 1960 season was pure Spielberg stuff, a legendary, aging Jedi warrior summoned in time of crisis ("Help us, Obi Wan. You're our only hope"). In that season, 40 years ago, that feels so far away to Philadelphians, the Force was with Philadelphia, and Obi Wan wore shoulder pads. And jersey number 60.

Today, Concrete Charley engages the world the same way he played football: head on and full contact. He has lived an eventful life. He battled Nazis from an altitude of 40,000 feet in World War II. He was a unanimous All-American at an Ivy League school. He was honored by the Maxwell Club as college football's top player. He finished second in the Heisman Trophy voting. He was picked number one in the 1949 NFL draft (*ahead* of Heisman winner, Doak Walker). He earned two NFL championship rings. He was honored as the NFL's Lineman of the Decade in the '50s. Chuck Bednarik, University of Pennsylvania legend, Philadelphia Eagle icon, is, unquestionably, the greatest football player in the history of Philadelphia. Despite all the glory that has been heaped on him, Charley's concrete has never cracked or chipped. It set long ago in the ethnic neighborhoods of a tough Pennsylvania steel town. Bednarik remains true to himself and true to his ideals. Unpretentious, candid, and outspoken, he embraces the same basic values he learned from a poor but loving family, in a time long ago that seems so far away from the world of the new millennium. To understand where Chuck's coming from, you have to know where Chuck came from.

"Concrete Charley" Chuck Bednarik (#60)

Charles Philip Bednarik was born on May 1, 1925, in the blue-collar, rough-and-tumble, south side of Bethlehem, Pennsylvania. His parents had come to America, separately, in the 1920s. Both originated from the Czechoslovakian area called Slovakia. Chuck's boyhood home was a row house facing Saints Cyril and Methodius Church, in a hilly Slovak neighborhood. Bethlehem was a city of ethnic neighborhoods, each anchored by a parish church. Everywhere the spires of churches pierced through the dingy clouds of smoke that belched over the city from Bethlehem Steel's mammoth smokestacks. Practically everyone in the Bethlehem of Bednarik's youth worked for Bethlehem Steel. Chuck's dad, Charles Albert Bednarik, toiled there for 38 years. He had arrived in America in 1921 at the age of 26, and settled into Bethlehem, which was later dubbed the Christmas City for no other reason than the obvious. He remained in Bethlehem for life. Chuck's mother, Mary Pivovarnicek, reached the new world in 1920, at the age of 14. Three years later, she married Chuck's dad. For life. Loyalty, family, and faith were the pillars of the Bednarik family. They remain the pillars of Chuck Bednarik's character. When Chuck married, he married for life. He was an Eagle for life. He has been a Catholic for life.

"I still go to church every day," he explains as he sits in his den in his Coopersburg home. "Eight o'clock mass. You know, on the Eagles, they used to call me The Bishop. I'd find a Catholic church whenever we played out of town, and then all the Catholic guys could go to mass on game day. The only thing I've got to watch, though, is my language. I'm working on it. You know, sometimes when I get mad, I'll use bad language. Like I used in that picture up there."

That picture. . . he points to it with that mangled hand. Chuck's fingers point every direction but straight out, a sobering testament to the brutality of NFL trench warfare. That photo is the most prominent photo on the wall in Chuck's den. The den wall, along with most of the other walls in Chuck's house, is a veritable Louvre of sport treasures. But the Mona Lisa of the Bednarik collection is *that* picture—the *Jig*, the photo taken seconds after Bednarik executed, so to speak, what is, perhaps, the sport's most famous tackle. He knocked Frank Gifford out cold. They called that photo, the *Jig*, in 1960 New York, accusing Chuck of dancing a jig over a fallen, unconscious superstar. Gifford was the Joe Hollywood guy of his era. He came from the West Coast. He had the looks, the endorsements. Though an unassuming type by nature, his image, nonetheless, was the epitome of New York uppitiness. Forty years after that photo of the *jig* was snapped, the image endures: Gifford, the fallen king, supine; Number 60, muddy and mammoth, gloating above.

"You know what I'm saying to Frank there," Bednarik explains, shifting in his easy chair as his family cat nestles in his lap. "I'm saying: 'This game is over,' except I added a word or two. That's what I mean about watching my language. But, I never knew he was out cold when that photo was taken. All I knew was that we won the game. I gave Frank a good clean shot. I didn't try to hurt him. And Frank always says that, too."

That photo belongs to the ages, and football's priceless archives. Like Franco Harris' Immaculate Reception, and Dwight Clark's "The Catch," Bednarik's *jig* freezes more than a moment. In stark black in white, it captures the essence of combat. Chuck is proud of that photo, and the others he has on display.

Bednarik gingerly sets aside the family cat who scrambles safely into the next room. Concrete Charley still knows how to set up a protective pocket. He rises from his chair to show the way around his den. Every step is a celluloid safari through the past. "That's me at Penn," he points out with pride. "We had some good players on that team. In those days when our men came back from the war, the ballplayers were older, more mature. They were a different breed back then."

Chuck recalled his war years. The stakes were as high as the altitude of his plane—much higher, much more final, than any stakes he played for, subsequently, on the gridiron.

"I flew 30 combat missions in Europe. We were in danger on every one of them. One time, our plane was hit with flak, and when we landed, the landing gear had been damaged. The plane started to veer off the runway, and I had to jump out. That was really scary, but actually, every single one of those missions was scary. I'm just grateful I survived. I kissed the ground when we landed after that final mission."

Bednarik returned from the war, no longer a provincial Bethlehem kid. He wanted to explore different options in life. He knew there were paths in life other than the one that seemed preordained for kids from the South side of Bethlehem– the "working-for-the-steel" path that his friends, family, and relatives had taken. Chuck turned to his high school coach who set him up with George Munger, then the head coach at the University of Pennsylvania. Chuck earned a scholarship to Penn, where he became everyone's All-American.

"You know, Penn used to outdraw the Eagles," Chuck points out. "When I was in college, they'd print news about the Eagles on page four or so in the Philadelphia *Bulletin's* sports section. The Penn game was always on page one. We used to get 60,000-70,000 people at Franklin Field for the college games, when the Eagles were struggling to get 20,000. I ordered four tickets for every home game at Penn. My parents would come down from Bethlehem with Emma (Chuck's future wife) and someone else, someone who had a car and could drive. My mom and dad saw every home game I ever played at Penn, but you know, they never came down to an Eagles game. I don't really know why they didn't. Penn was great, but I didn't expect to play football after I played at Penn. When I was in college, I never really thought too much about pro ball. I figured I'd end up coaching somewhere. Then I got drafted by the Eagles, and everything changed. But, the whole time I was in high school and college, I never once talked to a pro scout."

Chuck was a huge collegiate star at Penn, shining offensively and defensively. He also kicked extra points, punted, and even kicked field goals in a pinch. He was picked first in the 1949 draft. The home-town Eagles nabbed him as their "Bonus Selection". The Bonus Selection was an ill-conceived wrinkle in the draft system that was scrapped after a few years. Each franchise drew a piece of paper from a pile. All the pieces were blank, except for one. The team that walked away with that one piece that had a mark on it chose first, before the official draft began. In '49, the lucky team was the talent-rich, reigning NFL champs, the Eagles.

J.D. Smith, Chuck Bednarik (center) and Jim McCusker line up in practice.

The Eagles repeated as NFL champions in 1949, Chuck's rookie year. The ex-Penn star played linebacker on a defense that shut out the L.A. Rams in the championship game in Los Angeles. The rest of Bednarik's career, as they say, is history. Eight Pro Bowl selections, Lineman of the Decade, Concrete Charley, Hall of Fame, 60-Minute Man. Number 60.

"That second championship we won in 1960 felt great. It was a long time between championships for me. We had a lot of luck in '60, it's true. But you know, you make your own luck, and then you have to capitalize on the breaks that you get. Besides luck, though, we had the three things you need to win in this league: a great quarterback, a good running back, and good receivers."

Nowadays, they call that trio "The Dallas Formula," somehow ranking it up there with $E = mc^2$ for cosmic genius. It's amazing how sport constantly reaffirms the obvious. Bednarik's explanation for the success of the 1960 Eagles was echoed, independently, by his '49 Eagle mate, Bucko Kilroy. According to Bednarik and Kilroy, the Dallas Formula has been alive and well for years. It's the gist of basic, old-fashioned, winning football.

"You can't win without strength at those three spots. We had it. We had Van Brocklin at quarterback. He was great. We had Dean, Barnes, and Peaks to run the ball, and we had Tommy, Retzlaff, and Walston to catch it. Every one of those guys was a solid, quality player. Our team was also physically and mentally tough. We didn't give up, ever, when we were out there on the field, and we never gave in. The other big factor was that we avoided injuries. But, that's part of the luck I was talking about."

Injuries never stopped Concrete Charley. It took a catastrophe to keep Chuck Bednarik out of a lineup. Bednarik was like the model employee at "the Steel" who turned his sick time back, unused. He was the guy who packed his lunch day by day and earned his pay minute by minute. That was the Chuck Bednarik value system. It was simple. So he overlooked injuries. He was expected to play. And play he did.

"I missed three games my whole career with the Eagles. At Penn, I only missed one game. I had a cracked rib and a punctured lung. I was back in the lineup two weeks later. That's why I spoke out when Deion Sanders claimed he was an iron man 'cause he played offense and defense. Iron Man, my foot! I was in there banging every play, with no rest in between. Deion plays back there behind the line, not involved in any action unless the ball comes his way. He doesn't even come up to tackle. That's why I said he couldn't tackle my wife, Emma. Look, I played in 136 plays in that championship game. My nose was in there every play. I didn't sit back on anything."

By the time 1958 rolled around, Chuck actually was looking for a little less action. He was 33 years old at the time. Sensing his own gridiron mortality, he asked to be moved from linebacker to center.

"You take a lot less pounding at center. I was getting older," Chuck recalls, the years whizzing by like yardmarkers on a sideline sprint. "I was still in good shape, but I had to start thinking about extending my own career. When I played center at Penn, it was a different thing. In the single wing, center was the key position. The snap was crucial – remember, you were snapping to different guys in different positions back there in the backfield. But in the pros, in that T formation, center was a lot less punishing on your body than linebacker."

After the Eagles' horrid 1958 season, Chuck set his sights on retirement in 1959. He actually *did* retire in 1959. The Eagles gave him a "Chuck Bednarik Day," presenting their living legend with a television and a thousand dollar check.

"When I came out of retirement a few months later, I was worried they'd take that thousand dollar gift and TV back from me, but they never did," Chuck says with a wink.

Number 60 indeed came back. He had a storybook season in 1960. Then he tacked two more years on to his Hall of Fame career. Looking back, Chuck confesses that everything was not perfect. He has some frustrations, some misgivings, like the 1960 championship game.

"When we went into Franklin Field that day, I saw the new car they were giving the MVP of the game. I said to the guys: 'I'm going to win that car.' After the game, I thought I had won it. Nothing against Dutch, but he threw 9 for 22 that game. I played both ways, made that last tackle on (Jim) Taylor—I thought the car was mine. I thought I had an MVP season, too—playing both ways in all the big games, coming up with those hits on Triplett and Gifford, especially since I made those plays in New York."

New York. Bucko Kilroy says: "If Bednarik played in New York today, he'd be making $7 million a year. He'd be the biggest name in football. They'd love him up there." But he didn't play in New York. Chuck belongs to Philadelphia, and to a great extent, Chuck Bednarik is to the Philadelphia Eagles what Babe Ruth was to the New York Yankees. Both are poster players for their franchises, inseparable from their teams. Both were outspoken, controversial,

Chuck Bednarik (#60) in 1962.

and bigger than life figures. The feats of both are shrouded in legend. Did Ruth call his shot? Did he eat all those hotdogs? Did Bednarik ever play a full 60-minute game? Did he bring Jim Taylor down all by himself to win the title? The legends that each man carved are undoubtedly a few shavings short of fact. It doesn't matter. Whatever it is that they did not actually do, we figure they probably *could* have done, anyway. That's all that matters.

Another similarity between Ruth and Bednarik is that both endured some personal disappointments and hurts after retiring.

"I hardly go down to the Eagles' games now," Chuck continues, blitzing into the next topic. "It's not that I wouldn't go. It's just the crowds, the congestion. I haven't been involved with the team since Dick Vermeil was here in the late Seventies and early Eighties. When he came to Philadelphia, he called me up, and took Emma and me out to dinner. Dick said to me: 'Chuck, you're a winner. I want you associated with my Eagles team. You're Mr. Eagle. I want you on the sideline with my team.'

"I was honored. I was on the sideline when Vermeil coached, documenting plays, helping out. I wasn't a coach, but I participated in the decisions. I haven't done anything with the organization since then, but I am more connected to the team nowadays, since (current Eagles' coach) Andy Reid got here. The Eagles practice at Lehigh in the summer. None of the previous coaches ever asked me to drive over and talk to the team. Andy did. You know, I only live 12 minutes from the practice field."

Chuck Bednarik likes precision. He lives 12 minutes away – not *about* ten or 15 minutes away. Twelve minutes. Number 60 has always been a straight ahead, no-nonsense guy. Practical. Systematic. To Chuck Bednarik, a glass is neither half-full nor half-empty. It's twice as big as it needs to be.

Chuck directs you to his house with characteristic precision:

"Look, here's how you go. Go up Main street, and make a turn at the second light. From that point, go 2.4 miles till you reach a blue house, where you make a left-hand turn."

Two-point-four miles. . .That's the kind of precision I heard from the engineering students in college, not from centers or linebackers. But Chuck Bednarik is not typical. He's an American original. Precise, to the point, economic, specific, demanding. He has neither the time nor the patience (ask his wife, Emma, about Chuck's patience behind the wheel) to miss a turn because he strayed *point-one* mile beyond the turn. That's unacceptable.

Chuck tells you exactly how he sees things, exactly what's on his mind. As '60 teammate Jerry Reichow, puts it: "Chuck was such a strong personality, a great leader. The guy spoke and everyone in the locker room listened. Everyone knew that when Chuck demanded something of somebody, it was never anything Chuck didn't demand of himself. He had everyone's respect, and I guess a bit of fear, too. I lived in Hatboro (a suburb of Philadelphia) in '60, which wasn't far from where Chuck lived in Abington. We used to ride to practice together once in awhile, and sometimes I'd even feel a little intimidated by him myself. He was just a powerful individual."

Chuck and I had finished the chat and the photo safari. Literally hundreds of portraits, snapshots, and action photos salute old friends, old times, heroes and peers—Warren Spahn, Jimmy Brown, Timmy Brown … There were even a few shots of Sam Huff, reputedly Chuck's arch-enemy from the Giants rivalry. Every picture tells a story.

Emma returned from shopping. The bag brigade began immediately. Everything quickly and methodically found its rightful place. As I was leaving, Emma said, "Did you get all the information you needed?" I assured her I did. I thanked here for her hospitality. I told her there was additional information I was going to include. "It's material I picked up the first time I met your husband, 40 years ago," I said. She looked quizzical, until I explained.

"When I was a kid, my dad took me to Hershey every summer to watch the Eagles practice. One evening, as we were going home, we saw two huge guys walking on the other side of the street. One of them was your husband. The other turned out to be John Nocera. You remember him, Emma? Unfortunately John passed away a few years ago." Emma nodded, a shadow passing over her smile. "I was just a young kid, awestruck," I said, rushing back into a mistier past. "Of course, I was all set to run across the street for an autograph, but my dad stopped me. He was trying to be inconspicuous, telling me to let the two poor guys be. They were tired, they didn't want to be bothered … Then, all of a sudden, here comes Chuck Bednarik jogging across the street, dragging Nocera with him like a duffel bag. You know, I'd be lying if I told you I remembered even one thing Chuck said. It really didn't matter what he said. It was what he did. All I knew was that he made my day. Hell, he made my summer."

Emma just smiled, "Yeah, that's Chuck. That's the way he was brought up."

~ Chuck Doesn't Live Here Anymore ~

"Hi, Chuck. I'm writing a book on the '60 Eagles, and I was wondering if I could talk to you. Do you have some time?"

That's how I started the first phone conversation I had with Chuck Bednarik.

"I'm pretty busy," Chuck replied, still out of breath from his dash from the yard to the phone. "Besides, you'll have a tough time finding my place."

The voice on the other end of the line was big—not loud, not surly, not hostile. Just big.

"No, I can find my way around your area, Chuck. I used to go to Lehigh University," I fired back. For years, I've seen Chuck at Lehigh football games and

Concrete Charley—the last of the "60-minute men."

wrestling matches. I also knew that he grew up in the shadows of the university on Bethlehem's south side.

"You went to Lehigh!? OK! Then I'll find some time," Chuck said chuckling. There may have been a ring of relief in his voice.

"You know, Chuck, I lived off campus my last year at Lehigh," I continued, feeling more comfortable now myself. "The house I lived in was near your parents' home, I think. It was right across the street from St. Cyril and Methodius Church."

A short while later, I discovered the house I lived in that year was the house Chuck Bednarik grew up in. I'm glad my parents never knew that. They were always complaining that my roommates and I didn't put enough effort into housekeeping. Things would have been a lot different if they could have told Chuck Bednarik to stop by and inspect the house his dad worked hard to buy.

FourFour**Four**FourFourFour

Chocolatetown and Getting Ready

It's early July of 1960. The Pirates' pennant run vies with the Olympics for the spotlight on the national sport scene. Meanwhile, on the local Philly scene, spring hopes, as always, have morphed into mid-summer nightmares. The 1960 crop of Phillies' phenoms, like Ken Walters, Harry "the Horse" Anderson, and Tony Curry, have proved to be fleeting comets, whose April and May starlight was a cruel masquerade. Like an old dog circling down, tornado-like, into a favorite chair, the Phillies again settle comfortably into last place, a position they staked out in '58, and will occupy uncontested until the Mets and their 120 losses in 1962 flush them upward.

As for football, the sport lays dormant. July is baseball season. Last football season is forgotten. Next football season is a pennant race away. History records that the 1958 Sudden Death overtime championship game between the Baltimore Colts and the New York Giants drop-kicked pro football into national prominence. Nevertheless, in 1960, football, in many ways, fills the down time between baseball pennant races. In July, 1960 football coverage in U.S. papers is rarer than a rock concert in 1960 Russia.

Shortly after Independence Day, Buck Shaw returns to the Eagles' headquarters at 15th and Locust. Shaw succeeds in "coaxing his coaching staff back to their football *jobs* ahead of schedule," as a contemporary newspaper article expresses it. Training camp doesn't begin until July 24, and Shaw's coaches, like players in the '60s, depend on off-season jobs to supplement their relatively modest NFL stipends. Nick Skorich is one of Shaw's 1960 assistants. Skorich has been in professional football continuously since 1946 in one capacity or another. Memories of that July in 1960 are still vivid:

NICK SKORICH: "I was selling insurance in the off-season. It was a full-time job. I had all the same responsibilities as anyone with a full-time job. I had to make special arrangements with my employer to come back early like Buck wanted, before I was supposed to report. Coaching wasn't a year-round profession in those days. It wasn't easy to just come back whenever the club called you."

In addition to Skorich, Jerry Williams (defensive coach), Charlie Gauer (receivers coach) and Bucko Kilroy (chief scout and bottle washer, as Bucko describes his role) round out Shaw's staff—not a very large think tank by today's standards. Shaw's team is coming off a promising 7-5-0 season in '59. Anchored by Norm Van Brocklin at quarterback, the offense is set and solid at the skill positions. Running backs Billy Ray Barnes and Clarence Peaks, though not spectacular, are seasoned and reliable, each capable of occasional big gains and big games. Barnes and Peaks both catch the ball extremely well, adding versatility and fire power to the club's most potent weapon, its passing attack. Pete Retzlaff, Tommy McDonald, and Bobby Walston have developed into a respected, if not feared, receiving corps. They rank with the best in the business. The offensive line, on the other hand, is a huge question mark. The 1959 Eagles, despite their offensive production, ranked dead last in rushing yardage. Shaw and his staff fault the offensive line for the team's lack of rushing punch. The pass blocking is adequate, but spotty at times. A major problem has arisen as a result of Shaw's "three-teams" program to reconstruct the Eagles. Because of this scheme, the "team on the field" has never stayed around long enough to play together for an extended period, or at least not long enough to become a cohesive unit. Bednarik, at center, is the offensive line's most established star. J. D. Smith, a second-round draft choice in '59 (the Eagles lost their first-round pick to the Rams in the Van Brocklin trade), along with Jim McCusker, who came in '59 from the Cardinals, are the probable tackles. Two young bulls, Darrel Aschbacher, and Gerry Huth are vying for the guard slots,

Jim McCusker (#75) and J. D. Smith (# 76) line up at tackle for the '60 squad.

along with Stan Campbell, the only other veteran on the offensive line. In the entire group, Bednarik is the only one who has played for Philadelphia for longer than a year.

The defense is considered the club's biggest weakness. In 1959 the Birds' defense surrendered more points than nine of the 12 teams in the NFL. More jolting than their poor defensive ranking is the fact that the Eagle offense, which ranked third in the NFL in points scored, scored ten points *fewer* than the defense gave up.

Many defensive personnel scheduled to report to training camp are unproven, particularly if the team expects to be of championship caliber. Joe Robb, who came from the Bears in 1959, and Ed Khayat, return as defensive ends, along with Jerry Wilson, a second-round draftee of the Chicago Cardinals in '59. Jesse Richardson will be back at tackle; while John Nocera, Chuck Weber, and Bob Pellegrini return at linebacker. Tom Brookshier, Jimmy Carr, and second-year men Gene Johnson and Art Powell return for defensive backfield duty. Brookshier, who broke into the NFL in '53, is the dean of the defensive unit. Other than him, all the other defensive returnees, with the exception of Pellegrini and Campbell, have spent two years or less with the club (Pellegrini was an Eagle rookie in 1956, while Marion Campbell came to the club that same year from San Francisco). The defensive line has the same problem as the offensive line. There is no nucleus. At this point, only Brookshier's job is assured.

Shaw has some other big holes to plug. His kicker, Dick Bielski, is gone, swooped up by the new NFL franchise, the Dallas Cowboys, who debut in the NFL in 1960. The Cowboy roster is a patchwork of players from all the other NFL teams. In the off-season, each NFL team provided a list of players to Dallas. The Cowboys selected their roster from the lists.

Shaw talks about the Eagles' chances this year, and the difficulty he'll have replacing Bielski in a July 1960 interview:

"We could do better in the standings this year. But, we *do* have some question marks. Like, now that we lost Dick Bielski to Dallas, who's gonna kick off? Maybe we'll find a rookie with a strong leg for that. We've got 29 veterans reporting to spring training, and we think we've had a good draft. Those boys we have at the College All-Star camp might be real ballplayers."

~ Philadelphia Won't Have Dick Bielski to Kick Around Anymore ~

Dick Bielski, kicker, fullback, and tight end, remembers 1960 with mixed emotions: It was the year he left Philadelphia.

DICK BIELSKI: "I have no regrets about my career. If I hadn't gone to Dallas, the doors may not have opened up for coaching like they did, because Dallas is where I met the people who offered me the opportunities to coach. I knew something good was going on with the Eagles in '59. I had been with the club since

1955, and '59 was our first winning season. The guys on that team were my friends. Bobby Walston was my neighbor in Maple Shade, New Jersey. That guy took me under his wing as soon as I reached training camp in '55. Bobby was just a terrific guy. I was pulling for the Eagles all the way in 1960—well, I mean, as soon as the Cowboys were out of the race. I was there at the championship game—first pro game I ever saw from the stands. Pellegrini got me the tickets. As for my move to Dallas, Vince McNally called me on the phone and told me he had 'good news.' He said, 'You're going to the expansion team in Dallas.' I wasn't angry or bitter. I respected McNally. He knew football, and his plan in Philly certainly worked, even though I guess I didn't fit into it."

"Those boys" at the 1960 College All-Star camp are: Maxie Baughan from Georgia Tech, Gene Gossage from Northwestern, Bill Lapham from Iowa, and Ted Dean from Wichita State. The All-Stars are training for a game against the NFL-champion Baltimore Colts in Chicago on August 12.

The College All-Star Game is an annual affair that pits the college football's top graduates against the NFL champion. The game was inaugurated back in 1933, another brainchild of Arch Ward, the sports editor at the *Chicago Tribune*. Ward is also the guy behind baseball's All-Star game. The College All-Star series would last till 1976, before getting scrapped. As paychecks and bonuses rocket upward throughout the '60s, the owners grow increasingly apprehensive about injury. The owners don't want to risk losing a major investment for a frivolous cause. In a 1960 interview, coach Jerry Williams discounts the game for other reasons, saying: "I really don't think that College All-Star game is worth it. When I played (in the 1949 game, on the same team as Chuck Bednarik, versus the '49 champion Eagles), you know what I got for the game? A blanket, $100, and—I got to keep my uniform."

Maxie Baughn (#55) from Georgia was one of four college All-Stars on the 1960 Eagles team.

Shaw continues the roll call of missing faces. Dallas has gobbled up linebacker Bill Striegel and tackle Jerry DeLuca in the expansion draft. Both saw extensive action for the Eagles the previous season. Also missing will be Lee Riley, a 190-pound defensive back, who has been an Eagle since 1956. Riley was a top candidate for a defensive backfield slot but has been dealt to the Giants at his own request.

~ The Life of Riley ~

Lee Riley was an Eagle throughout the down years of the late '50s. He may have been a starter on the championship team, had he hung around long enough. However Riley, whose brother, Pat, coached the NBA Los Angeles Lakers in their glory years, had landed a good off-season job in real estate in New York. Lee's wife was a native New Yorker, so Lee campaigned to get closer to the Big Apple's core. He asked to be traded to the Giants. Lee got his wish. Unfortunately, as things turned out, he campaigned himself right out of a championship ring. It wasn't the first time Lee Riley left too soon. He made a career of it.

Lee Riley seems to have had the same impeccable sense of bad timing that cursed Pete Best. Best was the Beatles' drummer who was replaced by Ringo Starr just as the Beatles were about to cash in on the big money.

Three times in Riley's seven-year career, he left a club right before that club won either a division, or NFL, title. In 1956, Riley came to Philadelphia from Detroit, who went on to win the NFL championship in 1957. In 1959, Riley went to the Giants from Philadelphia, who immediately followed up with an NFL championship in 1960. And finally, in 1960, Riley went to the New York Titans, leaving the Giants, who went on to win the '61 Eastern crown.

Riley played his final two years with the lowly New York Titans of the American Football League. In his final season he intercepted 11 passes to lead the AFL.

Linebacker/guard Tom Louderbach, another stalwart who logged lots of playing time in '59, will be missing this year. Louderbach, who has been waived, ends up with Oakland in the AFL.

Shaw has been busily building his club, mostly via trades. After the Eagles '57 draft bonanza, the flow of draft talent into the club floundered significantly in '58 and '59. In '58, the Eagles had little luck signing their draftees. Of the 30 they drafted, they signed a league-low 11. That figure is, admittedly, slightly misleading, since Thereon Sapp, a '58 draftee, didn't graduate till '59. The process of drafting a player before his final year in college was called "red-shirting." Likewise, Bill Lapham and Gene Gossage were red-shirted in 1958 and would not join the club till 1960.

~ Madden Makes the All-Van Brocklin Team ~

"You know who used to be Dutch's gopher in Hershey?" Bucko Kilroy grins. "John Madden. I remember when Madden was in Hershey. The guy got hurt and spent all his time at camp hanging around Van Brocklin, soaking up all the football knowledge he could. Van Brocklin liked Madden. I think Dutch might have helped John get his first coaching job, although I'm not sure."

Madden came to Hershey in the summer of 1958 as an unsung 21st-round draft choice from California Polytechnic College (San Luis Obispo). He hurt his knee in training camp, and his ambitions for a playing career withered. Madden left Hershey in '58—most likely by bus—and ended up coaching at Allan Hancock Junior College in California. A few years later, he signed on as one of Don Coryell's (of "Air Coryell" fame) assistants. Eventually the demonstrative Madden went to the Raiders, where he became one of the most successful coaches in NFL history.

Despite their '58 draft woes, the Eagles didn't lose much ground to the competition. Of the 384 college players drafted in the NFL, only 181 were signed, while only 59 actually stuck in the NFL. One team bucked that trend. The Green Bay Packers, ravenously rebuilding because of their pitiful showings in the late '50s, signed 21 of 31 1958 draftees, including four lynch pins in their '60s dynasty: Dan Currie, Jerry Kramer , and Hall of Famers Jim Taylor and Ray Nitschke.

The Eagles fared better in the 1959 draft. Of the 31 collegians they drafted, they managed to sign 21. Three members of the '59 draft class: J. D. Smith, Gene Johnson, and Howard Keys, contributed significantly to the championship team's success.

The 1960 draft is more precarious and complicated since the American Football League has now entered the fray. The Eagles lose their first-round pick, Ron Burton to the AFL Boston Patriots. Burton, a Northwestern running back, gains a scant 1,536 yards in an undistinguished five-year AFL career. In addition, the Eagles lose third-round pick Curt Merz, who treks north to the Canadian League, along with fifth-round pick, Don Norton, who accepts the more lucrative offer of the AFL's Los Angeles Chargers.

Shaw's pre-camp session with the coaching staff ends uneventfully. The group watches a lot of film, and engages in a lot of discussion on what the team needs, but no clear direction is set. Shaw prefers to wait and see what this year's draft has wrought. He also plans to tap his team's versatility to fix whatever needs fixing. He has several players—Bednarik, Pellegrini, Walston, Powell, and others—who can play offense and defense. Thus, the answer to some of his problems may already be in uniform. They just may be out of position. As the coaching contingent heads for camp, they all agree on one thing. The Eagles are still a few players short of being full-fledged contenders.

PREPARING FOR CAMP

In mid-July, Equipment Manager Eddie Schubach putters into Hershey, Pennsylvania, and sets up in the Hershey Arena, which will serve as the dressing and training headquarters for the 54 athletes expected in camp. The 64-year-old Schubach knows the drill. He's done it for the Birds for the past 23 years. Schubach stocks the Eagles' bunker with 80 plastic helmets (at $30 apiece), 360 jerseys, 120 pairs of game pants (at $26.75 apiece), and 60 pairs of shoes (at $20 each). In addition, he stockpiles $1,600 of medical supplies and $1,000 worth of tape. In a 1960 *Philadelphia Bulletin* article, Schubach winces at such huge expenses, and reminisces about the simple life of days gone by.

"In the 1930s, Bert Bell owned the Eagles, and the players footed the bill for their own shoes and pads. They toted their own equipment around in duffel bags. When we played a pre-season game in New York, Bert would bus the team up to the city. Then, he'd feed every guy in this little cafeteria he knew near the railroad station. Bert held each and every one to a one-dollar limit. One buck, that's right! No more. A guy named Milt Romm worked for Bert. He'd canvass all the tabs before anyone could get out of the restaurant. After we all ate and everyone paid up, the players grabbed their duffel bags and hopped the subway to the Polo Grounds to play the game. Bert really squeezed that buffalo (referring to the buffalo on the nickel)!"

Training camp is no longer the Spartan ideal it was in the early years of pro football. In a 1960 interview, Chuck Bednarik recalls his first training camp in 1949.

"It was in 1949 at Grand Rapids, Minnesota—60 miles north of Duluth. I remember feeling a bit queasy when, before camp, they told me something about mosquitoes and bears. When I heard that, I didn't think it was going to be the greatest fun. But, the place where the camp was, was *so* far away from everything! There was nothing at all to do out there. The nearest movie was seven miles away. All they showed were double features—westerns—seven nights a week. The town loaned the team a school bus so we could all go to the movies together. We'd hop on the bus at 6:30 at night, and get back on at 9:30. I was there for a couple of months, right at the time that my daughter, Darlene, was born. I didn't get to see her till she was two months old. Yeah, that's the way it used to be, so the veterans nowadays all agree. Hershey is the best place to train."

In the same interview, Chuck also hits on the virtues of staying in shape in the off-season.

"I tell these kids in the game today that the most important thing to do is to work out off season, at least twice a week. Myself, I played squash and handball off-season, and golf in April. It's not easy to keep in shape when you're not playing football. Chuck Weber and I both worked a 40-hour week the whole off-season. But, two, three times a week, Chuck and I would get together and run and do push-ups. Chuck and I live near each other in Abington (a town in suburban Philadelphia), so it's good for both of us. We can push one another and keep each other motivated."

Eager to get started, Bednarik checks in early at Hershey. So does Pete Retzlaff —he of the much admired work ethic. Retzlaff is trying a new gimmick, special three-pound lead boots, Retzlaff explains their purpose in a 1960 interview:

"Tommy McDonald and I bought these contraptions. I read somewhere that there's a sprinter in Texas who used them, and he ran a 9.6 hundred, so I figured I'd give them a try myself."

Forty years after that interview, Pete still thinks those weighted shoes gave him an edge.

RETZLAFF: "They didn't increase my speed, though I'm convinced they helped me make sharper cuts. You know how I used them? Do you remember those diagonal lines they used to have in the end zones in that era? I used to practice by running across the end zone with those weighted shoes zig-zagging along the diagonal lines."

Only a few other Eagles arrive with the advance guard. As Ed Khayat explains:

KHAYAT: "We could never wait to get back to Hershey to see everybody again. But, remember, the ballplayers back then worked off-season jobs. That meant they had to wrap up their jobs, take care of their obligations at home, say good-bye to family and friends, pack up the car, and head off to Hershey, Pennsylvania, from wherever they lived. Guys made that trip from all over the country. Jet travel and air travel in general, weren't as common back then, so it took awhile to get there for some guys."

CHOCOLATETOWN

Hershey, Pennsylvania is beautiful. Milton Hershey conceived his Rockwellesque little town as a Utopia for the workers in his chocolate factory in the early part of the twentieth century. Utopian concepts somehow always manage to fall short, but Milton's experiment did produce a charming, spiffy little community, with street lamps shaped like Hershey kisses and an ubiquitous bouquet of chocolate in the air. Willie Wonka, eat your heart out. The town features an amusement park, a zoo, a world-class hotel, and several great golf courses. If it sounds like a resort, it is. Hershey has long been a favorite destination for Keystone State tourists. Best of all, as far as the Eagles are concerned, the townsfolk love the football players and vice versa. Eddie Khayat looks back with fondness:

KHAYAT: "What a great place Hershey was, and the people in that town were great, too! Years after I stopped going to Hershey, I still got cards from people who came to the practice field for camera day, or just to watch us practice. I can't think of a better place for football camp than Hershey."

On July 24, 1960, training camp officially begins. Nine Eagles—practically 20 percent of those invited—are no-shows. Defensive end, Jerry Wilson, and halfback, Tim Brown, are excused in order to finish up their summer-camp commitment for the Army. Both report a few days later. Marion Campbell is injured and awaiting surgery to remove calcium from his knee. A few others are still in transit, and expected a day or two late. Two of the offensive guards, however, are simply AWOL. Darrel Aschbacher, a free spirit from the University of Oregon, has decided to stay at the University for some summer classes. He telegrams the Eagles' brass to ask permission to *skip* training camp. Claiming he still wants to play for the Eagles (but, apparently, not quite yet), Aschbacher offers the Eagles an option. He suggests that he join the team at a more convenient time, on the west coast, one month after the start of camp, when the Eagles play the Rams in Los Angeles. After the telegram, Aschbacher goes incommunicado. Eddie Khayat reflects on his own efforts to bring Aschbacher back into the fold:

KHAYAT: "I knew, going into camp that year, that the Eagles were going to do it in '60! We had a good chance to win the title. I tried to convince Darrel and Paige Cothren, our place-kicker, to come back. Darrel was a good ball player, a real tough guy. He played for us in '59. Paige was good, too. But I couldn't get them to come back. Darrel wound up becoming a pilot for Delta Air Lines, I believe, and making a career of it. I understand he's retired now."

A second offensive guard, Stan Campbell, a 230-pound vet who earned two championship rings in a four-year tenure with the Detroit Lions, informs McNally that he won't be coming to camp because he's retiring. Forty years later, Stan Campbell explains his "retirement."

STAN CAMPBELL: "I had no intention of retiring! That's just what you did in those days. You had to say that to get McNally's attention. Before training camp, Vince and I had agreed verbally to a $12,500 contract. So, a week later, I get a contract in the mail—for $11,500. I send it back. Vince calls and says: 'Stan, you didn't sign the contract.' I said, 'That's right, Vince, 'cause it's not what we agreed to.' We talk it over again, and agree to $12,500 again. A week later, I get another contract—for $12,000.' I send that one back, too. Vince calls,

Veteran offensive guard Stan Campbell (#67), "threatened" to resign until his salary was raised to $12,500!

and tells me he can't give me what I'm asking, so I tell him I'm retiring. A few weeks later, we talk again, and he agrees to the $12,500, so I send him back the signed contract after I hand-wrote the correct amount on it. No, I didn't want to retire, not at all. I thought we'd win the championship in '60, and I wanted to be part of it. It's just that players didn't make much money back then, particularly linemen. I started out making $5,000 a year for Detroit in '52, and Detroit was a good-paying team. A lot of clubs didn't pay you for pre-season games and camp. Detroit did. They gave us 'laundry money,' as they called it—$25 a week during the pre-season. So, that talk of retirement in '60 was really just about money. You know, I added up all the money I ever made in my career from '52 -'62—and, remember, I played on three championship teams, and three second-place teams in that time—and I made a total of $110,000."

The Birds will be in Hershey less than three weeks before flying to Los Angeles for their exhibition-season opener against the Los Angeles Rams. In a 1960 interview at Hershey, Shaw talks about some radical shake-ups in the line-up that he's considering, and the improved line play he anticipates due to some somewhat scientifically questionable off-season, weight-adding programs.

"I'm going to try (tight end) Bobby Walston at deep defensive safety, and move Art Powell (a defensive back in 1959) to offensive end. I also want to prepare some guys, like Pellegrini and Bednarik, to play both ways this year. We can increase our depth by using both the offensive and defensive skills of some of our guys. We had lots of trouble on our line, offensively and defensively, last year. So, we tried some weight-adding programs off-season. The programs seem to have worked. Ed Khayat (a defensive lineman) has upped his beef from 225 last year to 255. Gerry Huth (an offensive lineman) has gone from 215 up to 228, and linebacker John Nocera is up to 230 from 215. Maybe that'll help bolster those lines some."

Khayat has indeed beefed up in the off-season. In a 1960 Hershey interview, he explains his "weight-adding" program, which was hardly cutting-edge stuff even for the '60s.

"I just ate. I forced myself to eat. I'm playing defense up here in the pros, so I need some meat. When I was at Tulane, I was an offensive end, and I was more interested in speed than bulk. It wasn't hard to force myself to eat. If that was my job for the off-season, it was better than some of the summer jobs I had in college. I used to load box cars of fertilizer. Northern boys couldn't handle the heat to do something like that, but we Gulf Coast boys are used to it. Eating was easier to do than that job."

On the second day of camp, Shaw trades fullback Walt Kowalczck for Jerry Reichow. Kowalczyk, the Eagles' second draft choice in 1959, never fulfilled the promise he showed in college. The 6-0, 205-pound Michigan State All-American rushed 26 times in 1959 for a paltry 37 yards. In Reichow, who plays end and quarterback, Shaw acquires a seasoned, versatile performer, who adds arms and legs to the coach's versatility strategy. A Philly sportswriter comments that the Eagles' trade is as lopsided in the Birds' favor as was "the purchase of Manhattan island from the Indians for 24 bucks."

~ Reichow Will Never Know ~

"Dutch knew I wasn't happy in Detroit," Jerry Reichow reflects from a hotel room somewhere in Arizona. The ex-Eagle end is a scout with the Minnesota Vikings these days. He's been associated with the Vikings in various capacities since 1961, when Vikings first-year head coach, Norm Van Brocklin, plucked him from the Eagles for the Vikings. "Back in '60, I knew Van Brocklin was planning to retire soon, so going to Philadelphia was attractive for me," Reichow reflects on the trade that brought him to the Quaker City. "I wanted to be a quarterback but in Detroit I was stuck behind Bobby Layne and Tobin Rote. Of course, when I got to Philadelphia, they had this red-headed guy named Jurgensen on the bench —so I moved over with the receivers."

Reichow was one of the veterans Shaw brought in at Van Brocklin's recommendation. The cadre of veterans brought balance and experience to the '60 team, which Reichow ranks as the tightest unit he's seen in almost a half-century of football.

"The first day I arrived in Hershey, I went out with the guys to a local place where they all hung out. I think the name of the place was Johnny Martini's. The whole team was there! I wasn't used to that. In Detroit, they didn't have the kind of togetherness Philadelphia had. Van Brocklin was the one that brought everyone together. He did the same thing every Monday during the season. Monday was our day off, so the whole team would spend the day at Donoghue's, near the Walnut Park Plaza. The Philly gang was really unique that way. I felt welcome and accepted immediately. Even finding a place to live went smooth. I switched houses with

End Jerry Reichow (#17), spent only one year in Philadelphia—that championship season.

Walt Kowalczyk, who I was traded for. We switched teams and we switched houses."

Reichow didn't catch a pass for the '60 Eagles. In '61, he made All-Pro as a Viking receiver. Reichow sums up the biggest frustration of his career this way: "I had some good years receiving in Minnesota. But even with the Vikings, I wanted to try my hand at quarterback. Unfortunately for me, they had Fran Tarkenton, who wound up in the Hall of Fame, too. Everywhere I went, they had a Hall of Fame quarterback – they had two of them in Philadelphia! I never did find out if I could play that position."

Reichow's arrival stuffs the Eagles' quarterback sack fuller. Besides Van Brocklin and Reichow, the Eagles have the still-unsigned Sonny Jurgensen, as well as Jack Cummings, a graduate of Lower Merion High School in the Philadelphia suburbs. Quarterback remains the Eagles' most solid position. There is no competition for the starting job, however. That belongs to Norm Van Brocklin.

~ Hoping for a Birdie ~

An early fissure in the '60s Generation Gap propagates in the Eagle front office during the Hershey camp. Sonny Jurgensen tells GM Vince McNally that he wants a contract with "more heat in it." The infuriated McNally blasts to the press: "I don't dig jive talk. Besides, 46 minutes!! ..." McNally is referring to the 46 minutes of playing time that Sonny Jurgensen has logged since he was plunked behind Van Brocklin two years before. The press is unsympathetic to Jurgensen. One Philly paper refers to him as "Van Brocklin's recalcitrant understudy."

In this battle, Jurgensen is more savvy than his old-line adversary, McNally. As Bob Dylan will soon write, the times they are a-changing—even in pro football. The fledgling AFL is luring quarterbacks away from the NFL, offering salaries between $11,000 and $15,000. Jurgensen can do the math. He may have played only 46 minutes in two years, but he has enormous market value. A legion of former NFL quarterbacks, dismissed as washed-up, mediocre, or marginal, like Jack Kemp, George Blanda, Dick Jamieson, Al Dorow, Babe Parilli, and Tom Dublinski, are finding new careers in the AFL. Jamieson was once an Eagle reserve, buried deep on the depth chart. Jamieson has found new life—and new cash—in the AFL. On the other hand, quarterbacks like Jurgensen know that a jump to the AFL is risky. Every professional football league in history, other than the NFL, has folded. Nonetheless, with the burgeoning television market, the prospects for this latest rendition of the AFL seem brighter than its predecessors.

Jurgensen's hold-out, according to the implications of the Philly pundits in 1960, prompts the Reichow deal. Reichow's ability to play quarterback makes Sonny more expendable. Apparently, the hubbub didn't phase Sonny at the time. Today, he doesn't even remember holding out in '60.

JURGENSEN: "I hadn't signed? I don't remember that. I imagine I just wanted more money. I thought you were talking about my other hold-out, the one in 1963. That one I remember 'cause it was kind of unique. I didn't hold out for more money for myself. I held out for more money for King Hill, our back-up quarterback. King and I both left training camp in Hershey together. It's not like we sneaked out or anything. The coaches knew we were going to do it. I told them! It shouldn't have surprised anyone. The Eagles sent Tommy Brookshier and Jack Whitaker, the announcer, out to find us. They caught up with us on the green at Merion Country Club. Brookie asked me what I was going to do, and I told him: 'Hopefully, I'm going to sink this putt for a birdie.'"

Future Hall of Fame quarterback, Sonny Jurgensen(#9), was Van Brocklin's back-up in 1960.

The Eagles appear to have an adequate punting game. Van Brocklin, along with running backs Clarence Peaks and Joe Pagliel can all punt, as can the rookie hopeful Cummings. Kicking-off and place-kicking are different stories. With Dick Bielski's departure, the Eagles have no one with "end-zone-reaching leg boom," as Buck Shaw terms it. Their 1959 place-kicker, Paige Cothren, a former Ole Miss fullback, has departed. Cothren was the first player in the club's history to place-kick exclusively. In the days of 36-man rosters, specialization like that was a luxury most teams couldn't afford.

Cothren came to the Birds via the Rams, who drafted him in 1957 in the 22nd round. The Ole Miss product nailed 14 field goals in his sophomore year to top the league. He led in field-goal percentage as well, connecting on 56 percent of his attempts. After his swap to the Birds in 1959, however, his production slipped calamitously. In 1959, Cothren connected on only eight of 18 attempts, for an accuracy of 44.4 percent.

Like Aschbacher, Cothren asks the Eagle management if he can miss a few weeks of training camp (Hershey seemed like the place *not* to be in 1960). The Eagles refuse, and release him even though they have no solid replacement on board. The candidates most likely to succeed are two vets: Bednarik, who has never kicked a field goal in the pros, and Bobby Walston, a place-kicker in past years whose leg is now considered dead.

As camp rolls on, another name drops from the active rolls. Darrel Aschbacher has indeed gone off to find the skies, never to suit up again. His retirement weakens an already shaky Philadelphia offensive line. Bucko Kilroy is touting rookie Gene Gossage to step in for Aschbacher when he joins the Eagles following the College All-Star game. Kilroy is in Chicago at the College All-Star training camp, where Gossage has turned out to be the fastest lineman in camp. Shaw is skeptical, though. He says he doesn't trust linemen with speed. In a 1960 interview, Shaw observes that fast lineman never seem to make it in the pro game. The Eagle chief prefers his linemen bulky, not fast. He feels they can't be both.

Fortunately, on August 10, with camp about to end, the Eagles get good news. Stan Campbell is back, his "retirement" ended.

The problems the Eagles have drawing their players to Hershey in 1960 belies the atmosphere of the camp. It is far from Devil's Island, as Theron Sapp remembers:

THERON SAPP: "I recall the first time I saw Hershey, with that park, and all the open spaces. It wasn't what I expected for a pro team's summer camp. I played under Wally Butts at Georgia. He was tough, and his practices were tough. When I got to Buck Shaw's summer camp, I was surprised. I thought to myself, 'With this pace, I can play a long time in this league!' But Buck was a nice man, a gentleman, and he knew what he was doing. He brought his team along so they peaked at the right time, and he didn't risk injuries."

The greatest dramas in camp take place between the defensive backfield

Running back Theron Sapp (#30), broke his hip during the Rams game and stayed in for another play.

and the receivers, where some great competitors lock horns daily in head-to-head competition. Jimmy Carr, generally acknowledged as the team's top prankster, recalls those sessions.

JIMMY CARR: "Brookie and the Baron (Retzlaff) played every snap like it was the championship. Neither one could stand having the other guy beat him. But then again, neither one could stand having anyone beat him. Then there was me and McDonald. I covered Tommy. Of course, Tommy never caught anything off me! I still tell Tommy that's why he caught all those passes in the games. He was starved for the ball after I shut him down all week at practice!"

THE EXHIBITION SEASON

The Eagles break camp and wing out to the West Coast to start their exhibition season. The Eagles open the '60s with a big win, embarrassing the Rams 20-7, in front of 39,480 fans at the Los Angeles Coliseum. Van Brocklin and Retzlaff steal the show. Retzlaff catches 11 passes. The Dutchman, pumped up by the standing ovation from his old fans, completes 15 of 24 pass attempts, good for 210 yards, and two touchdowns. McDonald chips in with a 33-yard TD pass

Left to right: Barnes (#33), Dean (#35), Van Brocklin (#11), Coach Shaw, and McDonald (#25), had high expectations for the 1960 season.

reception. Dick Christy, a Chester (a suburb of Philadelphia) native and Philly favorite, adds another score when he hauls a Van Brocklin pitch into the end zone.

In the euphoria of victory, the Eagles' weaknesses are masked. Even Shaw bubbles over afterwards, which is unlike the cautious Shaw:

"The defense was splendid, holding such a powerful offensive team to seven points while we were scoring 20. It was all the more surprising because we actually only had one real scrimmage in training camp. My, but we've got some tough kids on this team. That Joe Robb, what a blaster he is."

The Eagles use second and third stringers for almost two-thirds of the contest. The highlight for the players, however, is the 42-yard field goal that Chuck Bednarik boots for the final score of the game. Bobby Walston had kicked the team's first 3-pointer from 17 yards out, but Bednarik's field goal is the treat. It's his first as a pro.

Shaw tinkers with his lineup in the contest, hoping to discover some long-term solutions to his defensive problems. He inserts Joe Robb, who had never before played linebacker, at left linebacker. John Nocera starts at right linebacker. Nocera was used mostly as a fill-in at that position in 1959. Chuck Weber is the only starter who had played linebacker regularly in '59. As for the secondary, Shaw leaves the combination of Tom Brookshier, Jim Carr, Gene Johnson, and Art Powell intact, apparently scrapping his scheme about converting Powell to offensive end.

There are some unmistakable problems in the offensive backfield, however. Sonny Jurgensen, who has never been mistaken for Red Grange when he's forced to tuck the ball away, tops all Eagle rushers, gaining 32 yards on six carries. Furthermore, promising running back Theron Sapp breaks his hip in a collision with 290-pound Ram lineman Jon Baker. Shaw grouses that the three inches of loose infield dirt on the Coliseum surface caused the injury. In 1960, prior to the invasion of Astroturf, professional football fields are laid out on top of baseball diamonds, which are still being used for baseball in pre-season games. The infield area poses a constant threat of injury.

~ The Wave ~

"All I remember is that Baker fell on me, and it hurt. I ran into the huddle, and said, 'Don't give me the ball!'," Theron Sapp recalls, crunching back through the years. "You know the way Dutch was. I was worried he'd give me the ball, anyway, just 'cause I said not to. I stayed in for one play after that hit. Then I went off the field, and stayed on the sidelines the rest of the game. They didn't have doctors and medical care back then like they do nowadays. I went back to the hotel and didn't go out that night. All night long, I couldn't sleep. Next day, the team flew to San Francisco for our next game, and all the guys who were hurt, including me, were taken to Palo Alto Hospital. That's when they told me I had a broken hip."

Eddie Khayat laughs and adds another detail to Sapp's story. "Did Theron tell you Billy Ray waved him off after that play?" Khayat asks with a grin. "After Baker got up, Theron looked over at the sideline and motioned to Billy Ray Barnes to come in and take his place. Billy Ray just waved Theron off, and told him to stay in."

Sapp confirms the story. Barnes, his best friend and roommate at the Walnut Park Plaza, figured that getting your bell rung was a poor excuse to come out of a game.

"Of course, Billy had no idea I had a broken hip or that I was hurt seriously," Sapp concludes. "Then again, neither did I."

According to contemporary newspaper accounts, the Rams are not quite at full strength for their battle with the Eagles. One of the Rams' "better linemen," the paper reports, misses the game. On the day of the contest, the unnamed lineman, the paper continues, was "surprised at a friend's house, by the unexpected and ill-timed arrival of an irate boyfriend." Reportedly, he "sat down on a glass-covered coffee table and broke it." The big guy needs numerous stitches to close the wounds and never does make it to the stadium. Times have changed. That's boffo, story-at-eleven stuff in this millennium. His identity is not divulged in the Philadelphia papers, and the Eagles, 40 years later, don't even recall the incident, which had very little play in its day.

~ No Golden Gates ~

For today's generations whose autumnal Sundays are monopolized by the NFL, it may be hard to fathom that, in 1960, the NFL views the AFL as a clear and present danger. Because of competition from the AFL, the NFL in 1960, is scrambling to revamp its traditional way of doing business.

After one week of NFL preseason play, attendance is down drastically. That's a big hurt in the pocketbook. In 1960, the preseason is an economic necessity for professional football. Preseason gate receipts defray the cost of training camp, and anticipated gate receipts, for a variety of reasons, are in jeopardy.

Prior to '60, the NFL staged preseason exhibitions in cities like Denver, Boston, Buffalo, and Houston. The attendance had always been great, but now the

AFL has planted franchises in all those lucrative markets, effectively damming up a tried-and-true NFL preseason revenue stream.

Besides the threat of the AFL, the social forces of the '60s rock the sport's traditional *modus operandi*. In the '40s and '50s, teams like the Eagles scheduled blockbuster exhibition games in the fertile football fields of the south. By the '60s, however, more and more African Americans appear on more and more NFL rosters. Hugh Brown of the Philadelphia *Bulletin* writes in a 1960 article: "... Now, the Eagles and all other NFL teams, except the Redskins, have four to six Negro players. In order to spare these boys the humiliation of being barred from hotels where their white brethren are staying, the teams prefer to skip Southern cities, no matter how profitable they are. The Eagles are scheduled for one exhibition game in Norfolk, VA, but there will be no overnight hotel stay there."

The preseason money pinch is exacerbated on the West Coast. In 1960, the sport dollar does not stretch far enough to support baseball and football simultaneously. The baseball Giants and Dodgers are competing with four football teams: the NFL's 49ers and Rams, as well as the AFL's Oakland Raiders and Los Angeles Chargers. The Raiders, the San Francisco papers lament, are luring spectators away from the 49er exhibition games. In their opening exhibition match, the 49ers drew a measly 13,163 fans into Kezar Stadium, their smallest crowd since 1946. Attendance for their upcoming game against the Eagles is not expected to crack 20,000. The poor attendance in San Francisco is not just San Francisco's problem. It ripples through the rest of the NFL. Visiting clubs receive a percentage of the home-team's gate — the clubs use this cash to defray training-camp expenses. The Eagles' bean counters estimate that they need more than 39,000 spectators to show up for the San Francisco game just to break even for their trip west. It's a major cash outlay for an eastern club like the Eagles to cavalcade to the west coast in the '60s. Air fare costs $360 a person on a chartered plane. In addition, the club picks up the room and board for a coterie of about 50. And, then, of course, there's the new breed of players ... A Philly newspaper article denounces the "irresponsible spending of Eagle players" on the trip, grousing in one of its columns that: "A greedy 245-pound lineman actually signed for an extravagant $6.60 lunch, plus a 15% tip in Los Angeles."

John Wittenborn came to the Eagles after playing three games with San Francisco in 1960. Wittenborn remembers the financial and practical pinch that the transportation of the era put on the sport.

JOHN WITTENBORN: "San Francisco and Los Angeles used to schedule a whole series of games in the East or the Midwest so they wouldn't have to fly back and forth. Travel then wasn't like it is now. You didn't fly out to Philadelphia, play a game, and then fly back out West. It was an ordeal to go coast-to-coast. It took a long time, and it was expensive. San Francisco always scheduled away games in bunches—not only in the preseason, but in the regular season as well. In fact, I found out about my trade to Philly when we (San Francisco) were in the midst of our Midwest swing. After we had played our first two games at home, we flew out and played Detroit, Chicago, and Green Bay on consecutive Sundays. I never made it to Green Bay that year because of my trade to Philadelphia. I found out I had been traded when we were in Chicago. I didn't make it back to San Francisco. We weren't scheduled to return there for another two weeks."

There's a lot of talk as the Sixties break about the dilution of talent, now that there are so many professional teams. The NFL is sensitive to these accusations, and fears a wave of negative fan reaction to pro football's sudden expansion. The San Francisco papers, perhaps in reaction to the AFL-Oakland menace across the bay, lament that the NFL is "so thin in talent that *even* the AFL Oakland Raiders could make meal out of the Washington Redskins."

The preseason picture is disturbing. However, the good news is that regular-season ticket sales on the West Coast are booming. The Rams have already sold 30,000 season tickets (as of mid-August), and the 49ers are projecting sales in excess of 40,000. Both clubs feel that the poor preseason attendance indicates one thing: the average season-ticket holder can't afford to tack the cost of four exhibition games onto an already hefty regular-season tab. But that doesn't mitigate the current problem about how the clubs are going to cover preseason expenses.

The NFL is actively re-thinking the entire preseason system. Most NFL teams in 1960 play six exhibition games. In 1961, when the Minnesota Vikings are slated to join the NFL, the regular-season schedule will bump up from 12 games to 14. By mid-decade, the NFL plans to pump up the total number of franchise to 16, which will only exacerbate the preseason cash-flow problem. To address these financial concerns, there is a serious proposal on the table, in August, 1960, to count three of the six preseason games in the official final standings. Otherwise, economics may dictate that the preseason schedule be cut back to four games or fewer.

The Birds are confident and loose after the win over the Rams. On the flight from Los Angeles to San Francisco, Tom Brookshier zeros in on Eagle trainer Tom McCoy, who is terrified of flying. In mid-flight, Brookshier gets on the intercom, and announces that the number two engine is malfunctioning. McCoy bolts upright, food tray flying. The embarrassed McCoy dubs Brookie "Jimmy Piersall," after the colorful, tragic Cleveland Indian outfielder of the time, whose bouts with mental illness were dramatized in the 1957 film, "Fear Strikes Out." Brookshier, today, looks back on the incident, and adds:

TOM BROOKSHIER: "You know, we might have carried it a little too far. Some of the guys were pretending to get parachutes out and throwing them on the

On July 1, 1960, a beaming Tom Brookshier signed his contract. Head Coach Buck Shaw and general manager Vince McNally look on.

floor. We stopped clowning real quick, though. Chuck (Bednarik) had enough. Remember, Number 60 went through hell in the war, flying all those bombing raids. He grabbed me and told me to cut it out. You don't say no to Chuck. That ended it."

Brookshier is one of the most sought-after players in the league. The Eagles declare him untouchable, which doesn't deter the rest of the league from making offers for him. The Eagles, still negotiating feverishly for new players, nix a deal for Leon Clarke, the Rams' fleet 235-pound, offensive end. The Birds have long coveted Clarke, but the deal flops because the Rams insist on Brookshier in exchange. Clarke goes instead to the Cleveland Browns for linebacker Bob Long. Clarke probably reaps more notoriety (and money) from his marriage to the heiress to the Beechnut chewing gum and baby food millions than from his football skills.

The game against San Francisco turns into a spectacle. The Eagles' four College All-Stars join the team prior to the game, which Jurgensen starts at quarterback for the first time since Van Brocklin's arrival. The 49ers counter with John Brodie, their own talented backup quarterback to Yelberton Abraham (Y. A.) Tittle, a 12-year veteran, who, like Van Brocklin, is performing spectacularly in the twilight of his career. Jerry Reichow is another substitute, replacing Bobby Walston at tight end.

It's a strange night for the Birds, as the 49ers wallop them 45-24, in front of 17,677 at Kezar Stadium. History repeats itself as the two squads stage an extended free-for-all that turns increasingly ugly. The two teams had brawled in the 1953 regular-season game at Kezar Stadium, but this time it's worse. Even General Manager Vince McNally gets into the fray, according to contemporary articles. In his August 25th *Philadelphia Bulletin* column, Hugh Brown gives the following account:

"The spark that ignited the melee was touched off by 49er rookie Fred Williamson when he kicked John Nocera in the head while the Eagle linebacker was lying on the ground near the sideline. Then, the battle became general when 49er halfback Hugh McElhenny kicked the Eagle defensive lineman Ed Khayat on the head when he, too, was lying prone."

San Francisco's Williamson gains notoriety later that decade. San Francisco deals him to the Steelers, where he stays for a year, before finally settling down in Kansas City in the AFL. Proclaiming himself "The Hammer," before Super Bowl I, and promising to "hammer" the Packers, Williamson is the one who gets hammered—hammered and carried off the field. The Hammer heads for celluloid pastures and a career in films.

~ An Eagle to the Max ~

Eddie Khayat remembers the brawl in San Francisco. It started up right around him.

KHAYAT: "I got kicked in the head really hard. Next time I could see anything, I was in the end zone. I got a concussion and I had double vision. Everywhere I looked around that field, there were people scuffling. But old Maxie (Baughan), he was something. He chased McIlhenny for 40 yards and caught up to him. That McIlhenney could run, too, and don't forget, Maxie was a linebacker. That was the first time the Eagles met Maxie. He just came over and joined us from the College All-Stars before that game. But, when we saw him catch McIlhenney and get into it with him—well, Maxie became an Eagle that night."

It was must have been pretty impressive for Maxie to catch a back with McIlhenney's speed. He must have had some good jets himself.

MAXIE: "Oh, sure, I caught him within 40 yards, but the two main reasons for that were that, first, McIlhenney ran out of field at that point. He was in the end zone when I caught him. And, second, he was running backwards the whole time."

The Eagles' performance in the City by the Bay is not completely bleak. First of all, at this point in his career, Sonny Jurgensen is not the mature, unflappable Hall of Famer he later becomes. The 49ers "red-dog," or blitz him incessantly. By the time the ex-Duke star is lifted, the Eagles are facing a 24-7 deficit. But when Van Brocklin takes over at the helm, the Birds tack on 21 points in a half. Rookie halfback Ted Dean gambols 74 yards for a score on a pitchout in his first Eagle appearance. And the final ledger for total yardage favors the Eagles, 322 yards to 305. The offense has once again put points on the board. Shaw, however, is dissatisfied with the offensive line play. "Our pass blocking stinks," Shaw gripes.

After the game, the Eagles, in an unexpected move, place Art Powell on waivers, shrinking the squad to 42. Powell has been starting the entire preseason in the defensive backfield. In 1959, "King Pin," as Powell is nicknamed, ran 17 kickoffs back for 379 yards, and returned 15 punts for 124 yards. He would go on to a very impressive career, leading the AFL in receiving yardage in 1962 as a Titan, and again in 1963, as an Oakland Raider. Powell ends a 10-year pro career in 1968, amassing 8,045 in receiving yards, and earning a spot in the top 50 receivers on the all-time list for yards gained.

Powell's release is prompted by the emergence of two exciting newcomers to the Eagles: Ted Dean and Timmy Brown. Kilroy raves about Dean's stellar performance at the College All-Star camp. Meanwhile, Timmy Brown is daily dispelling naysayers who claimed he couldn't hold on to the ball. Brown was the 27th-round draft choice of the Green Bay Packers in 1959, but Lombardi axed him after the second regular-season game. In a 1960 pre-season interview, Brown explains why:

"Lombardi told me it was because I fumbled, but really, I never got a chance there. I wasn't the type of runner Lombardi likes. They liked power guys like Taylor, Hornung, Lew Carpenter, Don McIlhenny, and Howie Ferguson. I wanted to try to make it as a defensive back, but they had no place for me."

The Eagles rebound the following week, beating up conference rival Washington Redskins, 24-6 in Norfolk Virginia. Again, Jurgensen starts. Again the Redskins blitz the inexperienced Jurgensen into confusion. He plays the first half, leaving the game with the Eagles ahead, 7-6. The Rams, the 49ers, and now the Skins have made the young quarterback tentative and halting with the same tactic. Looking back at the era from today's vantage point, Jurgensen remarks:

JURGENSEN: "I was still green at that point in my career. Quarterback is a tough position to learn, and the only way you learn is by standing back there."

What is it that Sonny learned?

JURGENSEN: "Get rid of the damn ball! Don't hold on to it, or they'll kill you."

Billy Barnes, who makes a career of great performances against Washington, burns Foreman Field for 129 yards on only 16 carries. Barnes explains: "The folks back home (in North Carolina) only get to see me when we play Washington. I always put a little extra into that game, to give the boys back home a show."

~ The Tumbleweed in a Wind Storm ~

Billy Ray Barnes was the Eagles' top ground gainer in 1958 and 1959. His rushing totals increased from 551 yards in 1958 to 687 yards (his career best) in 1959. He made All-Pro his first three seasons in the NFL. His running style, which was likened to a tumbleweed in a windstorm, shortened his career. Barnes flung his body recklessly, scrapping for every extra inch of turf. He did not have a stellar season in '60. His individual statistics slipped significantly after 1959, yet Billy Ray was a central figure on the 1960 championship squad. Several teammates finger Billy Ray Barnes as the guy who most epitomized the heart, soul, and spirit of that championship squad. Barnes was fiercely loyal to his team and teammates. He still is. He was totally dedicated to winning each Sunday. And, in between Sundays, the ex-Wake Forest star was a bona fide character—a hard-living bachelor, always up for a prank, a good time, and a rock-'em-sock-'em football game. Everyone on the '60 Eagles has a Billy Ray Barnes story. Most have several.

Barnesy wore jersey number 33 with the Eagles—the same number he wore at his alma mater, Wake Forest, an academically respected institution. Billy Ray, who is still active at Wake Forest, tells a tale about a youngster who asked Billy what his score in the SAT's was when he applied to Wake Forest.

BARNES: "I said, 'Well, you know, son, when I went to school in the early '50s, we didn't really have the SATs. But that doesn't mean I don't know what it stands for. It means "Starting At Tailback."'"

Billy Ray Barnes (#33), was the Eagles' leading rusher in '57, '58, '59.

The Eagles move on to Norman, Oklahoma, home of the University of Oklahoma, to take on the Detroit Lions. In front of 32,500 screaming fans, Tommy McDonald seals a triumphant homecoming by catching seven passes for 202 yards, including a pair of TD's, to lead his team to a 40-10 laugher. Van Brocklin tosses 20 passes, completing 13 for 250 yards, despite missing practice all week. Dutch had been excused from practice so he could shoot a commercial in New York for Vitalis, a popular hair preparation product in the '60s.

In beating up on the Lions, Timmy Brown erases any anxiety about Art Powell's release. Brown hauls a first-half kickoff back 59 yards, reprising in the third period with a punt return of 46 yards.

Eagle confidence is swelling. Tom Brookshier, a spokesman for the club all year long, is quoted in the Philadelphia press: "We're a cinch to go all the way for an Eastern title."

Buck Shaw is not quite so optimistic: "Our blocking on running plays wasn't good, our defense was ragged, and if the Lions had anyone throwing besides Morrall, they would have had three more touchdowns." Obviously Shaw couldn't foresee the rest of Earl Morrall's career. The quarterback Shaw maligns that evening will go on to top the NFL in 1968 with 26 TD passes, in leading the Colts to a 13-1 season, and an NFL championship. Unfortunately, Morrall picked Super Bowl III that year to have one of the worst days of his career, and pave the path to immortality for Joe Namath and his Jets.

The Eagle contingent heads next to St. Louis. Their September 10 clash with the Cardinals will mark the first time the St. Louis Cardinals play in their new home. The Cardinals have just moved there from Chicago, where the franchise has been situated since the birth of the NFL. Joe Griesedieck, a midwest brewery tycoon, engineered the franchise's move to the Gateway City by guaranteeing season ticket sales of 25,000. As of late August, only 15,000 season tickets have been sold.

The Eagles' plane touches ground in the middle of a searing Midwest heat storm and drought. Shaw rejects every practice field the Cardinals offer him, because the ground, everywhere, is baked rock hard by ten straight days of torrid sun. The Silver Fox is convinced that hard surfaces ruin knees. Some of Shaw's old-world notions ring true. Had his opinion been more accepted in sport circles in the '60s and '70s, the number of knee problems among professional athletes for the past 40 years might have dropped significantly.

Eventually, Shaw finds a suitable field at Mercy High School. The school's Athletic Director had watered this field daily throughout the drought, rendering it usable. Shaw pushes practice time up to 10 AM to skirt the 98-degree afternoon heat. Suspiciously, 13 Eagles miss practice with injuries suffered in the Lions' game. Shaw notes that the hotel pool seems unusually crowded.

Right before the Cardinal game, the Eagles cut two Philly natives, Dick Christy and Jack Cummings. Christy, a graduate of St. James High School, signs with the Boston Patriots. Christy gains 363 yards in '60 with the Patriots. The following year, he joins the New York Titans, where he reunites with Art Powell and Lee Riley, and spends three productive years before retiring. Cummings, who fails to latch on with another pro team, leaves pro football.

~ Another Roundup for the Cowboys ~

The war for Texas is on, and Dallas is the battlefront. Though Texas is the largest of the contiguous 48 states, pro football has managed to cram two new franchises in one year into one Texas city, Dallas. The AFL Dallas Texans and the NFL Dallas Cowboys are grappling for the pro-football buck, and NFL Commissioner Pete Rozelle feels it's strategically important for the NFL to come out on top. It won't be easy.

The Cowboys' cross-town rivals, the Dallas Texans, are competing in the brand-new AFL, where they'll be much more evenly matched, and therefore more likely to draw fans. Texans love winners. To complicate matters, the fledgling Cowboys are plagued with injury problems. Only four games into the exhibition season, 12 of the Cowboys players are sidelined. Five of them will miss the entire season. Commissioner Rozelle decrees that each NFL team must now surrender yet another player to the fledgling Dallas Cowboys.

The Eagles lose the battle of the birds in St. Louis, as the Cardinals prevail, 34-13, in front of 25,000 at Busch Stadium. The Cardinals bounce back in this game, having been soundly trounced the previous week, 35-14, by the Packers. Inconsistency haunts the Cardinals all year. St. Louis is coached by Frank "Pop" Ivy, who has concocted a complicated, razzle-dazzle offense. Fans love it. Unfortunately, the offensive unit is often as baffled as the spectators. Ivy's offense tends to make bad things happen at bad times, as their 1959 league-leading 46 fumbles attest. That's an average of 3.83 fumbles per game.

Tonight, however, the St. Louis offense is humming, while the Eagles' is ho-humming. Baughan, Weber, and Van Brocklin all sit the game out. Baughan nurses an ankle he twisted when he stepped in a rut at the stadium in Norman, Oklahoma. Van Brocklin sits the game out with a cut on his thumb that he got while opening a soft-drink bottle the Thursday before the game. The cut required four stitches, so Dutch takes it easy.

The Birds' inability to run is alarming. They fail to gain a single first down rushing, and the top Philadelphia rusher, Billy Barnes, gains but 30 yards on nine carries. With Baughan and Weber both sidelined, Concrete Charley Bednarik, who is enjoying a sensational preseason, gets his first work at linebacker.

The day after the game, September 11, the *Philadelphia Bulletin's* Fall Football guide hits the stands. Photos of four area college coaches appear on the cover of this supplement, which is meager in content and coverage by today's standards. On the cover, there is no mention of the Eagles, the NFL, or pro football. Inside,

Hugh Brown, the *Philadelphia Bulletin* sportswriter assigned to the Eagles, writes every line of copy about the NFL, which amounts to three or four pages of material. The rest of the supplement is devoted, exclusively, to area college and high school football.

In the Guide, writer Brown forecasts the NFL finishers. Brown picks the Eagles to win the east—although he hedges, somewhat, with the caveat that they must remain healthy to do so. He picks the Packers in the west. Hugh Brown may be the only writer in the country to pick *both* the Eagles and Packers. Brown's are maverick choices. Nationally, the press vacillates between the Giants and the Browns in the East. The West is all but conceded to the Colts, NFL champs in '58 and '59.

BRIDLING THE COLTS

The Eagles were admittedly flat against the Cardinals. Feeling like bona fide contenders, the Eagles had looked beyond St. Louis to the Colts. Baltimore is football's elite, a great test of true mettle. The Baltimore defensive line, anchored by Big Daddy Lipscomb and Gino Marchetti, is the most famous and feared in football. The previous week, the Colts' defense showed they're still intimidating, throwing Redskin quarterbacks Eagle Day and M. C. Reynolds for 75 yards of losses. Quarterback Johnny Unitas remains the most recognized football name in the country. His corps of receivers: Lenny Moore, Raymond Berry, and Jim Mutscheller, are generally acknowledged as tops in the sport. Moore, Penn State's pride and joy, is the game's most exciting deep threat; while Berry is considered its most sure-handed receiver.

The Eagles' practice sessions become more spirited, prepping for the showdown against the Colts. Shaw decries his team's practice sessions of the previous fortnight, describing them as "patty-caking in shorts." The Oklahoma and Missouri heat left his team more lethargic than lethal. In an interview before the Colts' game, Chuck Bednarik agrees: "All the lads felt that way, like we haven't been practicing hard enough. We've been fooling around far too long in our underwear. The only way to practice is to put on our pads and sock away."

The intensity of the sessions picks up. Rookie Gene Gossage and Eddie Khayat have a minor scrape. Veterans like Bednarik and Pellegrini yell and stoke the team's fires for the big battle. Still, the Eagles manage to temper everything with a sense of humor. Offensive lineman, Jim McCusker recalls their practice sessions.

JIM McCUSKER: "Pellegrini was a fiery guy, a good leader. We knew how to get to him, though. He was the MVP in the College All-Star game after his senior year. When he gave his acceptance speech for the award, he said: 'I owe it all to my *dog*.' He meant to say 'to his *dad*.' So, whenever Pelly would make a mistake, or start yelling, the guys would start barking at him. It was just one of those things that kept us all loose."

The defensive line gets a big boost when Marion Campbell returns, his recovery from knee surgery complete. Selected for the 1959 Pro Bowl, the big, defensive end is considered the Eagles' best pass rusher. Van Brocklin also insists the Swamp Fox, as Marion Campbell is called, is the strongest man in football. His only competition, according to Van Brocklin, comes from the 49ers future Hall of Famer Leo Nomellini, who was born in Lucca, Italy.

~ Mr. Fox, I Presume ~

In 1983, Marion Campbell succeeded Dick Vermeil as the Eagles' 15th head coach. Marion had played his collegiate football at the University of Georgia, before being selected by the NFL's San Francisco 49ers in the fourth round of the 1954 draft. He was given the name "Swamp Fox" by Don McGill, a Public Relations guy at Georgia. No, the Swamp Fox, insists, he is not related to Francis Marion, the original Swamp Fox of the Revolutionary War. However, the nickname stuck. Pete Retzlaff recalls that, when one of the Eagles' rookie receivers arrived in camp, and Marion was introduced to him as "Swamp Fox," the rookie blurted out, in all seriousness: "It's a pleasure to meet you, Mr. Fox."

As for the Colts, they, too, are up for the game. Baltimore wants to roll into the regular season with momentum on their side. The Colts are striving to win three consecutive championship games. No other team has ever done that. The Packers won three consecutive titles in '29, '30, and '31, but in those years, there were no conferences, and no championship games. Teams were awarded the championship solely by virtue of their seasonal record.

The Eagles and Colts face off in Hershey Stadium. The condition of the turf is a pre-game concern. Two high school games and a scrimmage between Penn and Rutgers have been played in the two days immediately preceding the game. Nevertheless, the turf is in surprisingly good shape for the Eagles-Colts tiff.

The Eagles' performance this night quiets even the most cynical Quaker City fans, giving wing to the sentiment that "Maybe these guys are for real." Philadelphia humbles the proud champs, 35-21, before a record-setting Hershey Stadium crowd of 20,325. Van Brocklin is superb, outdueling his counterpart, Unitas, whose performance suffers without two of his favorite targets: Mutscheller and Lenny Moore. Notwithstanding their absence from the line-up, the Eagles display very few weaknesses in their most solid performance of the preseason. The most heartening sign for the coaching staff is the Eagle running attack, which rolls up an astonishing 279 yards—the Birds' highest total in years. Tacking on Van Brocklin's

Marion Campbell, the Swamp Fox, became the Eagles head coach in 1983.

242 aerial yards, the Eagles' offense looks unstoppable. Clarence Peaks, a former Michigan State All-American, enjoys a career night, piling up 144 yards on 13 carries. Ted Dean, hailed in the papers now as the "Rampaging Radnor Rookie," carries nine times for 80 yards.

Despite the elation of their big victory, the Eagles are still entering the regular campaign with some flagrant weaknesses. Their line play on both sides of the ball has been inconsistent. Their running game has been spotty and unreliable. Their pass rush has been anemic, though the return of Marion Campbell should jack up the line play. Shaw makes some last-minute adjustments. Prior to the Colts game, 245-pound Emmett Wilson is dealt to the Washington Redskins for Dick Lucas, a 215-pound ex-Boston College star and three-year Redskin veteran. Confident that the linebacking corps of Joe Robb, John Nocera, Chuck Weber, and Maxie Baughan is solid, the Birds put rookie backer Tom Addison on waivers. The release of Addison (who is picked up by the Patriots and enjoys an eight-year career in Boston) reduces the roster to 40. Two more bodies must be released before the Tuesday following the Colt game in order to reach the expanded league minimum of 38.

~ *Roster Schemes* ~

Times have changed. In September, 1960, Pete Rozelle increased the NFL roster limit from 36 to 38. That's ho-hum news nowadays, but in 1960, some fans were incensed about the new measure. The fans who had grown up in earlier decades when roster limits of 15 and 18 were legislated, considered a roster of 38 bloated. More important, to a generation that experienced the Depression, it was wasteful. Many fans back in 1960 resented paying a ball player $10,000 a year just to stand on the sidelines and do nothing. The sentiment was that these guys were not ballplayers, but spectators, and, therefore, undeserving of a paycheck. Some of the sport writers had a more sinister spin on the motive behind the measure. *Philadelphia Bulletin* columnist Hugh Brown explored that driving force in 1960 in a scathing article titled, "Kickoff of the Golden Years for Pro Gridders." Brown wrote:

"The roar of the sweet boy is being heard throughout the land. . . The NFL is expected to increase the maximum player roster from 36 to 38. Thus, with 13 teams in operation, a total of 26 sweet boys over the norm will have found a happy haven at the cashier's wicket."

Brown continues:

"In their plan to increase each roster to 38, the NFL padrones have not been motivated by pure altruism. Retention of two more broadbacks is expected to add about $20,000 to each team's payroll, but considering the benefits that will accrue, the money couldn't be better used unless it were sent to the income tax conscience fund."

Brown's charge, here, is that the owners will get their money back—and then some—by adding two more players to their 1960 rosters. The Minneapolis Vikings are slated to come into the NFL in 1961. The Vikings are required to pay each existing NFL franchise $60,000 for the three players they select from a list of players that each team must provide. The same process was used to create the Dallas Cowboys in 1960. Brown charges that, by increasing the squad size to 38, each team will have two expendable bodies to provide Minnesota. The owners will also, he goes on, reap a good payback by so doing. According to Brown's math, given that each team will receive $60,000 for the two extra players they surrender, each team will incur an added expense of $20,000 for carrying the two players this year. Since these guys don't really add value to the team, in Brown's mind, they have what amounts to patronage jobs. Brown concludes that there will be:

". . . a $40,000 profit for each gifter (team owner), which is fair enough considering the time and money spent in finding, baiting and training these players."

Some owners are opposed to the idea of a roster increase. The bell had not officially rung for football's enlightened era where every financial opportunity is siezed with gusto. Or maybe it had. How else can the Runner-Up Bowl be explained? In any event, some owners only see the added short-term expense. They don't want to pay the extra freight this year, even if it reaps them a $40,000 windfall next year. Of course, the owners in the '60s are basically the same group who owned the franchises in the '30s when passions revolved around roster *minimums*, not maximums. Those minimums were mandated to shortstop frugal owners from thinning rosters to such an extent that a couple of injuries prevented a team from fielding 11 players.

On Wednesday, before the season opener against the Cleveland Browns, a freak injury occurs that profoundly shakes up the entire defensive structure. Jimmy Carr, in a no-contact scrimmage, defenses Ted Dean on a swing pass. Carr puts his hands on Dean, leaps to avoid him, and catches his cleats in a rut. Carr tears ankle ligaments and is forced to the sideline for a few weeks, thus missing the opener. Carr remembers the incident well.

JIMMY CARR: You know what I was really doing? I was clowning around. I jumped real high, and came down on my ankle. I knew it was hurt pretty bad right away, but the guys wouldn't believe me. They thought I was still clowning around. Then the ankle swelled so bad in a couple of minutes, they had to believe me."

Suddenly, Shaw's entire defensive scheme is scrambled. Brookshier and Carr are his only experienced defensive backs. The other three, Gene Johnson, Bobby Jackson, and Jim Nieman have a combined one year's worth of pro experience. To address the situation, Shaw contemplates a complete shake-up that will alter both his offense and defense. He plans to move starting offensive end, Bobby Walston, to the defensive backfield, and return Bob Pellegrini and Chuck Bednarik to linebacker. Both Pelly and Chuck currently start on the offensive line. The coaches also consider trying offensive end, Alden Kimbrough and Timmy Brown as defensive backs.

Suddenly, the Eagle front office pulls a coup. They snag Don Burroughs from the L.A. Rams. The "Blade," as he is called because he "disappears when he turns sideways," is a seasoned 6'-4$\frac{1}{2}$", 190-pound defensive pick-off specialist who grabbed nine interceptions for the Rams in his rookie season in '55. A day after landing Burroughs, the Birds nab Bobby Freeman from the Green Bay Packers. Freeman, at 6'-1$\frac{1}{2}$," and 200 pounds, is a three-year NFL veteran, who spent two years with the Browns, and the previous year with the Pack. Freeman looks back now on his whirlwind introduction to the Quaker City.

BOBBY FREEMAN: "Vince Lombardi called me into his office on Wednesday or Thursday, and told me I was going to Philadelphia. He said Vince McNally of the Eagles had called him because one of their guys got hurt and the Eagles really need someone now. I asked Lombardi about money, so he called McNally up and said the deal was only on if the Eagles would pay one-half of my salary up front. McNally told Lombardi he'd think about it. I was sitting there in Lombardi's office, listening to the conversations between them. About 15 minutes later, McNally calls back and says he'll pay half my salary up-front. That's how it happened. I was on my way to Philadelphia, just like that.

"I sold my station wagon that day in Green Bay. I got to Philly on Friday, and arranged to rent Joe Robb's old house. Friday night, I went up to this big auto dealer that all the guys told me about. It was called Reedman's in Langhorne, and I bought a new car. We didn't practice on Saturdays, so the first time I played with the team was on Sunday in the opener."

Three weeks after Freeman lands in Philly, 12 trunks will arrive in the Eagles' office—one with a bicycle strapped to it. The trunks are all en route to his new apartment in Paulsboro, NJ. Bobby Freeman has officially arrived.

Season ticket sales boom in Philadelphia. The Birds, marketing with the uninspired slogan, "There's no football like pro football," are selling season tickets at a record clip for their six-game home season. The 17,230 season tickets they've sold so far exceeds the previous high of 12,151 set in 1956, and far exceeds the 11,806 season tickets they sold the previous year. As for season-ticket prices, they're selling for $25.50 in the North and South stands, and $15.30 in the East stands. Single-game ticket prices are $6, $5, and $3.

Before each game, the "Norm Van Brocklin Show," presented by Westinghouse, features announcer Bill Campbell and quarterback Norm Van Brocklin discussing Eagle strategy. Van Brocklin's slot is followed by a half-hour show hosted by former Bears' quarterback, Johnny Lujack, who airs highlights from the previous week's games around the NFL. Following each game, M. A. Bruder & Sons sponsors the Byrum Saam Show for a wrap-up of all the day's pro football activity. "By," best known as a Phillies play-by-play man, was also a voice in pro football.

The fans are oblivious to all the front-office scurrying and the domino effect that Carr's injury precipitates. Other than Carr, the Eagles are in tip-top shape for the Cleveland Browns. After the shellacking of the Colts, Philadelphia has gotten behind its Eagles, thinking good times, indeed, may have returned.

Pete Retzlaff, an emerging star throughout the turmoil of Buck Shaw's "three-teams" manipulations and prestidigitations, looks back today and feels the 1960 Eagles had finally gained the stability and strength they needed to win it all.

PETE RETZLAFF: "We left that preseason feeling confident. I don't think the rest of the league viewed us as a big threat. But, we were a different team after that big comeback against the Cardinals in 1959. We had team confidence, and we had a lot of players who were much better than they were given credit for."

Retzlaff was right. The 1960 Eagles had a long list of players who were underappreciated. Pete Retzlaff tops the list.

FiveFiveFive**Five**FiveFiveFive

The Baron

The Baron. Thirty-four years after his retirement, the nickname endures, pinned eternally to one man. Like his uniform number 44, Pete Retzlaff alone can claim it.

Nicknames like Lou "The Toe" Groza, and "Slingin'" Sammy Baugh, gritty and visual, talk football. They're Sunday names, tossed somewhere in the back of the locker with the helmets and the pads when the pigskins aren't flying. The Baron's handle, though, reaches out beyond the mayhem of Sunday's gridiron clashes, and into the mayhem of everyday life. If the word Baron connotes character and class, dignity and dash, then Palmer Edward Retzlaff wears his nickname well, in and out of pads.

There's an air of the extraordinary about the Baron. Talk to teammates and peers. They'll tell you. One after another.

The "Baron von Retzlaff" was a young gallant on the 1960 Eagles. The classic strong, silent type, Retzlaff was a poster boy for everything Cold War America thought our athletes should be. Retzlaff was a role model, shouldering and embracing that responsibility—a responsibility he considered paramount in his profession, more important than catching a football.

Time has little changed Pete Retzlaff. The Baron is substance without volume, confidence without bluster. As a player, he had a loping, athletic stride. His stride today, though less powerful, is no less purposeful. No matter what challenges he has taken on in life, he has succeeded via the measured strides of analysis, practice, and discipline. Teammate Tom Brookshier thinks back to the Baron's playing days, and marvels: "When Pete ran patterns, he was like a diagram come to life. He practiced every step, perfected every move. What an advantage that was to a quarterback like Van Brocklin. He knew he could release the ball before the defense sacked him, and the Baron would end up where he was supposed to be—under the ball."

Pete "The Baron" Retzlaff, spent his entire career with the Philadelphia Eagles.

Brookshier and the Baron go way back. Retzlaff recalls his early days with the Philadelphia Eagles, when the Baron moniker was born.

"You know Tom Brookshier gave me the Baron nickname, don't you?" Retzlaff asks. "I had just come to Philly from the Lions, and we were at training camp in Hershey. A bunch of us went over to Indiantown Gap (a military base in Pennsylvania). We ended up at the rifle range, firing rifles. I had been a First Lieutenant in the Army a few years before, and I was a decent marksman. When I hit the bullseye nine times in nine shots, Brookie started calling me 'The Baron.' It stuck."

It still sticks. Forty-some years later.

Retzlaff had and retains the physical traits of a baron: statuesque bearing, light hair, steely eyes. What's more, his ancestry is authentic. "I have more relatives in Germany than in the U.S.," he points out. But the Baron moniker sticks mostly because of the guy's character.

Defensive back Bobby Freeman says: "Pete was probably more serious-minded than the rest of us. But from the word 'Go,' there's not a finer person. He enjoyed a good laugh as much as any of us, but he just seemed to be on a different level than everyone else when it came down to discipline."

Pete relied on discipline and hard work to succeed. When he got to the pros, he was an unheralded college fullback, thrust suddenly into the roll of receiver, a position he had never played. Retzlaff looks back on those early days with Detroit:

"The Lions drafted me in the 22nd round out of South Dakota State. We were a small school, with a small football program. I probably wasn't given much chance to make the squad. When I came up in 1956, the Lions were overloaded with fullbacks, so they moved me over from fullback to receiver. The Lions really didn't know how to fit me into their plans, though, so they shipped me to Philadelphia."

"At, first, Philadelphia didn't know where to use me, either. The first action I saw as an Eagle was on defense. I played defensive back in my first pre-season game for the Eagles against the Lions at Norman, Oklahoma. Jerry Norton, the regular defensive back, went out of the game with a fractured bone, or, at least, that's what the doctors thought. There was a hair or something on the x-ray film, and they misread it as a fracture. As it turned out, he was fine. But they ended up pulling Jerry out of the game, and putting me in, and I came up with an interception. That was the first pass I caught as an Eagle—an interception."

Pete caught only 22 passes in his first two seasons. When Norm Van Brocklin arrived in 1958, he immediately spotted Retzlaff's raw potential and set about refining it.

"There's no question that Van Brocklin started me down the road to success," Pete admits. "Dutch thought I had potential, and just knowing that he felt that way made me start to believe in myself. The first time Van Brocklin saw me at Hershey, he told everybody: 'That guy runs patterns like Crazy Legs Hirsch.' 'Crazy Legs Hirsch!' I thought. 'That's great!' Hirsch was one of my idols at the time, and I gained confidence just hearing the comparison. Hirsch was a big name in the fifties, starring as himself in the 1953 film biography, 'Crazy Legs.' Van Brocklin also predicts: 'Watch that guy (Retzlaff). He's going to lead this league in pass catching.' Turns out, I did. I tied Ray Berry that year for most catches. I owe a lot to Dutch."

~ *The Maryland Connection* ~

Bob Pellegrini and Dick Bielski were teammates on the University of Maryland championship team of 1953. Bielski was drafted in the first round by the Eagles in 1955; Pellegrini was the number-one pick in 1956. Bielski and Pellegrini have remained close friends. Each is godfather to one of the other's children. Each, as Bielski points out, has a wife who makes terrific pasta. Each watched Pete Retzlaff blossom into a star.

From his Towson, Maryland home, where he owns and operates the Charles Village Pub, Bielski recalls Retzlaff's early days and how he, himself, contributed to Pete's improvement:

DICK BIELSKI: "When Pete got to Philadelphia, he was just a body beautiful guy—big and strong with a great physique—but he wasn't loaded with natural football talent. He didn't know how to catch a football. I told him: 'If you're going to make it in this league, you've got to be able to catch the ball.' I wish I hadn't said it. He wore my ass out. He made me throw passes to him for hours. Everybody else would be long gone, and the two of us would still be out there on the practice field throwing and catching. You could see Pete's determination, though. I spent 30 years in football, 21 of them as a coach for the Colts and Redskins, and Pete Retzlaff was the most successful self-made player I ever saw."

Retzlaff admits to having targeted linebackers to quarterback for him, noting: "You can *always* get a linebacker to throw you passes. They're all frustrated quarterbacks!" Bob Pellegrini was a bruising linebacker in the '50s and '60s. The ex-Marylander, who has worked for Showboat Casinos for years, shares the same recollections about Retzlaff as his crony, Bielski:

Pete Retzlaff, Tom Tracey, Maxie Baughan, and Chuck Bednarik visit the set of the popular TV show "Sgt. Bilko."

"Pete had that Joe Palooka body. He was one of the few players in those days with that kind of physique. In our day, we didn't work out like these guys do today. We didn't have trainers and weight programs. Pete worked on his own personal program. The guy worked hard at everything. That was his style. And, since he didn't catch the ball in college, he had to learn how to do it up here, which isn't easy. So, Pete was always looking for people to throw him the ball—guys like Bielski and me. I always felt Pete was the guy on our team who grew the most in every facet of life. He grew as a player, a person, a leader—everything. He commanded respect, without having to scream or yell. He could settle disputes in his own sort of Midwest, cornpone way. He turned into a terrific leader."

By 1960, Retzlaff had matured into a team leader. The Baron played a key role in galvanizing a diversified group of athletes into a winning machine. The Baron remembers that championship season as the apogee of his football career.

"We won the championship for a number of reasons, none of which show on paper. First of all, we had quality, intelligent players. So many members of that team became head coaches and assistants: Van Brocklin, Khayat, Marion Campbell, Carr, Barnes, Baughan, Weber. That's some of them, just off the top of my head. On paper, other teams had better talent. But the game isn't played on paper. I believe that 90 percent of the success in any sport is mental. That concept was never truer than in 1960. By mental, I mean confidence, I mean playing intelligently and having the discipline to avoid mistakes. The mental aspect of the game means toughness. It means not accepting defeat. That '60 team was mentally tough. A lot of teams *say* they're confident, but when their confidence is tested, when things go wrong, they fold. The 1960 Eagles never doubted themselves. Not once, not even after we got run over by Cleveland in the opener. Other teams lose faith when they fall behind. They point fingers, make excuses, come apart. We never did. We could be down by 20 points, and every guy on that sideline still felt we'd come back and win. Our whole team learned to look beyond statistics. We weren't intimidated by the great personnel on teams like the Browns and Giants. We just went out to win every Sunday. That's the mental part of the game—playing hard week after week, and not losing concentration. And, we had Norm Van Brocklin. Dutch knew how to win. He provided the focus and leadership. Every person on our team took responsibility for the team's success. We had so many different heroes that year! Has there ever been a team where so many different heroes popped up week after week? Everyone felt like he was part of the team, and that kind of spirit molded us into a tight unit.

"We had our share of 'characters' on that team, but most of all, we had team character. Buck Shaw had moved so many people in and out of the roster and lineup, searching for guys with the right character and chemistry. He knew what he wanted, and he eventually got it. The chemistry and camaraderie on that team was better than I've ever seen anywhere. Our guys hung around together, socialized together, did things together. Dutch gathered the whole team together every Monday at Donoghue's Bar. Those get-togethers promoted harmony and unity, and we jelled as a unit. We didn't have cliques. No one got down on anyone else, all season long. Instead, everyone was supportive. You put all those forces together, and you come up with something powerful that doesn't show on paper. It shows in results."

Pete still enjoys talking about the glory days. He enjoys occasional visits to the past, but he doesn't overstay. He has moved on to new challenges in the worlds of government and business, where he harnesses the same tools he used as a gridiron star. Pete Retzlaff's ticket to success was not blinding speed or flashy moves. His star hangs in a constellation of old fashioned virtues, like dedication, hard work, and fortitude. After all, Pete Retzlaff has been called dedicated and hard working even longer than he's been called the Baron.

CANTON DROPS THE BALL

Let's put it out on the table right now. Pete Retzlaff belongs in the Pro Football Hall of Fame. He is not a member of that exclusive fraternity, and no one seems to know why. His numbers are certainly convincing enough.

Number 44 called it quits in 1966 at the age of 34. At that point, only three players in the history of the National Football League had averaged more yards/

catch than he—a revelation to those who categorize Retzlaff, incorrectly, as a third-down, short-yardage, ball-control-type receiver. The Retzlaff name, at the time of his retirement, also appeared in the NFL's all-time top five in two other categories: number of catches (452) and total number of yards gained receiving (7,412). Since that time, he has cascaded down the list. But, then, so has Don Hutson. Retzlaff remains in the top 75 in each category, 35 years beyond his retirement.

At his retirement, Pete Retzlaff was the Philadelphia Eagles' all-time leader in five different categories: most career 100-yard receiving games (24); most passes caught in a career (452); most total yards gained receiving in a career (7,412); most yards gained receiving in a season (1,190); and most passes caught in a season (66). Thirty-five years later, he remains number one in most career 100-yard receiving games. He has dropped to runner-up in two other categories: most passes caught in a season, and most receiving yards gained in a career. Remember that these particular lists that Retzlaff tops—the all-time Philadelphia Eagle list—include two Hall of Fame receivers. They also encompass 68 years of competition—68 years during which only six Eagle jersey numbers have been retired. One of those jerseys, number 44, belongs to Pete Retzlaff.

If more than numbers is required for Hall of Fame consideration, what other qualifications does Pete Retzlaff have? Aside from numbers, what was Pete's impact on the tight end position?

Pete was a founding father of the tight end position. Prior to 1966, the *Pro Football Encyclopedia* (Maher & Gill, Macmillan, 1997) did not list "*tight end*" as a specific position. However, since 1966, the term tight end has rocketed into prominence. The tight end slot has become a key building block for every professional offense. So, what watershed event in 1965 or 1966 prompted the change in status? A convincing argument can be made that the 1965 Maxwell Club Award, which was presented to Pete Retzlaff, *Tight End*, gave the position its pedigree. Retzlaff had a fabulous season in 1965 as a tight end. To this day, no other tight end has ever won the Max-

At his retirement in 1966, Pete was the Eagles' all-time leader in five different categories. Here, he outmaneuvers Cardinal Hall of Famer Larry Wilson.

well Club Award. Quarterbacks win it regularly. That's hardly a revelation. Running backs win. There are a few scattered receivers on the scrolls, and a stray defensive star pops up now and then. But there's only one tight end.

Pete Retzlaff, arguably, had a substantial degree of influence on the perception of the tight end position. Now, returning to statistics, how does Pete Retzlaff stack up against the five tight ends who *did* make it to the Hall of Fame? Those five are Mike Ditka, John Mackey, Jackie Smith, Kellen Winslow, and Ozzie Newsome. Retzlaff and Newsome are tied for the lead in touchdowns in this pack. But rather than compare the entire group of greats, it may be more relevant to compare the three tight ends who played during the Baron's tenure. Those three are Retzlaff, Ditka, and Mackey. This trio did a yeoman's job in inventing and defining a new position, one that continued to grow dramatically in their wake. The pass-catching feats of their successors were bloated because of bigger schedules and pass-happy innovations like the West Coast offense, which presented opportunities that had not yet been explored or exploited in Retzlaff's day.

FIGURE 1

	RETZLAFF	DITKA	MACKEY
Years played	11	12	10
Years	1956-1966	1961-1972	1963-1972
Catches	452	427	331
Total Yards	7,412	5,812	5,236
Yards/Catch	16.4	13.61	15.82
TD's	47	43	39
Games	132	158	139
Years All Pro	5	5	5
Maxwell Club Award	1965	----	----

Drilling down a little deeper, it's revealing to narrow the Ditka-Retzlaff comparison down to the six-year stretch (1961-1966) when the two were both active. Ostensibly, the comparison should favor Iron Mike, since statistically that stretch was the most productive of his dazzling career. Mike was young and on his way up. Pete was aging and on his way out. Though Ditka averaged a few more receptions than his counterpart—Mike averaged 53; Pete, 49—Pete averaged 74 more yards per year (824 yards to 750 yards) than Mike.

Comparing that same '61-'66 period in Pete Retzlaff's career to John Mackey's 10-year career presents another compelling case for the ex-Eagle great. In only two of his ten seasons did Mackey exceed Retzlaff's *average* number of catches per year (49). And only once in Mackey's career did he gain more receiving yards than Retzlaff's *average* (824 yards) during the '61-'66 period.

Another persuasive set of data supporting Pete Retzlaff's Hall of Fame qualifications is the list of All-Pro selections while Retzlaff played tight end. The tight end position was not selected separate from the other ends in the All-Pro balloting until 1962. In 1962, which was Mike Ditka's sophomore year, three tight ends were selected All-Pro: Ditka, Ron Kramer of the Packers, and Preston Carpenter of the Steelers. Retzlaff was not a full-time tight end that year. Bobby Walston held that slot on the Eagles. However, from 1963 through his retirement in 1966, Pete Retzlaff was chosen All-Pro *every year*. Here are the year-by-year All-Pro selections for tight end while Retzlaff played it:

1963: Mike Ditka, Ron Kramer, and Pete Retzlaff
1964: Mike Ditka and Pete Retzlaff
1965: Mike Ditka and Pete Retzlaff
1966: Mike Ditka, Pete Retzlaff, John Mackey, and Jackie Smith

It's ironic that, in Pete's final year in the pros, he ended up in that group. It would have been ludicrous at the time this honor was bestowed to suggest that his three peers be inducted into the Hall of Fame and Retzlaff excluded. It is no less ludicrous today.

But again, such arguments rely on mere statistics. As the 1960 Eagles proved so definitively, success is not always reflected in statistics. So let's stray from statistics and examine Retzlaff's worthiness by talking to his peers, the guys who played the game. What better player to ask about Pete Retzlaff than Mike Ditka. Perhaps Ditka, tight end *extraordinaire*, is the man *most* qualified to judge Pete Retzlaff's impact on football and the tight end position that Ditka himself played so masterfully. Ditka had this to say in a February 1999 interview:

"If you're asking me, 'Do I think Pete Retzlaff belongs in the Hall of Fame?' Of course, I think Pete belongs in the Hall of Fame. Not only was he a great football player, I think he was a great credit to the game—the way he brought class and dignity to the game. And, *I think he helped revolutionize the tight end position.* The tight end position was kind of one thing when I played it, and, as Pete started playing it after he moved over from wide receiver, he turned it into something else. *I think that's where the game has gone now because of the tight ends that came in, especially Pete, and played the position the way he did.* It was a little bit different than the way I played it, but it was certainly very effective and he was a great player and had a great career, and he certainly belongs in the Hall of Fame."

Ditka, a fiercely proud man, is not given to trivial praise. He also possesses an astute football mind. An NFL coach for decades, he is tuned into the sport's nuances, and has witnessed each successive wave that has rolled across the gridiron for the past forty years. His opinion has the ring of authenticity that should rumble through the halls of Canton.

Mel Renfro is a Hall of Fame defensive back who shadowed Retzlaff around the gridiron. Renfro, a star of the great Dallas Cowboy teams of the late '60s and early '70s, entered the Hall of Fame in 1996. Renfro offered these insights in a March 1999 interview:

"I was a young guy coming into the league, and Pete was *the guy, the receiver* back in those days. He never said a lot about himself and was not a song and dance man, so nobody—none of the reporters—noticed his accomplishments on the field. Pete is just a great guy and a solid citizen who has done a lot on and off the field. I never heard anything bad about him."

Yes, in 1965, Renfro's sophomore season, Pete Retzlaff was "the receiver." He put together one of the finest seasons any tight end has ever had. Besides the Maxwell Award that year, he also won the Washington Touchdown Club Award, and the Wanamaker Award as Philadelphia's top athlete. Comparing Retzlaff's 1965 statistics to the most brilliant seasons turned in by any of the tight ends in the Hall of Fame, again strengthens Retzlaff's Hall of Fame case. The best individual single seasons by any of the tight ends in the Hall of Fame were turned in by Kellen Winslow in 1980, and by Jackie Smith in 1967. Winslow was with the San Diego Chargers, and Smith was with the St. Louis Cardinals. Below, their best years are compared to Retzlaff's best year.

FIGURE 2

	Yards	Yards/Game	Catches	Yards/Catch	TD's
Winslow 1980, 16 games	1290	81	89	14.5	9
Smith 1967, 14 games	1205	86	56	21.5	9
Retzlaff 1965, 14 games	1190	85	66	18.0	10

In this comparison, Retzlaff ranks lowest in only one category: total yards. In every other category, he is second, except for touchdowns, where he leads the pack. Raymond Berry, fabled receiver of the Colts' late '50s dynasty, praises Pete's 1965 season, while sharing these comments in May 1999:

"The 1965 season of Pete Retzlaff is the first thing that stands out in my mind (when I think about Retzlaff's Hall of Fame credentials). I remember watching him play that year. I would suspect he had statistically the best year any tight end has ever had. You'd have to check that (See Figure 2), but it was an incredible

Both teammates and rivals heralded Retzlaff as a "credit to the game," and one of the men who revolutionized the tight end position.

season. I would also be interested to see Pete's statistics and a comparison against other tight ends—John Mackey and Mike Ditka particularly (See Figure 1). I'm sure Pete deserves a place in the Pro Football Hall of Fame."

Retzlaff wielded significant influence on his profession off the field, as well. While still playing, he was a mover and shaker in the early days of the National Football League Players Association (NFLPA), serving as its President in 1962-63. Stan Jones, a Hall of Famer whose career spanned the years 1954-1966, feels that Pete's contributions to the Player's Association further solidify his Hall of Fame credentials. Jones said:

"I don't think I need to spend any time on his (Retzlaff's) athletic accomplishments. They speak for themselves. However, you mentioned his contributions to the game. I can speak firsthand that he personally saved the Player's Association. During the '62 season, Pete was injured and had some free time. He called me. I was captain of the Bears at that time. He asked if I could intercede with Coach Halas and allow him to speak to the Bears about the teams that were joining the Players' Association. We (the Bears) were the only team that was not a member. We had voted against joining in previous years. Pete said the other teams were threatening not to join if the Bears continued to avoid membership. I told Pete that we hadn't voted so far that year, but I doubted we would vote to join. George Halas had paid us during the pre-season games, unlike other teams (who did not pay their players for pre-season games), and we had no grievances against the Bears. Pete persisted. So, reluctantly, I said that I would ask Coach Halas if he'd allow Pete to come to Chicago to speak to the team. I spoke to Halas and, after a lengthy discussion, he gave me his permission. I told Coach Halas that I doubted we would join the Association. To make a long story short, Pete spoke to the team and, as a result, the team voted unanimously to join the Players' Association. Needless to say, Pete's presentation was impressive. If he could sell the Bears on joining, I thought he could sell just about anything. The toughest thing I ever had to do was tell Coach Haas that we had voted to join. In retrospect, it probably saved the NFLPA, but it cost me my captaincy, yet it certainly was the best thing I ever did as captain."

Halas, a visionary during football's first 40 years, started missing the mark by the time the '60s rolled around. He missed it on the union issue. Retzlaff did not. The Players' Association, once the '60s took hold, was an idea whose time had come.

Retzlaff's imprint on football did not cease with retirement. He served as the Philadelphia Eagles' General Manager from 1969-1972. His GM tenure allowed him to unleash perhaps his most profound strength: remaining unflappable when dealing with conflict. He shifted from the head of the player's union to General Manager with the same ease he exhibited shifting from split end to tight end. Following his GM stint, Retzlaff joined the broadcasting team at WIP radio and WCAU-TV in Philadelphia for awhile.

Off the gridiron, Pete Retzlaff's character and life were, and remain, of Hall of Fame caliber. His '60 teammates tout him as a role model. Jerry Wilson, who was dealt away from the Birds in the midst of the 1960 championship run, sums up the team's sentiment nicely: "Pete made a lasting impression on me—I mean, a life-long impression, as to what it takes to be an All-Pro. I learned by watching him. I learned not only the mental and physical attributes required for success, but also the necessity of hard work and dedication."

For years, Pete Retzlaff has devoted himself to the Pennsylvania Special Olympics, also chipping in with a stint on the International Board of the Special Olympics. He's

As Eagles' general manager from 1969-1972, Pete Retzlaff remained unflappable in the face of conflict.

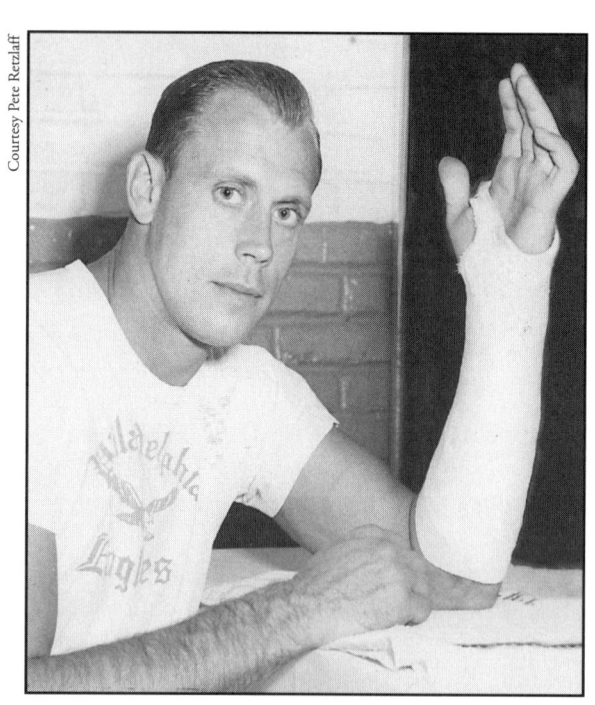

During the '62 season, Pete Retzlaff played with a broken wrist.

currently serving on the Boards of the Pennsylvania Environmental Defense Foundation, the Montgomery County (Pennsylvania) Open Space Commission, and the Montgomery County Lands Trust Board. In addition, locally Pete is an Advisory Board member of both the Paradise Watch Dogs and the Perkiomen Watershed Conservancy. The Perkiomen group awarded him their Director's Award on March 5, 1999.

In the business world, Pete serves on the Board of Directors for several successful companies, like Teleflex, Harleysville National Bank, and Paris Business Products. He is also the President of Southwest Grain.

All things considered: statistics, endorsements from peers, role in shaping the modern game, impact on the field, impact off the field, personal character, citizenship, life successes … how is it that Pete Retzlaff falls short of qualifying for the Hall of Fame? If he doesn't have the right stuff, what does the right stuff look like?

Retzlaff's esteemed colleague, Mike Ditka, was renowned for lugging the pigskin for crucial extra yardage in his playing days. He did the same thing with his comments on the Baron:

"You know these things (getting into the Hall of Fame) sometimes become popularity contests. Sometimes (you don't make it) if you're not popular enough or people don't bring your name up. And, the other thing that happens, too, is that people have a tendency to forget just how good the players were back then, because they're so caught up in the present."

Stan Jones summarizes the overwhelming sentiment about Pete Retzlaff whose singular nickname, the Baron, captures the essence of a man who ennobled his profession. Smith says:

"I cannot think of any senior player I would recommend higher than Pete. I have tremendous respect for Pete Retzlaff as a player and as a man. The Hall of Fame could not select anyone more worthy of enshrinement."

SixSixSixSix**Six**SixSixSixSixSix

Humiliation

Logically, the past should have little effect on the present in sports. Players change. Management changes. Football changes. There is no tangible continuum. But somehow over the years, in defiance of all logic, the past and the present *do* link. And, the links to the past that some franchises lug around are as woeful as Jacob Marley's.

Take, for example, the Detroit Lions and the Washington Redskins. The Lions have *never* won a game in Washington, D.C. Both these teams have been around since the Roosevelt administration. Yet, through all the decades, all the eras that each of these franchises has fielded teams, no Detroit Lion team, in 20 tries, has left victorious from the Capital City. So logically, we can say the past doesn't matter. That each game is a new game. That each contest was played independent of all the other contests. That a contest that took place pre-TV has nothing to do with a game that's played post-home computers. Logically, that's correct. But if a coin flip comes up heads 20 straight times—well, there are more things on heaven and earth than are dreamt of in our philosophy.

Cleveland owns the Eagles-Browns series. Through 1959, the ledger is not as lopsided as it is in the Skins-Lions series, but it's not that far off, either. The Browns rule 15-5. Ten years, almost to the day, have passed since the two teams first met in the 1950 opener, which Cleveland won 35-10.

The faces have changed completely in the ten intervening years. Chuck Bednarik is the sole survivor from that first clash at Philadelphia's Municipal Stadium. Lou Groza played in the '50 game for the Browns, but Groza is retired in 1960, at least for the moment. He will not compete today. Paul Brown, the Cleveland coach, was on the sideline in 1950, masterminding the rout. He was a relative unknown in the NFL as the '50s dawned. By 1960, Paul Brown is famous. He enters Franklin Field in September, 1960, as the most successful coach of the most successful team in pro football history.

- A Little Brown History -

The Cleveland Browns were formed in the mid-'40s as one of the charter franchises in professional football's new All-American Football Conference (AAFC). The new league had a vision, born of post-War America's hope and prosperity, to grow and compete with the established NFL, and someday to battle the NFL for the title of world champ in a joint, postseason tournament. The AAFC founders didn't know it at the time, but their dream came two decades too soon. Twenty years after the AAFC was founded, the first Super Bowl took place, pitting the AFL against the NFL to decide the world championship.

The AAFC consciously crafted a similar look to the NFL, shamelessly replicating the senior circuit's structure down to the most minute detail. The AAFC went so far as to name Jim Crowley, a former member of Notre Dame's Four Horsemen of the '20s, as its first Commissioner in order to match—or counter, as the case may be—NFL Commissioner, Elmer Layden, a fellow Horseman.

The Cleveland franchise was owned by Arthur (Mickey) McBride, who ran Cleveland's Yellow Cab Company. McBride hired Ohio State head coach, Paul Brown, as his head coach. The Cleveland Browns, under the tutelage of Paul Brown, quickly became the most ardent and energetic organization in professional football. Brown and his band set about recruiting with missionary zeal in an atmosphere that was, essentially, no holds barred. Brown took advantage – something he was adept at doing both on and off the gridiron. The new league did not create its teams via a draft. Furthermore, they enacted virtually no regulations governing the signing of players. Paul Brown lured graduating seniors away from the NFL with big salaries. He combed military bases for talent. As the armed forces wound down after World War II, the military ranks were swelled with young athletes awaiting reentry into a society that was reinventing itself. Professional sport was poised to zoom into a new age. The Cleveland Browns were riding the crest of that new age. They offered big money. They wooed players away from the NFL. And, they gobbled up more prospects than their rosters could hold. They didn't want to lose this roster overflow, so they kept them gainfully employed till there was room on the roster. This crew marked time with jobs in owner McBride's taxi company, thus giving football the still-surviving term, "taxi squad."

When competition began, the Browns had no competition. Paul Brown's team blew away the rest of the AAFC. In the four years they played in the league, the Browns' records, by season, were: 12-2-0, 12-1-1, 14-0-0, and 9-1-2. The Browns drew modern-magnitude crowds in their first year of existence. Twice that first season, they topped the 70,000 mark. They averaged a startling 57,137 spectators per home game. The 1946 AAFC championship game drew 41,181 faithful who witnessed the Browns outlast the New York Yankees, 14-9. Unfortunately, few of the other AAFC franchises shared the Browns' success at the turnstiles. The league floundered financially from its founding.

The Browns flat-out dominated the AAFC. They followed up their 1946 championship with championships in 1947, 1948, and 1949. By 1949, however, even Cleveland fans stopped showing up. Average attendance tumbled to 29,553. In fact, only 22,550 showed up for the 1949 championship game, which was hosted by Cleveland. That championship game turned out to be the league's final game. Naturally, Cleveland won it, scoring a 21-7 victory over Buck Shaw's San Francisco 49ers. Granted, the NFL championship game that year, which pitted Los Angeles against the Eagles, drew even fewer onlookers (22,245). But the NFL match was played in a driving Los Angeles rain storm. Furthermore, the NFL was more established and financially secure. They were capable of weathering such a disappointing turnout.

The Browns didn't fold with the demise of the AAFC. They stormed into the NFL in 1950, along with the San Francisco 49ers and the Baltimore Colts. The Browns took the NFL title their very first year, outscoring the LA Rams, 30-28 when the two met for the championship in front of a sparse Cleveland home crowd of 29,751. The Browns continued to roll, taking Divisional honors for the next three years ('51, '52, and '53). However, in all three of those years, they lost NFL title games—first, to the Rams in '51, and twice to Buddy Parker's Lions, in '52 and '53. In '54 and '55, the Browns got their revenge against both clubs, beating the Rams in '54 and the Lions in '55 for back-to-back NFL titles.

Smarting from the departure of Otto Graham, who quarterbacked Cleveland from the team's inception in 1946, Cleveland suffered its first losing season in 1956. Like a true champion, they rebounded back on track in 1957, when the Jimmy Brown era was ushered in. Brown won the NFL's Rookie of the Year Award in 1957, as the Browns again topped the Eastern Division. The Lions, however, put a big exclamation mark on the final match-up between the two '50s giants, by embarrassing Cleveland with a 59-14 flogging.

To close out the '50s, the New York Giants twice captured the Eastern Division's crown, but the Browns were right on their heels, finishing second both years.

Paul Brown had been Cleveland's one and only coach for their entire glorious history. He was a great coach. He was not a great front man for the organization. Brown was sometimes tactless in handling the press. A proud man, he still harbored resentment for the disrespect and snubs the press shot his way during his tenure in the AAFC. Neither he, nor his team, nor his league were taken seriously during the late '40s. Consequently, Brown blasted into the NFL with a chip on his shoulder—a chip that remained even after the 1950 drubbing he inflicted on the Eagles. That 1950 opening-day win was not sufficient vindication. Brown taunted the Eagles in the 1950 return match. Intending to silence the naysayers who dismissed Cleveland as a one-dimensional team that could only pass, Brown ordered his Hall of Fame quarterback Otto Graham not to throw a pass. Graham followed the order to a "T," and the Browns won the game, 13-6, entirely on the ground. Interestingly, Graham lost the passing crown that year by a small margin to a Los

Angeles rookie named Norm Van Brocklin. Had Graham thrown his normal ration of passes against the Eagles in that rematch, Graham might have worn the NFL passing laurels.

Brown's contributions to the professional game place him among the sport's top innovators and thinkers. Sometimes called the Father of Modern Football, Brown changed coaching into a year-round profession. The success of his Browns, along with the complexities and demands of the modern game, eventually made his peers work year-round, as well. Brown's system integrated the activities within a football organization, like recruiting, training, and scouting. He took a more academic, scientific approach to the game than his counterparts. His players carried play books and participated in skull sessions and classroom practice sessions. He signed African Americans immediately, without hesitation, in his first year of operation. He introduced his own system of play calling. Brown called the plays from the sideline, shuttling "messenger guards" in and out of the game on alternating downs. Controversial in its day and disdained by field generals like Norm Van Brocklin and Bobby Layne, the Brown play-calling method was, nonetheless, the precursor of today's systems. Bobby Freeman, defensive back with the '60 Birds played for Paul Brown in 1957 and 1958. Freeman looks back at his former mentor's endless quest to gain the advantage on an opponent.

BOBBY FREEMAN: "Paul Brown was a great coach, a great thinker. I guess you could call him a scientific thinker—always looking for an advantage. He started a program when I was playing with Cleveland where everybody was taking vitamin pills. They were supposed to make you less injury-prone. I don't recall exactly how they worked, but the pills were supposed to build up amino acids. The theory was that the amino acids enabled you to produce more oxygen, and ultimately they made you less injury prone. I think that was the basic theory. Some of the older guys on that team, the ones who had played on those great Cleveland teams from the late '40s and early '50s, were really committed to the program. They were looking for ways to prolong their careers at that point, and some of them wound up taking 40-50 pills a day."

Chuck Weber, the Eagles' middle linebacker in 1960 was one of Paul Brown's assistant coaches with the Bengals. He remembers Brown as a shrewd football man.

CHUCK WEBER: "Brown was one of the smartest football men I've ever been around. He was probably the most analytical guy in the game."

Since the moment the Browns left their first cleat mark on NFL turf, they have dominated Philadelphia—starting, of course, with their 35-10 upset victory in 1950. In half of the ten seasons that followed—from '50 through '59—the Browns have swept the season series. Even in 1956, when the Browns endured their only losing season in 15 years of competition, they swept the series. Two of their five wins came at the expense of Philadelphia. Twice in the decade the Browns have held the Eagles scoreless.

From the beginning, there has been an edge to the rivalry. In 1953, it was the Eagles who thwarted the Browns' bid for an unprecedented, undefeated season. Cleveland entered the final game of the 1953 campaign with a perfect 11-0 record. Though the game was meaningless for Philadelphia, the Eagles thumped the Browns, 42-27, to blemish Cleveland's otherwise perfect regular-season record. But worse than that, the defeat broke Cleveland's momentum and sent them into a tailspin at the most inopportune time. Two weeks later, the Lions squeaked out a 17-16 victory over Cleveland to earn the NFL title. The following season, Philadelphia extended Cleveland's frustration, clubbing the Browns in the 1954 opener to extend the Browns' losing streak to three.

In 1957, a big brawl erupted, resulting in the ejection of seven players. Besides disliking Philadelphia's team, Paul Brown has a score to settle with one of the Philadelphia players. Brown remembers vividly that Norm Van Brocklin quarterbacked the Los Angeles Rams to a comeback victory over his Browns in the 1951 title game. Van Brocklin had entered the game in relief of Bob Waterfield, and threw a 73-yard touchdown pass to Tom Fears for the winning score.

As the two teams prepare for the 1960 match-up, history definitely favors Cleveland. One link to the past, however, favors Philadelphia. The last time the Eagles opened against the Browns in Philadelphia, the Eagles won, 28-10.

THE LINE-UPS

The 1960 Browns are an impressive bunch. Their roster is generally acknowledged as the most talented in the East. Their backfield duo of Jimmy Brown and Bobby Mitchell is sensational. Though they've only spent three years together, the two form one of the finest running tandems ever. The Mitchell-Brown tandem comprises arguably the most explosive inside-outside rushing combination in the league's 40-year history. Both men are future Hall of Famers, although Mitchell will be remembered mostly as a receiver. The Cleveland quarterback is Milt Plum, a Delaware Valley native who graduated from Woodbury High School in New Jersey and Penn State University. Overshadowed by the flashy exploits of his backfield mates, Plum quietly fashions a career season in 1960, easily winning the NFL passing crown. To this day, Plum's 1960 season ranks 19th on the all-time list for highest average yards per passing attempt (9.2 yards) for a single season.

Cleveland's offensive line, led by future Hall of Famer Mike McCormack, (who will become the Eagles' 13th head coach in 1973) is superb. McCormack joins Jimmy Ray Smith, John Wooten, Gene Hickerson, and Dick Schafrath to form a deadly front wall that rips open gaping holes for its marquee backs. The receiving corps of Gern Nagler, Ray Renfro, Leon Clarke, and Rich Kreitling is

82   **1960** *Philadelphia Eagles:* **Nothing but a Championship**

September 17, 1961 Franklin Field. With Jim Carr in the opener against Cleveland, 1961 is a different story. The Eagles win 27-20 at Franklin Field. Here, Bednarik downs Ray Renfro as Carr (#21) closes.

underrated, but effective. The pass catchers are a lot more dangerous, however, because of the attention that Brown and Mitchell command.

Cleveland's kicking game, long the dominion of Hall of Famer Lou Groza, now belongs to Sam Baker, a worthy successor to "the Toe." Baker will finish the '60 campaign with 12 field goals. The following year, Baker will relinquish the booting chores to Groza when the latter comes out of retirement.

The Cleveland defense is spearheaded by five-time Pro-Bowler Walt Michaels at linebacker. Dave Lloyd is also in the linebacking corps. Lloyd will be traded to Philadelphia in 1963 and play there until his retirement in 1970. Bernie Parrish headlines a strong defensive backfield that will intercept more passes in 1960 than the Eagles—the only squad in football that can make that claim. Parrish ends up snagging six interceptions himself, returning them for a league-leading 238 yards (that's an average return of almost 40 yards per interception). The defensive line is anchored by Floyd Peters at tackle. Philly fans will get to know Peters better in the latter part of in the decade. Peters closes out the final six years of his career ('64-'69) as an Eagle. Paul Wiggin at defensive end is another solid block in a stingy defensive line.

The Browns have few, if any weaknesses.

Overall, the Eagles enter the tilt with few major changes, offensively, from

1959. Van Brocklin, Barnes, Peaks, McDonald, Retzlaff, and Walston comprise an offensive machine that is tested and true. The offensive line, at this point, is somewhat suspect. Bednarik, at 35 years of age, starts at center. Even though Chuck is an all-time great, his age makes him a question mark. Bob Pellegrini, Stan Campbell, Jim McCusker, and J. D. Smith fill the rest of the slots on an offensive line that has not proven it can block effectively for the run.

The defense holds the key to victory. The Eagles face the Herculean challenge of assimilating some key personnel into their defensive scheme with less than a week's orientation. With Carr's injury and the sudden introduction of two new faces—Burroughs and Freeman—the defensive stability of the unit is questionable. Their defensive backfield, which could hardly be called cohesive at this point, may prove vulnerable. Bobby Jackson, second-year man from Alabama, recalls the general mood going into the game:

BOBBY JACKSON: "When they introduced the teams before the game that day, they elected to introduce our defensive team That's because Jimmy Brown was on the offensive team for Cleveland. He was such a big name, the brass liked to call his name and introduce him 'cause they knew the fans were there to see him. I have to admit, I was really nervous that day myself. I almost didn't make it out. The fans were packed into Franklin Field. Everybody in the place was excited. I remember Buck Shaw telling us in the locker room: 'Look at all those people out there. They're only here for one reason—that's to see you win. So, let's give them what they came here for.' Well, that day, we sure didn't give them that. For some reason, we were nervous. We never loosened up."

The Eagles start Don Burroughs at safety. Bobby Freeman fills Carr's vacated corner position. Burroughs had only practiced with the team from Wednesday to Friday, and Bobby Freeman didn't even practice. He didn't arrive in Philadelphia till Friday. Tommy Brookshier and Bobby Jackson round out the backfield. Gene Johnson also sees extensive service in the defensive backfield. Jesse Richardson anchors the defensive line which also features Marion Campbell, Eddie Khayat,

Rookie back Bobby Jackson (#28) remembers that the Eagles were not ready for Cleveland in the opener.

and Don Owens. Rookie Maxie Baughan, Joe Robb, and John Nocera form the linebacking corps.

September 26, 1960 is a warm, sunny Sunday. Summer still lingers in the air, as 56,303 believers, skeptics, and hopefuls push into Franklin Field—the largest Philly football crowd since that day, ten years ago, when the Browns paid their first visit to the Quaker City.

The home crowd winces through a disastrous day. Every weakness of the 1960 Eagle team is laid bare and rubbed raw. The defense surrenders a whopping 329 rushing yards, as the Cleveland backs stage a track meet worthy of the Penn Relays. To heap more problems on an already-beleaguered coaching staff, the offense is spotty, and the running game is inconsistent.

MITCHELL AROUND RIGHT END

The Eagles receive the opening kick-off. Two plays later, Bernie Parrish picks off a Van Brocklin aerial and runs it back to the Eagle 31. On the Browns' first play from scrimmage, halfback Bobby Mitchell scoots all 31 yards around right end for six points. On the day, Mitchell gains a whopping 156 yards on a mere 14 attempts. Backfield mate Jimmy Brown tacks on 153 rushing yards on 24 carries.

After the Browns' lightning-like score, the Eagles again receive. For a second time, Van Brocklin is picked off—this time by Don Fleming, a rookie defensive back out of Florida. Fortunately, the interception doesn't translate into Cleveland points. The Brown offense fizzles, and Sam Baker fails on a 34-yard field-goal attempt. However, as soon as the Eagles get the ball back, they turn it over again. For the third consecutive series, Van Brocklin is picked off—again, by rookie Fleming. This time, Fleming laterals the ball to linebacker Galen Fiss who hauls it all the way to the Eagle 8-yard line.

Fleming came to Cleveland in 1960 via the then-Chicago Cardinals, who had red-shirted him out of the University of Florida in the 28th round of the 1959 draft. The rookie will finish a promising inaugural season with five interceptions. Sadly, the young star dies in 1963, having snagged a total of ten interceptions in an abbreviated, but superb career.

Following Fleming's second pick, the Browns make good. From the eight, the Eagles are penalized half the distance to the goal line, where Jim Brown scores on his second center lunge.

The Eagles enjoy their first possession of the game that does not abort on a Van Brocklin interception. Advancing mostly on the ground, Philadelphia reaches the Cleveland 14, before sputtering to a halt, and settling for a Walston field goal, as the first quarter ends.

After Baker kicks a 15-yard Cleveland field goal, the Eagles pull off a slick 73-yard scoring drive. McDonald makes a sensational grab of a 24-yard TD pass to pull the home-towners within seven points of the visitors at 17-10. From then on, unfortunately, Philadelphia's afternoon deteriorates rapidly. The Browns rumble for another second-period score, stretching out their advantage to 24-10. Then, after Parrish recovers a McDonald fumble, the Browns embarrass the Birds by traipsing 71 yards on only three rushes. Brown covers 37 of them on a pitchout. Then, the big Cleveland back grinds out four more on a center smash, before Mitchell scurries the final 30 yards on another scamper around right end. After Baker tacks on his second field goal for the Browns, the Eagles respond with their own TD—a 36-yard scoring pass to Bobby Walston that brings the score to 34-17. Immediately afterward, the Browns respond with their own touchdown, upping their tally to 41 and icing the victory.

In a fourth-quarter mop-up role, Sonny Jurgensen engineers an impressive, but inconsequential, 74-yard scoring drive. The ex-Duke signal-caller completes five of six passes, capping the drive with a five-yard scoring toss to Retzlaff.

The final reckoning is: Cleveland 41 — Philadelphia 24.

The Eagles are humiliated. "I never saw a professional team look worse against a running attack," Buck Shaw grumbles in the gloom of the post-game locker room. "The defensive line was awful, the linebacking was awful, and, except for Tom Brookshier, the defensive backfield wasn't any help. It's too bad we haven't some place to reach for help. The defense, though, wasn't the only culprit. It was a lousy day for everybody."

The Eagle coaching staff is beside itself. Defensive coach Jerry Williams muses: "The defensive strategy was sound, but the assignments weren't carried out. The whole team wasn't aggressive. The linebackers were waiting for Mitchell and Brown to come to them, instead of shooting the lanes and going after them."

Mitchell and Brown were unstoppable. The previous year, both men finished up the season among the NFL's top five rushers. That feat has not been accomplished since. A few backfield mates have managed to finish in the top five within their own division or conference, but not in the NFL as a whole.

Mitchell and Brown are the story of the day. The two Cleveland stars run over, around, and through the Eagle defense. Both are gifted athletes. Mitchell possesses world-class-sprinter speed, although Chuck Weber, who played with both men in his days as a Brown, recalls that Jimmy Brown could actually beat Mitchell in a sprint.

CHUCK WEBER: "Both of them could fly, but Jimmy Brown was an amazing athlete. I think he beat Bobby in a 40-yard dash with pads on. That shows how dangerous Brown was—a guy that powerful with that kind of speed. He was the hardest guy in the league to bring down."

Mitchell and Brown are completely different personalities. Mitchell, the greatest runner to come out of Illinois since Red Grange, rooms with Brown, who is the first in a long line of Ben Schwartzwalder-coached Syracuse backs to star in the NFL.

~ Orange Crushers ~

Jimmy Brown was the first in an amazing succession of running backs who came out of Syracuse University, when Ben Schwartzwalder coached there in the '50s and '60s. After a stellar collegiate career, Brown rolled up 12,312 yards in nine years as a professional. His record is all the more amazing, considering that the regular season consisted of only 12 games in Brown's first four seasons. In his last five years, the NFL schedule expanded to 14 games. Brown's career totals have been eclipsed by runners who played 16-game seasons. In Brown's entire career, only once did he fail to lead the NFL in rushing. Only twice did he not gain more than a thousand yards in a season. Brown could have tacked on several thousand more yards to his lifetime total, but he chose to truncate his career several seasons prematurely. The twentieth century ended with ESPN's selection of Jimmy Brown as the fourth top athlete of that century.

Brown's successor at Syracuse was Ernie Davis. Davis, a fleet, powerful running back, led the Orangemen to a Cotton Bowl victory and their only national championship in 1959. Davis tragically succumbed to cancer and never played pro ball.

In '65, '66, and '67, Syracuse pumped out three great backs in rapid-fire succession. Jim Nance came into the AFL with Boston in 1965. In his sophomore year, he became his league's premier running back. Nance was the AFL's only 1,000-yard rusher in 1966, topping his circuit both in carries, with 299, and in rushing yards, with 1,458. Meanwhile, over in the NFL, his fellow Syracuse alumnus, Jim Brown, led the senior circuit in each of these categories. Nance repeated in 1967, again leading the AFL in both rushing categories. From '67 onward, his skills slowly diminished till his retirement in 1973.

Floyd Little was the next great Syracuse back to pop out of the Schwartzwalder chute. Little played his entire nine-year career with Denver. The ex-Orangeman is still one of the all-time leading ground gainers for the Broncos, with 6,323 yards. His best year was 1971, when he gained 1,133 yards on 284 carries to lead all NFL rushers.

Larry Csonka graduated from Syracuse in 1967 and toiled 12 years in the NFL. He missed the 1975 season, which he spent in the employ of the ill-fated World Football League, along with two of his sidekicks from the Miami Dolphins' 1973 Super Bowl championship team: Jim Kiick and Paul Warfield. In his NFL career, Csonka racked up 8,081 rushing yards, while posting three 1,000-yard rushing seasons. He remains the all-time leading rusher for the Dolphins.

Mitchell is an easy-come-easy-go, devil-may-care sort, who explains in an interview after the game how he psyched himself up for the Eagle contest.

"My trouble," Mitchell expounds, "is that I just can't get mad enough for pro football. I concentrate on one guy, usually before a game, imagining dirty things he might say to me. But today, I saw right off those Eagles were out to win, and it got me mad all over."

Jimmy Brown, in contrast, is reserved and introspective, sometimes avoiding interviews altogether. Together, Mitchell and Brown, in 1960, are as potent on the gridiron as Mantle and Maris are on the diamond.

Notwithstanding the dazzling exploits of Mitchell and Brown, Shaw blames poor tackling for the debacle. The Browns had exploited the inexperience of defensive backs Bobby Jackson and Gene Johnson, each of whom had seen a lot of action. Shaw contends that Jimmy Carr, a sure-handed, hard-hitting tackler, would have slowed the Cleveland ground attack. Carr, Shaw contends after the game, knows how to turn Mitchell in and how to prevent him from escaping outside, as Mitchell had done on his two 30-yard-plus touchdown runs around right end. Paul Brown, over in the opponents' locker room, disagrees.

"We've scouted the Eagles for the past four weeks, says Brown, "and we've discovered that their defensive line plays a tight four-man front. We successfully destroyed this defensive alignment by pinching in the Eagle line. That's what sprung Mitchell on pitchouts."

Coach Shaw is normally discreet. He doesn't name names to the press. However, after the game, the Eagle coach targets big Jesse Richardson as a major scapegoat. Jesse is a native of Roxborough, an old-line Philadelphia neighborhood, and very popular with the home-town fans. Shaw is already talking of replacing Jesse with John Riley Gunnels, a rookie from Georgia. Assistant coach Skorich supports the head coach's rant in an interview he gives during the week following the game: "We were very disappointed in Jesse's showing. He has not been moving as well as last year, and he did not look good in any of the preseason games. The films didn't show him making a single tackle on Sunday."

Shaw, himself, assumes part of the blame for the loss, offering this closing thought in the morose twilight after the game: "I think what may have happened is that, unconsciously, we brought ourselves to the heights against the Baltimore Colts last week in the exhibition. When we beat the Colts, we gave everyone the false impression that we were a helluva ball club. So much was expected of us that our ballplayers froze completely in the ball game."

Forty years later, guard Gerry Huth endorses Shaw's summary:

GERRY HUTH: "I can't explain that first game, why we were so flat. We came off that big victory over the Colts the week before, and we had a good exhibition season. To be honest, I just don't feel we were ready for the Browns in that opener. And, another thing, I think the Browns came here thinking: 'Maybe these Eagles are for real,' because we had beaten Baltimore. They really bore down against us, more than we were prepared for. I remember that they were really intense right from the opening kick-off in that game."

Eddie Khayat, a veteran coach himself, points out what he feels was one of Buck Shaw's defining strengths:

EDDIE KHAYAT: "Buck Shaw knew how to get his team ready for Sunday. His teams were physically and emotionally set to play when game time rolled around. That's not an easy thing to do, but Buck had the knack. He and Raymond Berry were the best guys at bringing a team along like that I've ever seen."

Coach Shaw was off his game for that opener. But, what was more disturbing was that his quarterback was off his game, as well. The Dutchman ended the day with a statistically impressive 251 passing yards, but his accuracy was a mediocre 16 for 35. The three early interceptions he tossed away dug his team an enormous hole—too big to crawl out of in a miracle finish. Nick Skorich, in a post-game interview, observed: "Van Brocklin was tight. He wanted to win so badly. You'll never see the Dutchman throw so poorly again."

Looking back over the years, Gerry Huth also agrees with Skorich's post-game assessment:

GERRY HUTH: "You can say a lot of things about Dutch, but he would admit when he was wrong. He gave a lot of hell to people, but, when he made a mistake, he didn't back away. I remember him after that opener. He stood up in that locker room and told everybody, 'I stunk. I take responsibility for losing this game. But we're still going to win it all this year. That was only one game.'"

To add insult to injury, the day after the Cleveland pasting, the season's first paychecks arrive—paychecks lightened by deductions for pre-season fines. Somehow, all those bedroom sneak-outs, curfew violations, classroom mistakes, and assorted other misdemeanors don't seem as funny now as they did at the time.

"It *cost me* ten bucks to play in 'Frisco," whines Billy Ray Barnes. Commissioner Pete Rozelle had fined Barnes $60 for his fisticuffs in the San Francisco pre-season game. Eagle players were only paid $50 for the game. Questioned

Van Brocklin took responsibility for losing the Cleveland game.

about it 40 years later, many of them claim that Commissioner Rozelle revoked the fine, and no one ever paid it. However, Billy Barnes, 40 years later, maintains that he was indeed fined and docked real money unjustly.

The game leaves doubters in its wake. The sunshine patriots who once considered the Eagles legitimate contenders now write them off. Serious doubts crop up about Van Brocklin. His performance, at age 34, may signal erosion of skill. The Eagles cannot contend without Van Brocklin. Behind Sonny Jurgensen, the offense had sputtered against San Francisco, St. Louis, and Washington during the exhibition season. At this stage in Sonny's development, he doesn't have enough experience to carry this team all the way.

The Eagles prepare for Dallas, putting the Cleveland calamity behind them. Charlie Gauer adds: "We told the defense to watch Jimmy Brown and Bobby Mitchell. They did. They watched them better than the people in the $6 seats (*the most expensive seats at the time*), but mostly from the rear."

Van Brocklin, for his part, tackles the task of rallying his team. He starts the process the following day, surrounded by tables instead of turf.

SevenSeven**Seven**SevenSeven

Slow Start:
Face Breakers, Game Breakers, and Game Faces

The Monday morning quarterback

To many of the 1960 Eagles, a key date in the march to the 1960 NFL championship begins the next day—the Monday following the Cleveland catastrophe. It begins, not on the gridiron, but in a little taproom, or "tappie," as bars are called by Philadelphians in the '60s. The name of the tappie is Donoghue's. Bob Pellegrini recalls those Monday get-togethers:

BOB PELLEGRINI: "Dutch would gather everybody together every Monday at Donoghue's. It wasn't a formal meeting, and it wasn't mandatory. But, practically every guy on our team will tell you how important those Mondays at Donoghue's were to our success that year, and to our coming together. Practically every guy showed up every Monday, and we grew more and more tight-knit as the season went along. You know, if a team has overwhelming talent, you can have cliques and still win. But, we didn't have that kind of talent. Some guys on the team tried to form cliques, just like they do everywhere. The difference here was that Dutch wouldn't have it. He wouldn't let them. He'd tell guys to stop griping, or stop carousing, or stop doing whatever they were doing that might interfere with the team's harmony, or their own concentration. He'd tell everybody that we had a championship to win, and we needed everyone to win it. After that Cleveland opener, Dutch kept everyone at an even keel. He assured everybody that it was just one game, just one loss. 'We're still going to win the championship,' he told everyone. The Eagles put that one game behind us that very next day, on Monday at Donoghue's. And we went on a tear after that. We won all those games in a row. It was like the opener never happened."

In the late '50s and early '60s, the Walnut Park Plaza is action central in the Philadelphia sport scene. Johnny Callison, Don Demeter, and several other Phillies live there, as do some of the Philadelphia Warriors (Philly's NBA basketball team at the time), and some of the Philadelphia Ramblers ice hockey team. Van Brocklin and his family lived at the Plaza when the Van Brocklins first relocated to Philly from the West Coast in 1958. His daughter, Kirby, eight years old when the Van

Brocklins moved east, fondly recalls riding endlessly up and down the elevators, energized by the bustle of hotel life, while she and her family familiarized themselves with the east coast and a strange new city.

KIRBY VANDERYT: "My sisters and I had fun at the Walnut Park Plaza. We were all younger than eight years old at the time, and we had fun running around the hotel, with all the people around and all the activity. There were lots of Eagles living there, and they were always real nice to us, so we got lots of attention. But, it was so different coming to Philadelphia from Los Angeles where we had grown up and were used to living. I know now it was hard on my mother to make that change."

By 1960, Van Brocklin has relocated his family to a new home in King

Bob Pellegrini (#53) played offense and defense for the '60 gang, but was hampered by injuries all year.

of Prussia, in 1960 still a pristine Philadelphia suburb. The Dutchman's daily ritual during that championship season is to drive his three daughters to Friend's Central school, and then blast out in his Thunderbird to the Eagles' office at 15th and Walnut before practice. Mondays, however, are off days in the Buck Shaw regimen. There is no practice. So, instead of driving to the club offices as he does the rest of the week, Van Brocklin heads to the Walnut Park Plaza each Monday. Once there, he telephones the resident Eagle bachelor contingent: Barnes, Burroughs, Sapp, Baughan, and others, and asks them to get together. Sapp recalls Dutch's Monday morning ritual.

THERON SAPP: "Dutch felt that it was important for the team to get together informally— just the players, without the coaches. He wouldn't take no for an answer. So, he'd call up to our rooms, and we'd drag ourselves downstairs to the lobby, no matter how tired we were, or how little sleep we had. Monday was our day off, so Barnes and me and others usually went out the night before. But when Dutch called, we came down, no questions asked."

Call it bonding, call it goofing off, call it anything you want. But don't call it trivial. Asked why the Eagles won the '60 championship, Marion Campbell—a head coach in the NFL for nine years—replies without hesitation:

MARION CAMPBELL: "Those Mondays when our whole team got together were the single most important thing that brought us success that year. We won that championship as a team, and because we were a strong team. And it was all Van Brocklin's doing. He insisted on people spending time together. Dutch really functioned as a coach that year, every bit as much as a player."

The Eagles have a good week of practice despite their lopsided loss. They're still loose, and they're still confident. John Wilcox, a rookie in 1960 who now lives near the Walla Walla River in Oregon, recalls the indomitable spirit of the '60 Eagles:

JOHN WILCOX: "The veterans made it easy to feel like you were part of that team. Those guys were so loose! Especially Barnes and Brookshier. Those two always had something going on. They made every bus trip to the practice field an adventure. Daily. You know, we had to take a bus from Franklin Field over to Murphy Field (where the team practiced) every day. Everyone always had to hustle and stay awake, because those veterans would make that bus driver take off before the stragglers got back on the bus."

The team flies out to Dallas for its Friday night game against the Cowboys. The two teams are meeting for the first time ever. The Dallas Cowboys, the first new franchise to join the NFL since the Baltimore Colts in 1953, are the NFL's first-ever cut-and-paste franchise. In prior years, new franchises, like the Frankford Yellow Jackets in 1924, the Eagles in 1933, and the Browns in 1950, were already assembled and competing in other leagues before entering the NFL. Not so with the Cowboys, whose roster was synthesized from the most expendable players on each NFL roster.

Dallas, as a viable marketplace for professional football, was considered risky in 1960. A defunct franchise called the Dallas Texans had played one NFL season in 1952 before folding due to lack of fan support. That Dallas Texan team became known as the "Homeless Texans," when their franchise folded, and they lost their stadium in mid-season. The league had to take them over to finish out the season. Since they had no home stadium, all their home games had to be played on the road. They established Hershey, PA, as their home base, but vanished for good the next year. In 1953, their spot in the Western Conference was taken by the Baltimore Colts.

The Dallas area has traditionally been college football territory. The Texas Longhorns and Southern Methodist Mustangs have gigantic local followings. The smart-money guys up north are skeptical that Dallas, with a 1960 metropolitan population of only 700,000 people, can support two professional football franchises, particularly when they're both competing in a marketplace where the Longhorns and Mustangs rule. Both the NFL and the AFL are trying to establish franchises in Dallas in 1960. The AFL team is the Dallas Texans—no relation to the defunct NFL franchise with the same name. The Texans are trying to identify with the local college scene by signing up big-name Texas college talent. Cotton Davidsen, from Gatesville, Texas, who had been a quarterback at Baylor, is inked as the Texans' quarterback. Jack Spikes, of Texas Christian, is another local whose name appears on the Dallas Texans' roster.

So far in 1960, neither the Cowboys nor the Texans have nestled deep in the heart of Texas. Two Texas millionaires—Lamar Hunt for the Texans and Clint Murchison, Jr, for the Cowboys—lock horns in a battle for the Lone Star State. Each man uses a different approach. The Dallas Texans give away the store, stuffing free game tickets into potato chip bags and cigarette cartons. They include free game tickets with $10 purchases of groceries. They inflate their attendance figures. The Cowboys, in contrast, do little in terms of freebies.

Since the Longhorns, the Texans, and the Cowboys all share the

John Wilcox (#71) played one year and earned a championship ring. Brother Dave, a Hall of Famer, played 11 years and never won a championship.

same facility, the Cotton Bowl, the competition between the AFL Texans and the NFL Cowboys on home-game weekends is fierce. The Eagles-Cowboys match, of necessity, has to be played on Friday night. The Longhorns will take the field on Saturday, followed by the Texans on Sunday. The gate gimmick the Texans have dreamed up for their upcoming Sunday game is billed as "Friend of the Barber" Day. Everyone who shows up at the Cotton Bowl in a white jacket gets in free (I would pay gobs of money to see the marketing department's pitch meeting for that promotion). And, in case you don't have a white jacket hanging in your closet, any high school student who brings in a torn ticket stub from a high school game can also enter free.

The Dallas Texans crow about the success of such gimmicks. The previous Sunday, they boast, 42,000 people—I hesitate to call them fans—allegedly spun through the turnstiles at the Cotton Bowl. The Texans defeated the Los Angeles Chargers that day, to wind up in a tie with the Denver Broncos for the AFL lead. Everything sounds like it's coming up yellow roses for the Texans, except that only 10,000 customers—that's less than one in four—actually paid to get in.

The Cowboys, on the other hand, have remained relatively gimmick free, holding fast to their original ticket prices, which range from $2.75 to $4.60. The Texans have already dropped their ticket prices from $2.75 to $1.

The Dallas papers have allotted the two new pro teams equal coverage, right down to the last agate line, as Hugh Brown of the *Philadelphia Bulletin* points out in one of his 1960 columns.

Both the Cowboys and the Texans are plagued by a provincial quirk. The city of Dallas is what is termed in 1960, a "gate town." Freely translated, that means that spectators do not pay to get in till right before game time. Consequently, weather—fickle, at best in Dallas—has enormous repercussions on earnings. The Cowboys had anticipated a gate in excess of 45,000 for their Saturday-night opener against Pittsburgh the week before. Unfortunately, rains came the night before the game, and continued, unabated, till 3:00 PM on Saturday. The ticket sales plummeted accordingly, dropping off to a disappointing 30,000.

As for their football team, the recently assembled Cowboys are an unknown. Their coach, Tom Landry, played for the Giants in the '50s, before joining Jim Lee Howell's coaching staff. Landry was the Giants' offensive coach in the late '50s, serving on the same staff as defensive coach, Vince Lombardi.

The Eagles' primary fear is quarterback Eddie LeBaron, who gave them fits in his days as a Redskin. Washington dumped LeBaron to clear the deck for Ralph Guglielmi, the former Notre Dame star. Thus far in 1960, however, Guglielmi has been a disappointment.

In LeBaron's first game, Dallas' opener, the Cowboys came close to upsetting the Pittsburgh Steelers. The 5'-7" LeBaron, a cagey NFL veteran out of the University of Washington who is renowned for his ball-handling wizardry, completed 15 of 28 passes for three touchdowns and an imposing 345 yards (a higher total than Van Brocklin will hit all year). Unfortunately, it wasn't enough. His team lost 35-28.

LeBaron has an impressive corps of receivers in Fred Dugan, Dick Bielski, Jim Doran, Ray Mathews, and Billy Howton. They're all reliable and experienced. Dugan will finish the '60 season with 29 catches, before being traded to Washington in '61, where he snags 53. Doran, who played on all three Lion championship teams in the '50s, has averaged 27 catches a season from 1955 to 1959. Mathews has caught 230 passes in eight years as a Steeler. (In 2000, he still ranks in the top 50—directly ahead of Tommy McDonald on the all-time list for average gain per catch). The 1960 season will be his last. Billy Howton, who started his career with Green Bay in 1952, has had a stellar career. In 1960, he suffers through his worst season, with career lows for catches (23), as well as yards gained (363). He rebounds in 1961 with a career-high 56 catches, enjoying two more good years before retiring. Howton's career statistics are gaudy. He ranks ahead of Tommy McDonald in career catches (503 to 495), and yards gained (8,459 yards to 8,410 yards).

On game night in Dallas, it's 84 hot and muggy degrees when the Eagles take the field in front of a skimpy Cotton Bowl crowd of 18,500. The game is not broadcast on TV in Philadelphia. Philly fans are forced to tune into WCAU on the radio to follow the action.

The two teams play dead even all night long. Each scores three touchdowns. Each kicks two field goals. The Eagles roll up 16 first downs; Dallas, 17. The Eagles rush for 162 yards; Dallas, for 154. The Eagles pass for 139 yards; Dallas, for 194. The Eagles intercept five passes; the Cowboys, four. The difference in the game is two blocked extra points. Bobby Freeman blocks them both.

Van Brocklin completes 11 passes in 23 attempts for 139 yards. Again, he tosses three interceptions. Again, two of them come in the first period. Both are picked off by Dallas linebackers. Tom Braatz nabs the first and Jack Patera the second. For both Patera, who hails from the Dutchman's alma mater, Oregon, and Braatz, 1960 marks the end of their careers.

Besides Freeman, the Eagles' big hero is Chuck Weber, the middle linebacker from Abington High School in suburban Philadelphia, who attended college at nearby West Chester College (which is now West Chester University). Weber intercepts three passes, and, in doing so, saves the Eagles' season.

~ The Wrestler ~

"I was the first guy ever from West Chester to wrestle in the NCAA National Championships. That was back in 1953," Chuck Weber recalls. "I almost won. I won't make excuses, but I was in the AAU Tournament the week before and I pulled my latissimus dorsus muscle. The match was at Penn State, and I had the guy down, 3-0, but I let him up. Then, I had nothing left."

The loss didn't deter West Chester University from selecting Chuck as the greatest athlete in the school's history. Chuck starred in wrestling and football at West Chester. He made Little All-American at offensive guard, but he didn't get drafted. He joined the Marines and ended up playing football in the service. He also coached baseball and wrestling. Weber was voted the "Most Outstanding Player" in football, which resulted in offers to try out for some NFL clubs, including the Eagles. He picked the Cleveland Browns, despite being a Philadelphia area resident all his life. Chuck explains why:

CHUCK WEBER: "I heard that Paul Brown gave people the best opportunity. That's what I needed. I needed a fair shot, since I wasn't drafted, and I didn't have a big name. I still remember when the Browns made the last cut. I was

Eagles linebacker Chuck Weber was a standout in both football and wrestling at West Chester University in the early '50s and was later named that school's greatest athlete.

sitting outside Brown's office, waiting to see him. He had scheduled appointments with a few of the guys that were candidates for getting cut. I remember going up to his secretary, and asking: 'Hey, did the guy ahead of me look sad when he left?' Anyway, Brown kept me, and we won the title in my first year."

When he got to the Eagles in '59, Chuck was the unsung guy who ran the defense. As his teammates assert, Chuck Weber was one tough guy. Maybe it was the Marine training. Chuck tells a story about Jesse Richardson when Jesse and he were with the Boston Patriots.

CHUCK WEBER: "I was the Patriots' defensive line coach in '64, and I'd work the guys pretty hard. We were doing this 'hit and spin' drill that Jesse hated. He kept complaining over and over, 'You're taking years off my career.' I'd say, 'No I'm not, Jess. I'm doing you good.' Next year, doesn't Jesse get that job, and I become Defensive Coordinator. I look over one day, and there's Jesse running everybody through the same drill. They're telling him the same thing—it's taking years off their careers. And, Jesse's saying: 'No, no, I'm doing you good.'"

Chuck played in pain practically his whole time in Philadelphia. He hurt his ankle in the final exhibition game against the Rams in 1959, and it was never right again. Chuck has lived in the shadow of the Eagles' "other" Chuck for years. Contrary to popular belief, Chuck Weber, not Chuck Bednarik, was the Eagles' middle linebacker in 1960. Chuck explains further:

CHUCK WEBER: "People are always saying Number 60 was our middle linebacker. I'll tell you, I was really happy to read a *Sports Illustrated* interview with Chuck Bednarik a few years back. Chuck explained that he practiced with the offense that year. I was the one who called the defensive signals, so, when Chuck played defense in those big games, I was the one calling the assignments."

Like the team's "other" Chuck, people listened to Weber. The ex-wrestler, ex-Marine was a rough and tumble guy, who knew how to take care of himself. Chuck laughs about his tangle with Mike Ditka, one of the game's celebrated tough guys.

CHUCK WEBER: "When Mike was a rookie in '61, he was the Bears' big threat. Jerry Williams put me on Mike, and told me not to let him get off the line of scrimmage. So, I didn't. I was all over him, grabbing him, holding him. One play, I grabbed his neck and shoulder pads and dragged him down, like a wrestling move. When the Bears were in the huddle, I told the ref, 'Watch this Ditka guy, he's grabbing me.' Next play, out comes Mike, swinging away. The ref sees him and throws a flag. Well, now, it's years later, 1985, and I'm coaching in San Diego, and Mike is coaching the Bears. Before the game, you know, the coaches sometimes get together and talk. I went walking over to Mike, and said, 'Hi Mike, I'm Chuck Weber.' Mike just looked at me, and said, 'I know who you are,' and walked away!

Besides his interceptions, Weber also spearheads the Birds' defense with four unassisted tackles and seven assists on tackles. Chuck has a banner year in 1960. He picks off six interceptions, which accounts for more than half the interceptions over his entire seven-year professional career.

Against Dallas, the Eagles once more fall behind early. Van Brocklin's second interception leads to a Dallas field goal from 31 yards out, giving Dallas a 3-0 advantage. Walston kicks a pair of field goals, and McDonald catches Van Brocklin's only scoring pass of the evening, a 16-yarder lofted into the end zone, where Tommy has left ex-Penn Stater, Fred Doelling stranded. Bobby Freeman then intercepts a pass at the Dallas 23. The Eagles' offense drives to the 8, only to turn the ball over when Barnes flips an interception into the end zone on a halfback pass. LeBaron comes right back with a 75-yard scoring toss to Frank Clarke, a play that leaves Bobby Freeman red-faced, beaten one on one. The Eagle defensive back recalls that play 40 years ago:

In 1960, Chuck Weber anchors the defense from his middle linebacker spot.

BOBBY FREEMAN: "Frank Clarke was a great receiver. I just got turned around, and, yes, my mistake did kind of spur me on to block the extra points."

On the extra point, Freeman hurls himself at the ball and knocks it down, providing the Eagles a narrow 13-12 margin. The Eagle offense again stagnates after a Weber interception, and Philadelphia is forced to punt. Then, Burroughs picks another one off, and the Eagles convert the opportunity into a TD on a Billy Barnes 10-yard scoring jaunt. With a 20-12 lead, the Birds kick off, and Timmy Brown fumbles on the 3. LeBaron sneaks in for a score. On the ensuing extra point, Freeman once more breaks through for the block, making the cushion 20-18. The Eagles score again on a 23-yard Barnes TD. In the end, Freeman's blocked PAT's decide the outcome. As Tommy Brookshier says today:

TOM BROOKSHIER: "Ask Bobby *how* he blocked those kicks. He blocked them with his face! The rest of the defensive backfield used to get all over Bobby about that—tell him that's why he wasn't as good looking as the rest of us. Believe me, Bobby Freeman was one tough football player. He was out to win any way he could. He typified the toughness of that '60 team."

After the game, Buck Shaw calls the contest the "longest 60 minutes I ever spent in football. I knew we were a better team, but I was afraid all the way through that we would pull some boners and hand the game to them." Shaw zeroes in on the offensive line's "terrible blocking," and the defensive line's "leaky defense against the run." Cowboy backs, L. G. Dupre and Gene Babb, tore through the Eagle line with reckless abandon. The Eagles have now surrendered almost 500 yards on the ground in two games.

Tom Landry credits the Eagle coaching crew, claiming he was outcoached. Landry feels the Texas team would have scored more except that the Eagles' 3-5-3 defense caught Dallas totally unaware. After the game, Landry has this to say: "They destroyed our short passing game in the first half by rushing three linemen against LeBaron and dropping five linebackers back in the middle. I had to change our whole offense in the second half to get anywhere."

The Eagles suffer one major injury. Howard Keyes, their big offensive lineman, is carried off the field in a stretcher after knocking Cowboy Bill Butler out cold on a kick off.

THE BARON BUSTS LOOSE

The .500 Eagles return to Philadelphia with a squad that's dead last in the NFL in four defensive categories: most points given up (66), most rushing first downs surrendered (26), most yards given up against the rush (482), and highest average gain against the rush (6.3 yards). The upcoming Cardinal game does not bode well for the Birds.

First of all, the Cards dealt Philly its biggest setback of the preseason. Sure, Van Brocklin sat out the entire contest; but Dutch has been horrible so far in 1960. His accuracy is a mediocre 50.9 percent, but, statistics aside, the four first-quarter interceptions he has surrendered have devastated his team. His six interceptions double the number of touchdown passes he's thrown.

Second, the Cards have one of the football's best running attacks. The image of Cleveland backs sprinting around Franklin Field is all too vivid in coach Shaw's memory. Shaw makes some adjustments intended to bolster the defense against the Cardinals' tricky single-wing. He moves 230-pound Joe Robb from linebacker to defensive end. Robb had never played linebacker before this season. He is more comfortable on the line, more natural and instinctive. Weber, Nocera, and Maxie Baughan form the new linebacking corps. Baughan has impressed everyone so far, as Shaw notes: "Linebackers are a breed apart, and I think Maxie is a member of that breed. He's fast and moves instinctively. Weber isn't fast, but he's an old hand and isn't fooled easily. Nocera does some things right and some things wrong, but we are hoping for improvement. Last year, we had Tom Catlin in that spot. He was old and past his physical peak, but he wasn't fooled."

For a change, history is on the Eagles' side. Philadelphia holds a 17-10 edge in the series. Recent history is even more propitious. In 1959, the Eagles beat the Cards twice.

The weather on game day cooperates. However, despite the warm and pleasant Sunday, attendance dips down to 33,701 a considerable drop from the 56,303 zealots who showed up for the opener. Some Philly fans, who were euphoric about their team three weeks earlier, have already cashed in their hope. But, the attendance today suffers more from competition with the World Series, which is being televised, than from anything else.

The football game is a see-saw affair from start to finish. For the third game in a row, the Eagles' opponent draws first blood. The Cardinals, after a couple of futile exchanges, march 62 yards on six plays. They eat up 42 of those yards in one gulp on a pass reception by John David Crow. Crow, the 1957 Heisman Trophy winner, destroys the Eagles all day long, rushing for 134 yards, and tacking on 65 more yards on three pass receptions. For the third game in a row, the opponent outgains the Eagles, 364-293 yards, while piling up 20 first downs to the Birds' 14.

The Eagles match the Cardinals with a first-quarter TD. After Don Burroughs intercepts a pass from Cardinal quarterback John Roach, the Eagles take over at the St. Louis 21. On the first play from scrimmage, Van Brocklin hits Retzlaff for a TD. The Baron is the first Eagle receiver in 1960 to bust out with a huge day. His final tally against the Redbirds reads seven catches for 132 yards. On the Eagles' next possession, Van Brocklin fumbles, and the Cardinals recover. Chuck Weber promptly picks off another Roach toss to stop a Cardinal drive at Philadelphia's 25. The Dutchman flips an interception right back to the Cards. The ex-Eagle, Bill Koman, nabs it, and the interception leads to the Cardinals' second score, a 23-yard halfback pass from versatile John David Crow to Joe Childress. Two minutes later, the Eagles drive to even the score at 14. The big plays of the Eagle advance are a 40-yard burst through center by fullback, Clarence Peaks, and a 13-yard pass to Retzlaff in the end zone.

As the first half winds down, Tom Brookshier intercepts yet another Roach pitch and hauls it back to the 37. Again, Van Brocklin finds Retzlaff, who makes a leaping catch on the one-yard line, and bounces into the end zone for an apparent touchdown. The officials incorrectly rule that the ball should be on the one-yard line, which forces Clarence Peaks to bull his way to paydirt with two seconds left in the half. The rules at the time state that an offensive player can get up and run with the ball if he has not made contact with a defensive player. Nobody touched Retzlaff on his catch and slide, so it should have been a touchdown. Fortunately, Philadelphia scores and takes a 21-14 advantage into the locker room.

Less than two minutes into the final quarter, the Cards knot the contest at 24. With 5:52 remaining, St. Louis surges ahead on a Jerry Perry field goal from the 33. Retzlaff again performs his heroics on the next possession, keeping a faltering

John Nocera's (#29) fourth-quarter sack and fumble recovery helped to derail the Cardinal offense.

drive alive when he catches a first-down pass in a third-and-25 situation. Philadelphia proceeds to score via a Van Brocklin to McDonald 11-yard pass. Nevertheless, the game scuffles to a tense close. Nocera sacks Roach, who fumbles, and Nocera recovers the ball. However, Walston blows a chance to put the game away when he misses a 33-yard field goal. The Cards take the ball and thunder from their own 20-yard line down to the Eagles 26. With 20 seconds left, Joe Robb, working from his new defensive end position, jars Roach as he releases the ball, allowing Don Burroughs to camp under it for an interception, which he returns 25 yards to seal the victory.

The day after the game, Shaw gripes about his team's poor fundamentals: "There was no nourishment in watching the game films. Our blocking was horrible. Starting Wednesday and continuing on Thursday, we are going right back where we were in training camp. We're going to put on the pads and hit the dummies and the charging sled too."

The most alarming part of the loss is that another opponent has chewed up the Eagle defense with its running game. John David Crow, en route to his greatest year, churned through the rag-tag Eagle line for 134 yards on 16 carries. Furthermore, the Eagles' "bomb" squads, as special teams were called in the '60s, were weak. Ted Dean filled in at halfback most of the game for the injured Billy Ray Barnes. The wear and tear on his legs caused him to kick off short consistently, which was a source of consternation to the Eagle coaches.

Shaw is growing impatient at this point with his team's inability to stop the run. He speaks as though he's ready to set his "three-teams" carousel in motion again. He complains to the press: "Our bomb squad coverage has developed a tendency to let someone else do the tackling on those collisions of massed bodies. Last year, our bomb squad performances were uniformly good. But at that time, we had a lot of rookies who weren't sure they had made the team. Now, maybe some of them are too sure."

Shaw wastes no time in declaring war on complacency. He peddles 6'-4," 255-pound Don Owens to the Cards. St. Louis needs Owens to replace Frank Fuller, their top defensive lineman, who was injured in the game against the Eagles. In return, Philadelphia receives a 1961 draft choice. Owens has fallen out of favor in Philly, as Shaw explains after the trade: "The deal could help Owens. He'll be playing in his home town. He didn't help us much. I think he figured he had it made with this club after three years. No professional player should figure that way."

THROWN AGAINST THE LIONS

The winless Lions meow into town. The Eagles are favored to win by a touchdown, since Detroit, in two games thus far, has rushed for only 166 yards—a 2.9 yard per-carry average—and scored only 19 points. Still, the Eagles' 2-1 record is shaky at best. Philadelphia's victories have come over teams that, thus far, have a combined 1-5 log. Opponents have outscored the Birds, 93-82.

Detroit was an unimpressive 3-8-1 in 1959. Despite the fact that their powerhouse squads of the early and mid-'50s are history, the Lions' personnel are still top-notch. Three future Hall of Famers appear on their '60 roster: Yale Lary, Dick "Night Train" Lane, and Joe Schmidt. Several other big-name stars pepper the line-up, like Alex Karras, Wayne Walker, Nick Pietrosante, and Roger Brown. The Lions feature a stalwart defensive front wall, anchored by Karras and Brown. Detroit surrendered a mere 95 yards in its last game against the vaunted San Francisco running attack, featuring J. D. Smith, Hugh McElhenney, and Joe Perry.

As for the Eagles, physically, they're in great shape. Jimmy Carr, recuperating from his ankle injury, is almost 100% recovered. Barnes has fully healed from ankle and hip injuries he suffered against St. Louis, and guard Gerry Huth is finally healthy enough to play a full game.

History favors the Lions in this one. Against Detroit, Philadelphia has managed only three wins against nine losses in past encounters.

The weather is warm and sunny as the number of Philly spectators, 38,065, creeps slightly upward from the Cardinal turnstile count. For the first time all year, the Eagles score first, and then hold the lead throughout the match. The final score reads 28-10, Eagles' favor, as the defense shines. Lion quarterbacks Jim Ninowski and Earl Morrall complete only 14 of 37 passes. Van Brocklin is accurate on only nine of his 19 attempts, but two are scoring strikes—one to Walston, the other to Dean. He also completes a 51-yarder to Tommy McDonald, who is held to one catch, as is Retzlaff. Clarence Peaks, almost inconspicuously enjoying his finest season, is the offensive star, chugging 88 yards on 14 lugs.

Maxie Baughan is awarded the game ball for his 15 tackles, 10 of which are unassisted. Joe Robb again stars at defensive end. He and Marion Campbell team up for the first potent Philadelphia pass rush of the season. Robb, Campbell, and the Eagle defensive wall throws the Lion quarterbacks for losses of 40 yards. When the Lions do get a pass off, four attempts are intercepted. When linebacker John

Clarence Peaks

Nocera is injured, Concrete Charley Bednarik joins in the defensive fun for the first time in 1960. Bednarik snags a Morrall pass and makes a couple tackles in the two defensive series he's on the field.

The Lions' offense is stifled. Detroit's sole touchdown comes when Joe Schmidt returns an interception all the way, rolling up the first points in his Hall of Fame career.

Turnovers are the big difference in the game. The Lions cough up two fumbles and four interceptions, effectively killing any offense they mount. In the cheerful aftermath, the Eagle staff overlooks the fact that the Birds tallied only two more first downs than Detroit, yielding 154 rushing yards in the process. That's only 12 yards less than Detroit gained on the ground in *two* previous games.

The Birds do not dominate the Lions. As late as the fourth quarter, the score was only 14-10. Jimmy Gallagher, one of the Eagles' front office guys in 1960, recalls that some Detroit players were taunting Tom Brookshier as the Eagles left the field. "Wish we could play you guys again!" they were yelling. Brookshier shot back: "You can—just win your division, 'cause we're going to the championship game!"

That theme, expressed by Detroit, nags the Eagles all year. The 1960 Eagles are not dreaded by opponents. In their first four games, Philadelphia hasn't had a single impressive performance. All they have are three wins. Still those wins have come against teams with a combined record of 1-10-0. The Eagles, themselves, are ranked last in team defense and last in team defense against the run. No Eagle back has rushed for 100 yards in a game. In contrast, three opposing backs have topped the century mark against them. But the Eagles have already learned to look beyond statistics. They put their game faces on and come to the stadium to play ball. Others may not take this team seriously, which is irrelevant. The Eagles take themselves seriously. They have nurtured a healthy team attitude. They don't care about statistics or style, only about the final score. Ted Dean comments on the team's attitude:

TED DEAN: "We weren't cocky, just confident. I know that, every time I was on a football field, I believed that I was going to perform well. We had a whole team that felt that way. We always thought we would win, no matter what was happening. It didn't phase us if another team was running the ball on us. We didn't worry about that. We knew we'd just have to figure out some other way to win."

Despite their .750 winning percentage, the Eagles find themselves in third place, behind the 3-0-0 Browns and the 3-0-1 Giants. The Giants were surprised in their last game when they only managed a tie against Washington. Redskins' quarterback, Ralph Guglielmi, was at his best before the Giants' home-opener crowd of 60,625. Down 17-3 at half-time, the Redskins came back to tie the Giants on the strength of Guglielmi's 13 for 16 passing. Meanwhile, over in Cleveland, the Browns are starting to look invincible. They lead the entire NFL in points scored (remarkable, since the Browns have played only three games, while most of the league has played four), and fewest points given up.

~ *The Blade* ~

Don Burroughs was, unquestionably, the most unlikely looking football player on the '60 squad. At 6'-4 1/2" and weighing 180-something, the Blade's "look" in pads was more Fred Astaire than Knute Rockne. Van Brocklin nicknamed Burroughs the Blade when the two met at the Los Angeles Ram's summer camp in 1955. Dutch couldn't believe that anyone that skinny could be that good.

Actually, the Blade tried to make it as a quarterback with the Rams that year. The Blade recalls:

DON BURROUGHS: "That was in 1955, my first year. The rookies got to camp first, ahead of the veterans. I threw the ball with the rookie quarterbacks for ten days or so, until the veterans came to camp. Then, who comes along but Dutch, Billy Wade, and ex-USC star, Rudy the "the Rifle" Bukich. I didn't throw the ball again."

In 1951, as a quarterback for Colorado State, Don Burroughs led all NCAA passers by completing 68 percent of his passes. Burroughs' running back in that Colorado State offensive backfield was Jack Christiansen. His top receiver was Jim David. All three of these Colorado State backfield mates wound up on the other side of the scrimmage line in the pros. They all became defensive backs. David and Christiansen spent their pro careers playing alongside one another. The two of them teamed with Yale Lary in Detroit's secondary. The trio of David, Christiansen, and Lary played on all three of the Lions' championship teams of the '50s. David finished his eight-year career with 36 interceptions. Christiansen picked off 46 passes in an eight-year career, which began in 1951. Twice he led the NFL in interceptions, snatching 12 in 1953 and 10 in 1957. Christiansen's exploits earned him a spot in the football Hall of Fame, along with his Detroit backfield mate, Yale Lary, who grabbed 50 career interceptions. Lary is tied for 14th on the all-time career interception list with two others. One of those others is Don Burroughs. The Blade, with his 50 career interceptions, trails only 21 others in picking off

Don Burroughs

passes. The Blade put up Hall of Fame numbers but has never received commensurate recognition.

Burroughs, like his teammate McDonald, was always battling perception. His two college mates, David and Christiansen, were both drafted by the pros. He, on the other hand, was passed over. The Blade went in the Army, and reported to Fort Ord where he played on the same team as Ollie Matson and Don Heinrich. He was noticed by an NFL scout during his stay at Fort Ord and earned a look by the Rams. The Blade recalls:

DON BURROUGHS: "After we played the Rams, their General Manager, Tex Schramm signed me. He was good to me, that Tex Schramm. But I wasn't happy with the rest of the management in Los Angeles. Dutch knew I wasn't happy, and he knew what kind of ballplayer I was. He worked to get me to Philadelphia, and I was glad he did. I really loved playing in Philly. The fans were great, and so were the media—compared to Los Angeles. The papers there would pick you apart."

The Blade had started off sensationally with L.A. As a rookie defensive back, he picked off nine passes, a career high he matched in 1960 as an Eagle. He picked off seven for the Rams in 1958, but his total plummeted to zero in 1959, which made him expendable. The Eagles picked him up for a draft choice. What a deal!

As backfield mate, Tom Brookshier, puts it:

TOM BROOKSHIER: "The Blade's looks were so deceiving. He looked like a good wind would knock him over, but he was a tough competitor. Blade was never afraid to stick his helmet in there and mix it up. But I still say that's how he got all those interceptions. Those quarterbacks couldn't see him when he turned sideways."

~ *Six, Maybe Seven, Eagles Quarterbacks* ~

The Eagles actually have seven quarterbacks on their squad in 1960. Van Brocklin and Jurgensen, obviously, head the list. But in a pinch, the Birds could also call on Jerry Reichow, Don Burroughs, Bobby Jackson, and Bobby Freeman. Reichow was a quarterback at Iowa, while Burroughs was the NCAA's most accurate passer in 1951 at Colorado State. Bobby Jackson who was a single-wing quarterback at Alabama, admires for the way his friend, Bobby Freeman, played the position:

BOBBY JACKSON: "In those days, a lot of times, the best athletes were the quarterbacks. Remember we all ran the option in that era. I played for Bear Bryant at Alabama, and I played both ways—quarterback on offense and cornerback on defense. Bobby Freeman played for Vince Dooley over at Auburn. Let me tell you, that Bobby was really talented. He was a great college quarterback. You know, he won the MVP at the Senior Bowl the year before I graduated—really put on a show. Bobby could run. He was probably the fastest guy on that '60 team. I played in that Senior Bowl the year after Bobby and roomed with Theron Sapp from Georgia. Theron won the MVP that year. But in those days quarterbacks did a little of everything. They threw, ran, punted, place-kicked. Dutch punted for the Eagles, and Bobby Layne kicked field goals, punted, and passed for the Lions in the early '50s."

Who's the seventh quarterback? It's linebacker Bob Pellegrini, who claims he was a quarterback in high school. But then, considering what Pete Retzlaff says about linebackers being frustrated quarterbacks, Pellegrini is a dubious addition to the list.

The Eagles are learning how misleading statistics can be. Statistically, one of their shining stars is not lighting up the league. He's not among the leaders in any receiving category—save one. Thomas Franklin McDonald is one of the leaders in touchdowns scored. He hasn't caught many passes—at least not enough to satisfy him. However, when he catches one, it's usually at a critical time, and it usually goes for a touchdown. Philly's favorite flanker finishes the championship season with 39 catches. One-third of those catches terminate with McDonald celebrating in the end zone—a sight that gets Philadelphians right where they live.

EightEight**Eight**EightEightEight

Touchdown Maker

In the hearts of Philadelphians, that's where Tommy McDonald lives. When athletes are measured in terms of heart, guts, and determination, the name Tommy McDonald pops up. No matter how hard he got hit by defensive backs, no matter how woozy he was from collisions with linebackers or goal posts, McDonald popped right back up to his feet. I mean, he popped *right back up*—an instantaneous, fast-forward, in-your-face, kind of right back up. His pop-up routine captivated the heart of the hometown fans. It infuriated opponents.

The greatest part of the McDonald pop-up-when-you're-nailed saga is its constancy. No one in Philadelphia old enough to have licked Green Stamps or traded Raleigh coupons recalls a single instance when Tommy did *not* pop right back up after a hit. No amount of manhandling could slow him down. His legend of indomitable toughness is Philly history.

These days, talking with Tommy McDonald about churning cleats and feats of reckless abandon brings a smile to his face. McDonald's grin shows a few more wrinkles than it did in 1960, when his number 25 was the third-down cynosure of all eyes at Franklin Field. But the essential Tommy remains pretty much unchanged.

"I just wanted to show the defense they couldn't intimidate me cause I was small. I made that pop-up my trademark," he admits. "Even when I got pounded and didn't know where I was, I popped right back up so those tacklers wouldn't know I was hurt. I wouldn't give them that satisfaction."

As a 176-pound flanker, McDonald absorbed an enormous amount of pounding. He made his living galloping into dangerous turf—a gazelle taunting lions and other assorted predators ready to pounce and pummel.

"I remember one time when Dick Butkus tackled me. Boy, he was a tough hitter. When I looked up, Butkus was holding my one leg, and another guy was holding the other one. Butkus looked at him and said, 'Go ahead. Make a wish.'"

Tommy McDonald was one of the game's most enthusiastic players.

Talking to Tommy, you get the impression that he is in awe of many of his peers. He never utters a negative word about them. He comes across as a guy who's tickled pink to have had the chance to play in the halcyon era that grew football into today's mega-success.

Thomas Franklin McDonald, in his youth, never dreamed of becoming a pro football player. His hometown, the tiny New Mexico hamlet of Roy, isn't even a speck on a lot of maps. The Hall of Famer remembers the days of his youth vividly. He speaks with a faraway fondness about the vistas of the southwest where he grew up. Though Philadelphia has been his home for several decades, somewhere back there in the dust, that same small town is still a big part of Tommy McDonald.

"Roy was a little farming community. There were only a 1000 or 1400 people in the whole town. There were two grocery stores and a red light. Yeah, basically, that was about the size of it. My folks planted wheat, and my grandfather owned cattle. Actually, my dad was an electrician. As a kid, I helped him do electrical work, which I always felt strengthened my hands for catching footballs later on. You don't realize it, but turning screwdrivers and the like—you have to have a strong grip to do that kind of work. You're constantly squeezing. I really think working with my dad gave me good hand and wrist strength. The school I went to in Roy was a combined elementary and high school. There were maybe a 100, 125 kids there all told. I enjoyed those early years in Roy, but, you know, if our family hadn't moved, I'd probably be a farmer myself today. That's why I'm dedicated to the Big Guy Upstairs. There's nothing wrong with farming, but the Big Guy gave me the opportunity to do some other things. He always seemed to put me in the right place at the right time, 'cause, when we moved away from Roy, that's when things kind of opened up for me."

Things did open up. Tommy McDonald, football star, got his engine revving in Albuquerque, where his family settled after eighth grade. Tommy came under the tutelage and influence of Hugh Hackett, his high school track and football coach. Hackett set the fleet, young, southwestern jackrabbit off and running. In his senior year, McDonald won five gold medals in the state track finals. That same year, he set a new standard for New Mexico high school basketball by scoring 595 points in a single season. Coach Hackett not only encouraged his young athlete, he championed him for some prestigious college football programs.

"Coach Hackett recommended me to Oklahoma. I was so impressed with Coach Wilkinson there. You know what I liked most? He emphasized education. He told me: 'You're coming here for an education. Football is secondary.' I was approached by some other fine schools, like Southern Methodist, Texas Christian, and the University of New Mexico. But Coach Wilkinson impressed me most because he really seemed to care about me. He had a way of putting things in perspective. You forget how much a young kid needs that. Not only that, he was a wonderful football coach. He never hollered or raised his voice, but he sure could motivate. He was a great X's and O's type of guy who understood the game, and he had a great eye for talent."

Tommy McDonald appreciates people blessed with an eye for talent. Traditional footballers harbored a natural bias against McDonald. Only the gifted few who could look past size and bulk foresaw McDonald's pro potential. But then, Tommy was always getting overlooked—no pun intended—by those blind to the inner fire at the core of a true winner.

~ "All he does is score touchdowns"—a Philly tradition ~

Tommy McDonald came to town for the same reason that Cris Carter left town over 30 years later. All they did was score touchdowns.

In 1956, Tommy McDonald, one of college football's brightest luminaries, languished in the NFL draft until round three. The Sooner star, who finished third in the Heisman voting that year, was passed over for only one reason. He was considered too small for the pro game.

If credentials were the sole determinant, drafting McDonald in the first round was a no-brainer. He starred on both offense and defense on an Oklahoma team that swept through the collegiate ranks with more gusto than the original Sooners swept across the Oklahoma territory. In McDonald's entire career at Oklahoma, the Sooners never lost a game. In his senior year, only four opponents even *scored* on the Sooners. Tommy McDonald was Oklahoma's marquee player. In the Heisman voting in 1956, McDonald racked up more first-place votes than the winner, Paul Hornung, of Notre Dame. Yet, when draft day came, Tommy's accomplishments were dwarfed, so to speak, by his lack of size. Kilroy and Jimmy Gallagher influenced the Eagles to take a chance on McDonald.

"We used to study films of all the major colleges, and Oklahoma was the top team back then," Kilroy recollects. "Week after week, all I'd see was this guy McDonald scoring touchdowns. So, we drafted him. The rest is history."

Gallagher recalls draft day, November 27, 1956, at the Warwick Hotel in Philadelphia.

"The first few rounds of that 1957 draft took place in late November of '56, before the regular season was over. Later on, in January of '57, we picked the remaining rounds. We picked the early rounds in November so we could beat the Canadian League to the punch. Their season ended sooner than ours, so they held their draft before we did. They were starting to take a lot of our good players, because they drafted ahead of the NFL. Anyway, in November of '56, the Eagles were ahead of the Browns in the standings. The Browns were 2-7, and we were 3-5-1. So, Cleveland picked right ahead of us, and took Jimmy Brown. We were hot on Brown! But Cleveland had first shot, and we lost him. Had that draft taken place in January, *we* would have had first shot at Brown, 'cause we finished behind Cleveland. But at least we got Clarence Peaks, a good runner, in place of Brown. Actually, Cleveland delayed for a half-hour themselves. They were hung up deciding between Clarence and Brown. As for McDonald, Bucko and I had seen this highlight film on him. All Tommy did was score touchdowns in it! I mean he looked sensational in the film. Every round, when the Eagles' turn to pick came up, I sounded like a broken record. 'Pick McDonald,' I'd say. 'All the guy does is score touchdowns!' I think they got tired of listening to me, and finally, in round three, we drafted him."

Years after Gallagher had convinced the Eagle brass that there was value in a guy who only scored touchdowns, Eagle coach Buddy Ryan released receiver Chris Carter. His reasoning? "All Carter does is score touchdowns," Buddy informed the Quaker City. Carter, after leaving the Eagles, crafted a long, distinguished, sure-fire Hall of Fame career. He's caught a lot of passes, and, yes, he *has* scored a lot of touchdowns. The Minnesota Vikings do not, apparently, hold his touchdown habit against him, just as the '56 Eagles did not hold McDonald's mania for TD's against him. Scoring touchdowns is what brought McDonald to Philadelphia, even if it's what got Carter kicked out.

"Even Mr. Wilkinson had doubts about whether I could make it in pro ball," Tommy remembers. "When the Eagles went down to Oklahoma for a preseason game in my second year as a professional, he told me that he was glad I was still with the Eagles. He confessed to me that he wasn't so sure I'd make it at the pro level because of my size. I didn't doubt myself. I always figured I could hook on somewhere with a pro team. If I didn't make it on offense, I thought I could make it as a defensive back. I knew it was going to be tough for me to run the ball up here. When I got to the pros, Billy Barnes and Clarence Peaks were in camp as rookies. They were bigger guys than me, and they could drag tacklers with them. I couldn't do that."

One thing's for sure, Tommy McDonald did not receive a banner welcome to the NFL, the Eagles, or the Quaker City. His first disappointment was the College

All-Star Game, which he watched mostly from the bench. He was in good company, though. Jim Brown sat out with him.

"I've never really investigated, but that crop of rookies in 1957 had to be the best ever. There was Sonny Jurgensen, Jim Brown, Len Dawson, Johnny Majors, Clarence Peaks, Billy Ray Barnes, Don Bosseler, Jon Arnett, Abe Woodson, Jim Podoley, Ed Sutton, Ron Kramer, Jerry Tubbs, Jim Parker, Paul Wiggin, Henry Jordan, Jack Pardee, Don Shinnick, and Terry Barr. Hey, those names are right off the top of my head. Did I miss any? I guess I shouldn't have been disappointed that I didn't play much in that College All-Star Game, but I was. I couldn't help it. The Eagle coaching staff had flown over to Chicago from Hershey just to watch me, and I hardly got in. I felt good, though, when we got back to Hershey. They put me in to play defense in practice, and I intercepted two passes."

That memory underscores the man's pride. McDonald could fill 50 scrapbooks with great moments from his college and professional career, yet his voice pops with pride over an inconsequential practice session in Hershey, simply because it proved to doubters that he was a player.

A month later, Tommy found the road into Philadelphia just as rocky.

"There was a robber or criminal at that time called the Kissing Bandit. This woman thought I looked like the artist's sketch of this character. She called the police, and next thing I know, they take me to the police station. I'm telling the cops that my name is Tommy McDonald and I play for the Philadelphia Eagles. Of course, I was brand new. No one in Philadelphia knew me at that point. So, these cops are looking at me, and I'm just a little guy—and of course, they're thinking: 'Yeah, right. Sure you play for the Eagles.' I had just arrived in town, didn't know anyone and didn't know my way around. So, I called Mr. McNally (the Eagles' General Manager at the time), the only person I could think of, to come down to the station and speak on my behalf. He came down and straightened things out. Anyway, that was my introduction to Philadelphia."

In his rookie year, the Eagles didn't know exactly what to do with their ex-Oklahoma star. Other than returning kicks and punts, the kid from Roy saw limited action as a rookie. It wasn't till coach Charlie Gauer recalled an old Oklahoma Sooner play that the Eagles decided to try McDonald as a pass-catcher.

"At Oklahoma, we had a play where I would fake into the line, then go downfield and they'd throw to me. You know, I only caught four touchdown passes in college, and one of them was a 55-yarder that Jimmy Harris threw to me on that play. Jimmy was drafted by the Eagles in '57, too. He was one of the guys we traded to bring Norm Van Brocklin here. Anyway, Gauer remembered seeing that particular play. He thought I caught the ball pretty well and wanted to try me out at receiver."

That's when the name Tommy McDonald started to pop up all around Philadelphia and all over the NFL. Tommy proved Bucko Kilroy and Jimmy Gallagher right. It *did* seem that all he did was catch touchdown passes. As it turns out, one of every 5.9 passes McDonald caught went for a touchdown. But that's not all Tommy did. He played every down—catching, decoying, and blocking, all-out, all the time. He studied his position. He knew the opposition's strengths and weaknesses, and he worked every advantage. He got more dangerous as the game wore on.

"Tommy McDonald was the best fourth-quarter receiver I ever saw," teammate Tom Brookshier adds. That's a convincing endorsement. Brookshier has seen them all in his 50-or-so years around the sport. "It was almost like, late in the game, Tommy had you figured out and was going to catch you. What a tough guy, and what a competitor! He'd do all the little things, anything he could do to beat you."

The little things. . .ironic that a guy considered too little to play this game beat the opposition doing the "little things" they overlooked. Tommy cites one of these little things, a little trick he had up his sleeve.

"When I was playing, it was real popular around Philadelphia for kids to cut off their jersey sleeves like I did. Everyone thought I did that to show off, or to act tough, or something like that. But, that wasn't the reason at all. I could stretch my arms out farther with the sleeves cut off. You know, football jerseys bind your arms a lot more than you think. I wanted to be able to stretch my arms out as far as I could. Every extra inch of reach counts. It might make the difference. I think cutting off those sleeves worked, too. I got my hands on the ball more than a few times because of it."

Yeah, it's a game of inches. Just sit around the draft table and you'll find that out.

Tommy did get his hands on more than a few footballs. At the time of his retirement, he was ranked in the top five, all-time, for career receptions, yards receiving, and touchdowns. Even today, Tommy is in the top 10 for touchdowns.

"And, you know, it's a different game today," Tommy says, as the discussion breaks into the open field. Tommy's a natural in this territory.

"I was really blessed in having two all-time greats like Norman Van Brocklin and Sonny Jurgensen throwing to me. But football was still more of a run-oriented game when I played. Nowadays, these teams throw all the time. I'd fit right into this era. I'd love to be playing today."

Like many of his teammates, Tommy McDonald has some mixed emotions about missing the glitter and glory of the modern sport. He loved his days in the sun—and the rain, and the drizzle. He has no regrets. Yet, he's well aware that he and his peers were a warm-up act—a much lower paid one, at that—for today's megabuck extravaganza. Current fans tend to see Tommy's heyday in a different light. They peer at dim black and white images. They listen to the crackling soundtracks, punctuated by the stark John Facenda voice-overs. Some neophytes from today's generation don't make a connection between Tommy's era and the glitzy, high-energy, high-tech modern game. Today's game looks like '50s football on steroids. It looks like Arnold Schwartzenegger compared to Charles Atlas. But, McDonald is no fossil from a defunct world. Tommy, the master of the crossing pattern, was a cross-over player. In an age when America's heroes were self-effacing and stoic, Tommy was demonstrative and spontaneous, often hopping into teammates' arms after touchdowns. In an inhibited era, he was one of the few to emote. He was an original, as all his teammates will attest. And originality is a claim that most of the moderns can't make.

So, what does Tommy think about today's end-zone choreography, those modern-day gyrations that link more to the Rockettes than to Rockne?

"I think the kids are just having fun out there. They don't have fun playing football like we did, you know. I played with a lot of enthusiasm, myself, just 'cause I loved playing this sport. And I was always thrilled to score. That's just me. That's why I did that little routine at the Hall of Fame, when I brought my boom box on stage. That's why I was chest bumping the other inductees on the podium. So many people have told me they loved the whole routine I went through. Believe me, I was just excited about being there. The Big Guy Upstairs has been really good to me. I've been fortunate, and the whole Hall of Fame thing was the thrill of a lifetime for me. I just wanted to show everyone how honored and happy I was. Every year, they make a little bet about who'll break up, who'll cry, first. But, they didn't bother making the bet the year I went in. Everybody said, 'Forget it. No sense betting this year. McDonald's a sure thing.' So, I was just trying to loosen things up, 'cause I knew I would get emotional. I guess some people didn't think it was dignified enough for the occasion. But so many other people have actually thanked me for it. They say: 'Hey, Tommy, what you did was the best thing we ever saw at an induction ceremony.' I went up for the ceremony the following year, and people came up to me, saying: 'It's dull this year, Tommy. Really boring. We need you up there again.' So, no, I don't have problems with the ballplayers today celebrating. I'd be out there doing it myself."

No one ever enjoyed his Hall of Fame induction more than Tommy McDonald.

Never one to linger around in one zone, Tommy dashes off to other subjects, like his family, his grandkids, and his portrait business. Tommy McDonald, entrepreneur, runs a successful portrait painting business in King of Prussia. He juggles his family and business commitments with a hefty slate of speaking engagements and personal appearances. He's always been popular as a speaker because he gives off such energy and comes across as such a nice guy.

Tommy McDonald: nice guy. No, Tommy hardly looks the part of the tough southwestern hombre who played for years without wearing a face mask. To make matters worse, the little flanker chattered constantly when he was between the lines. According to teammates, rather than lay low, Tommy taunted and baited defenders into hitting him harder. Grizzly posses patrolling "the middle" were always gunning to shut this little outlaw up for good.

"He was a tough guy," recalls Clarence Peaks, Tommy's 1960 teammate. "Tommy was just a great old country boy. I don't think the guy ever dropped a pass. He had the greatest hands. And, I'll tell you what else he had. He had heart. Didn't matter how hard you hit him. He was right back up on his feet, and begging Van Brocklin to throw the ball his way next play. The guy never got tired, always wanted the ball."

Jim McCusker, offensive lineman on the '60 squad, calls Tommy the toughest guy, pound for pound, he ever saw.

"One day, Tommy had an abscessed tooth. His head was so swollen he couldn't get his helmet on. Fortunately, it was easy to find Tommy a bigger helmet, since he had the smallest head on the team! Anyway, he put this other helmet on, and couldn't even buckle the chin strap. Of course, I don't know if you know this or not, Tommy never buckled his chin strap anyway. But he had to play that whole game in excruciating pain. He wound up playing a great game, too. But that's the kind of competitor he was. You couldn't keep him off the field."

So what does Tommy think of the "tough" homage paid him by his peers?

"Well, I am proud that I only missed three games because of injury in my entire career. I guess some of that 'tough' stuff is because I didn't wear a face mask. I wasn't trying to be tough, though. I didn't wear a mask for the same reason I cut off my sleeves. I could see better. That bar cut off my field of vision. That was really the only reason I didn't wear the face mask. The Big Man Up There was watching over me, I guess, so I didn't get hurt. Then again, I always stayed in good shape, to reduce the risk of injury. I didn't get hurt at Oklahoma, either. Of course, maybe you just don't feel any pain when you're winning."

Oklahoma, where the win comes right behind the pain. That's where the fleet game-breaker first started getting popped by the big guys. But, like the Rebel, Johnny Yuma, the southwestern hero of a popular TV western of the era, McDonald was panther-quick and leather tough. No matter how viciously he got whacked, he popped up, all set to hurt you on the next play where it really mattered—on the scoreboard.

Tommy McDonald broke sport paradigms with the same deftness that he once broke pass patterns. As a prankster and quipster, Tommy hardly fit the classic image of a football tough guy. Today, he is a proud grand-pop. But he's not the typical ex-jock pressuring his little ones into following his own footsteps. After all, Tommy never listened to footsteps.

"You know, my grandson plays for the King of Prussia Longhorns. Seems funny, 'cause that was my first team as a kid, the Roy Longhorns. That's special for me. It really is. I mean, here I am a grandfather, and my grandson is playing football for the Longhorns—half a country away from where I grew up. He's doing real well, too, but I don't want to steer him toward football. That kind of thing has to be his own choice. I love him just the way he is, no matter what he does."

That's the way Philadelphia loves Tommy McDonald. The way he is. Still, it would be great to have the name, McDonald, pop up on Philly gridirons in the new millennium. The kid'll have to know, though, that Old McDonald is one tough act to follow.

The thrill of a lifetime—Tommy McDonald scores the first TD of the championship game.

NineNineNineNineNineNineNine

Double Dutch and Red Dogs

While the Eagles enjoyed their first, somewhat convincing victory of the season, the Browns were coloring another opponent black and blue. Another meager Texas crowd of 28,500 watched Brown and Mitchell, along with backups Prentice Gautt and Jamie Caleb, trample the hometown Texan tenderfoots, 48-7. Mitchell ran unfettered, scoring first on a 30-yard dash and later on a 90-yard kickoff return. With the cushion up to an insurmountable 28-0 by half-time, coach Paul Brown mercifully yanked Mitchell and Brown from active duty. Their replacements, Jamie Caleb and Prentice Gautt, continued the assault, rumbling an additional 129 yards on the ground, and tacking on a touchdown apiece.

The Cleveland running attack isn't new news. The new news is the potency of Cleveland's less heralded weapons, like the NFL's top-rated passer, Milt Plum, and the NFL's top-rated defense. In three games, Cleveland has yielded just 51 points. The Eagles defense has surrendered more than twice that many, albeit in four games.

So, where are the Eagles' heads, as they await their rematch with the same team that walloped them 41-24 in the opener—a team that just ambushed the Cowboys 48-7— those same Cowboys who played Philadelphia dead even, except for two blocked PAT's? Stan Campbell reflects:

STAN CAMPBELL: "Did Cleveland beat the Cowboys that badly? No, I didn't remember the Dallas game was that close when we played them in '60. I guess it was. But I only remember that we won. We won all those games in a row after the opener. How many was it? Nine, ten? As for Cleveland, we never worried about the other team, or who was on the other team. We just went out every week to win. We always figured we'd win, no matter who showed up across the field, because, well, we just had confidence that we would. We did it enough times. Really, it's that simple."

"I only remember we won." Focus … Focus was the twelfth man on the '60 Eagles—a twelfth man who suited up every week and played every down. *It's that simple.* Interviewing the '60 Eagles is time-travel from today's information-glutted age to yesterday's don't-overload-me-with-data mentality. Sometimes the old notions work. Data are numbers, not facts. It is not a *fact* that Cleveland's number-one-ranked defensive team was superior to Philadelphia's last-ranked defensive unit. It's *data*. And, though it might be an interesting piece of data to some, it meant nothing to this Eagles bunch. Ask any of the Eagles whose defensive unit they'd rather have on the field when a game was on the line. Ask any of the Eagles whose unit they'd bet on if you needed a game-saving tackle or a killer turnover. For the Eagles, there *is* only one answer to those questions. And their answer flies in the face of data.

BOBBY FREEMAN: "We had a bunch of ordinary people who did extraordinary things, some of them for only that one year. That's what that '60 team had. I don't know why or how it happened. I never experienced the same feeling on any other team before or since. Maybe it was the mix we had—veterans, young guys, and great leaders like Dutch, Brookie, the Swamp Fox, Eddie Khayat, Retzlaff, Peaks, Chuck Weber—so many guys who injected their personal style of leadership into a whole big mix. We had some truly great players, and we had some ordinary players. But we were all like equals on that team. We socialized together, did things together. And on the field, we played for only one thing: to win every week. No one was ever jealous of anyone else's success, and we wound up with a different hero just about every week."

Going into the Cleveland contest, the Eagles boast not a single leader in any individual category. Their team statistics are mediocre at best. Various guys who are not household names, like Freeman and Weber, save the season with their Dallas heroics. Retzlaff, Robb, and Burroughs come up with the game-saving plays against the Cards. Versus the Lions, defensive back Gene Johnson makes two interceptions, Peaks gains 88 crucial yards, and Maxie Baughan bags 15 tackles and his first game ball. It's a bit like the Yankees' formula of the era. The Yankees always feature a line-up packed with stars and superstars, but, when those big Series games come along, someone like Bobby Richardson or Billy Martin or Don Larsen, or one of their lesser lights would shine.

MAXIE BAUGHAN: "I was only a rookie, and in those early games still worried about making the squad and staying on the team. I knew Buck Shaw had shipped a lot of guys away on trades over the past few years. I didn't want to get traded, so I just concentrated on doing the best job I could. I didn't get caught up in the spirit that something special was happening around here until they gave me that game ball after the Detroit game. But what I think was so special about this team was how unselfish the whole group was. I played pro ball a long while and never saw a gang with this team's chemistry. Everyone put the team ahead of himself. We went a long way on that spirit alone. And we always seemed to come up with a big play when we had to."

Like that big third-and-25 pass that Retzlaff snagged against the Cardinals. Without it, the Eagles would be 1-2, and dangerously lagging behind the leaders. Jerry Reichow sees the Eagles' penchant for those big plays as breaking some new ground in the NFL of 1960.

JERRY REICHOW: "With McDonald, Walston, and Retzlaff, and with Dean and Barnes coming out of the backfield, we had a big-play team, a term that really hadn't been popularized at that point. But that's what we had. Running still dominated the game in '60, but our team had a pass-oriented attack, and a quarterback who could come up with big plays anywhere on the field. Our defense was the same way. They were a big-play bunch, with lots of interceptions and turnovers at key points."

Big plays, big turnovers, and multiple heroes—different guys stepping up every Sunday. And every Sunday, everyone's head was in the same place. Just like every Monday, everyone's body was in the same place—at Donoghue's near the Park Plaza. The Eagles were in sync, in rhythm. There's no data to measure that, except in the win column.

MUMBLES' WOBBLER

The Eagles are 13-point underdogs going into the Cleveland rematch. A throng of 70,000 is expected at Cleveland's lakeside theater of intimidation known as Municipal Stadium. The Eagles hope to contain the Browns' high-powered running attack this time around. Jimmy "Gummy" Carr is back. The Birds are convinced that Gummy stops the run better than any other defensive back in football, with the exception of his mate, Tom Brookshier. Eagle linebacker, John Nocera, will sit the game out with an injury. Bizarre that the Birds count an injury to a starter as a plus; however, most feel that Nocera's replacement, Bob Pellegrini, who has started every other game at offensive guard, strengthens the linebacking. Aside from Nocera, the Eagles are at full strength. So are the Browns, except for flanker Ray Renfro. None of their other starters will miss the game.

Game day is chilly and overcast. The Eagles have not won in Cleveland since 1952, and the Browns' win streak over the Eagles has climbed to seven.

On the game's first play from scrimmage, Pellegrini is taken off the field. Badly hobbled and removed from the fray, Pellegrini is unable to return. The Eagles send in 35-year-old Concrete Charley—the same guy Shaw said was "too old for linebacking" a few weeks earlier. The 12-year veteran is assigned double duty for the day. He toils 59 minutes, leading the charge on the offensive line, while leading all defenders with 15 tackles, 11 of which are unassisted.

From the opening kick-off, the rematch has a different feel. For the second straight game, Philadelphia scores first. On the home team's opening series, the Eagles stand fast. Then, with the ball at Cleveland's 49, the Birds' offensive unit trots onto the field for the first time. On the first Eagle play from scrimmage, Van

Brocklin strikes deep to "closed" end (as tight end is often called in 1960) Bobby Walston, who hauls it in at the Cleveland 10-yard line and strolls in untouched for six points.

Cleveland responds with five unanswered scores. A tough Eagle goal-line stand forces Cleveland to settle for a field goal. Sam Baker adds two additional field goals. The Browns manage to reel off a couple of big plays, including a long TD pass to Leon Clarke in the first half and a 71-yard TD run by Jimmy Brown early in the second half, to stretch the Cleveland lead to 22-7.

After Brown's scores, the Birds soar back for successive touchdowns. The second TD comes on a 57-yard Van Brocklin strike to McDonald that lets the Eagles creep to within one point of Cleveland, 22-21. The Eagle defense again stiffens and halts the Browns before Van Brocklin takes over for the Birds and engineers a drive that culminates with an 8-yard swing pass to Barnes for a score.

The Browns get the ball back and immediately march 88 yards to retake the lead. With time almost out, the Eagles embark on a final drive that starts at their own 10-yard line. Van Brocklin tosses 27 yards to Retzlaff, and pushes 12 yards further downfield with a pitch to McDonald. A pass interference call on Cleveland defensive back Vince Costello marks the ball at the Cleveland 31, where Bobby Walston kicks a 38-yard field goal with less than 21 seconds remaining in the contest.

The Eagles win their fourth in a row.

Jimmy Brown has another big day, grinding out 167 yards on 22 attempts. However, as Jesse Richardson marvels in the postgame glee: " He's a terror. He just knocks you over." Forty years later, Tom Brookshier has this to say about Jimmy Brown:

TOM BROOKSHIER: "JB was the greatest runner ever. He was so powerful and fast. You know, people don't know it, but I'm in the Hall of Fame, and Jimmy's the one who got me there. I'll tell you what—if you push the button on one of those little display stands they have in front of his bust, you'll see me. I'm number 40, and I'm chasing JB into the

Veteran tackle Jesse Richardson was born and raised in Philadelphia. He led the defense against the Redskins.

end zone. So, I *am* in the Hall of Fame. Me and Jimmy Brown are in there together."

Unlike the opener, the Eagles completely shut down Bobby Mitchell, holding him to 35 yards on 14 carries. Defensive coach Jerry Williams says: "We simply turned Mitchell in, something we didn't do in the first game." After the opener, Browns' coach Paul Brown had pooh-poohed this as an excuse, saying that Cleveland outsmarted the Philadelphia defense by spreading out its own offensive line. Williams is vindicated. Paul Brown is silent. Robb, Bednarik, and Carr stifle the fleet Mitchell all day. D-back Jimmy Carr looks back:

JIM CARR: "We didn't let Mitchell get outside. We noticed in the film that, every time Cleveland pulled a guard, they ran the ball. We reacted accordingly. Jerry Williams had us really prepared for the Browns."

Cleveland again wins the statistical battle. The Browns have the edge in first downs, 21-18; rushing yards, 202-136; and total yards, 451-428. The day, however, belongs to the three oldest Eagles—Chuck Bednarik, Norm Van Brocklin, and Bobby Walston.

Bednarik is simply amazing. After the game, Chuck calls it "my greatest victory ever, and I've had a lot of good ones." Bednarik talks of how much he wanted this win to avenge the opening-day 41-24 humiliation the Browns laid on Philadelphia. And Number 60 had a personal score to settle as well. Bednarik elaborates in an interview after the game:

"I lined up for a play with their slotback on one side of me and that end, Gern Nagler, on the other side. The Browns have a cute little thing they call 'The Clip.' Bobby Mitchell comes around end, see. The slotback makes a feint toward me. While I'm watching him, that end came from my blind side and hit me so hard I somersaulted in the air and landed on my feet. Somehow I staggered over and helped Jimmy Carr tackle Mitchell. Then, I'm getting up and I see Paul Brown. He's laughing at me. He says something like: 'Bednarik, you're too blankety-blank old for this game.' Listen, I admire Paul Brown, but my own father couldn't laugh at me at a moment like that. I told him off good."

In his home near Bethlehem, PA, Chuck Bednarik reminisces all these years later about his relationship with the Cleveland coach:

CHUCK BEDNARIK: "I have nothing but respect for Paul Brown. He certainly was a fine coach. He coached me in the Pro Bowl in 1954, when I won the MVP. I ran an interception back for a touchdown and punted four times for him in that game. I know he respected me. But, that day in '60 in Cleveland, he just really got to me, telling me I was too old. We went at it the whole game."

Chuck elaborated on his own physical state after playing both ways, in an interview he gave in 1960, after speaking at the Maxwell Club lunch the Wednesday after the Cleveland game. Chuck said:

"I was numb for 24 hours. I couldn't eat. I couldn't sleep. People have asked me if I celebrated Sunday night. I was home in bed and my poor wife was rubbing my left thigh—the thigh where I pulled a muscle."

The Eagles' other "old man," Norm Van Brocklin, is sensational for the first time in the regular season. He completes 17 of 26 passes for 292 yards and three touchdowns. The Dutchman rips the Cleveland defense apart. Paul Brown, at the post-game press conference, gushes: "As for Van Brocklin, he is one of the finest football players of all time."

Bednarik himself heaps praise on the Eagle quarterback after the game: "Van Brocklin was never greater. He called at least ten audibles. The first touchdown he threw to Walston was an audible. But the smartest call was a pass Dutch didn't even try to complete. Thirty seconds left, and Dutch comes in the huddle and says, 'When I call, 'Set' give me the ball and I'll throw it out of bounds.' Pete Retzlaff went over to the sideline, but Dutch threw it over Pete's head to stop the clock. That set up the next pass, the interference penalty, and Walston's kick. Bright, huh?"

Nick Skorich, who is spending the new millennium near Princeton, New Jersey, can still recall Dutch's brilliance all those years ago. He also recollects his single-mindedness.

NICK SKORICH: "Dutch was ahead of his time, all right. He could read defenses better than anyone in those days. Charlie Gauer and I had some plays we thought would work, and we wanted Dutch to use them. The trick with Dutch was to get him to think your idea was his idea. We tried to convince him the whole first half to call certain audibles that Gauer and I figured would be effective against particular defensive sets that Cleveland used. Charlie and I had really studied the films. But we couldn't get Dutch to use them. Then, in the second half, Dutch did call them and they worked. Of course, after the game, Dutch never mentioned in the interviews that Charlie and I had given those audibles to him."

Assistant Coach Nick Skorich understood the psychology of working with "Dutch" Van Brocklin.

Jerry Huth adds that Bednarik isn't the only Eagle harboring a personal vendetta with one of the Browns. Dutch set his sights on Don Fleming.

JERRY HUTH: "Dutch didn't forget that opener, and that rookie, Don Fleming, who intercepted him twice. That kid had taunted Dutch in the first game, yelling over to him: 'Hey, number 11, throw me another one!' I don't think

Fleming knew who number 11 was at that time. I'm sure he knew after the second game."

Besides Van Brocklin and Bednarik, Bobby Walston, a nine-year veteran who had just turned 32, has a remarkable day. In addition to his 49-yard touchdown reception, Walston leads all receivers with 94 total yards. However, it's not his receiving, but his gut-wrenching, game-saving 38-yard field goal that becomes perhaps the biggest play of the season.

When the Eagles fly into the Philadelphia Airport, hundreds of fans greet the team and carry Walston through the lobby. Local papers crow that fans haven't been this excited since Dick Sisler hit his home run to win the 1950 National League pennant for the Phillies.

~ Mumbles ~

So much justifiable credit for the 1960 title has been given to the "old" Eagles, Norm Van Brocklin and Chuck Bednarik, that another veteran of arguably comparable merit seems smudged out of the story. Robert Harold Walston is one of the greatest Eagles of all time. He is, it appears, history's most forgotten Eagle.

No one on the '60 Eagles forgets the guy they called "Mumbles," "Blackie," Cheewah," and the "Sheriff." His ex-roommate, Tom Brookshier, applauds a gifted natural athlete and one of the squad's unusual characters:

TOM BROOKSHIER: "The guy was a machine, never gained a pound, just lean and tough. You know, Bobby was a boxer when he was younger. Nobody would mess around with him, except that he was really a party guy—always looking for a good time. I guess people that didn't know him well didn't recognize that side of him, 'cause he had that funny way of talking. That's what got him named "Mumbles." We called him Cheewah, too. He was part Indian, Bobby was. And, what a football player Bob Walston was! He was the guy who made our biggest play, I think. That kick against Cleveland that won the game. I don't think it would have happened without a big gust of Lake Erie wind. But Bobby did it, and we were off to the championship from then on."

The kick … a lot of Bobby's teammates shake their heads about *the* kick. The wobbler. As legend has it—or perhaps, wants it—the pigskin did not clear those Municipal Stadium uprights on leg power alone. So give Lake Erie an assist. But give Bobby the credit.

In the general euphoria following the 1960 season, the entire Philadelphia team cited the Walston kick in Cleveland as the pivotal play of the year. The gusts and swirls of 40 intervening years have slightly reshaped the collective memory. Today, different alumni single out other moments and key plays. Nevertheless, the importance of Walston's boot cannot be diminished. When that ball split those uprights, the Eagles transformed. Hope became resolve. Faith became belief.

And Bobby Walston was vindicated. He had been considered marginal when the 1960 season began. Management had written him off, or, at least considered him a question mark.

Walston started his career with a bang. He had won the NFL's Rookie of the Year Award in 1951, catching 31 passes for 512 yards, and scoring 94 points for the 4-8-0 Eagles. In 1954, he set the Eagle record for most points in a season with 114. He kicked only six field goals but snagged eleven touchdowns for the second-place Birds. Nevertheless, by 1959, it appeared that Bobby Walston was being eased out of the Philadelphia picture. For the first and only time in his career, he didn't boot a field goal. The Birds had hired Paige Cothren for that chore. However, Cothren was so disappointing that the brass cavalierly cut him loose in 1960, opting, hesitantly, to take a chance on Walston. As for receiving, Walston's friend and New Jersey neighbor, Dick Bielski, was being groomed for Mumbles' "closed" end position. Bielski had come up as a fullback in '55, but was being systematically eased into the tight end, or closed end, position in '58 and '59. In '59, Bielski caught only one less pass than Walston, whose total had slipped to 16. In comparison, Bobby had averaged 32.5 receptions a year from 1951 to 1956. That average halved from 1957 through 1959.

Cheewah's teammate, Chuck Bednarik, and Bobby seemed to be on the same path in the late '50s. Bednarik had been selected All-Pro every year from 1950 through 1957. However, Chuck's name disappeared from the scrolls in 1958 and 1959. He, like Walston, seemed to be in decline.

Their rescaling of the heights in 1960 was a major reason for the team's success. Walston scored 105 points in 1960, second best in the NFL, and a personal second best. In 1954, Walston set the Eagles record for points in a season—a mark that lasted 30 years, till kicker Paul McFadden broke it. Walston's mark still ranks third on the Eagles.

Bobby Walston stands alone atop the all-time Eagle scoring list. His 881 points almost doubles what Sam Baker rung up. Baker is in second place with 475 career points for the Eagles. Ironically, Baker was Mumbles' successor during the Birds' declining years in the '60s.

MUZZLING THE PITT BULL

The Eagles have two weeks to recuperate, since they draw a bye the week after the Cleveland battle. As expected, Cleveland bounces back the next week with a 32-10 win over hapless Washington. Surprisingly, the powerhouse Giants lose to the Cardinals, leaving Philadelphia and Cleveland with matching 4-1 records atop the Eastern standings. Fittingly, as far as Philly fans are concerned, New York tumbles into second the same day the entire country tunes into the TV show, "The Violent

World of Sam Huff." In this special, Giants' middle linebacker, Sam Huff, was wired up with a 10-ounce box containing four batteries, a maze of tubes, and a microphone—all of which was placed under his shoulder pads. The Huff documentary booms the sights and sounds of gridiron combat into American living rooms. Huff's "Violent World" spectacle blasts football's popularity higher than ever, while simultaneously boosting the renown of the New York Giants.

As for the Eagles' image, Philadelphia is viewed more as a curiosity than a menace by the national pundits. Pittsburgh Steeler publicist Ed Kiely blurts to the press: "The Eagles are pretty much the same kind of club as us (the Steelers are 2-3-1 thus far). They have a top passer, three fine ends, but not much of a defense. The difference is that the Eagles have been getting the right bounce from the ball." The Steelers are the Eagles' next opponent.

Preston Carpenter, recently traded to the Steelers from Cleveland, piles on to Kiely's remarks: "We can beat the Philadelphia Eagles two games this year. We are just as big as they are, and we have a better coach, too." Kiely, scrambling now to do damage control, says the ex-Cleveland receiver was misquoted.

The Steelers are feeling snakebit. They fumbled six times and lost a close game, 19-13, to the Packers on the Eagles' bye week. Their fumbling fiasco came on the heels of a heartbreaking 28-21 loss to the Browns. The difference in that game was a Steeler TD that was called back, along with the Steelers' failure to score from the Browns' 6-inch line.

Birds' coach Nick Skorich voices his concern about the approaching battle with the Steelers: "Buddy Parker's teams always get better in November." Skorich is resurrecting the embarrassing specter of the 31-0 drubbing the Steelers laid on Philadelphia the previous November.

The Eagles plot an air assault against Pittsburgh even though, almost imperceptibly, running back Clarence Peaks is putting together the best season of his career. In 1959, Peaks finished 15th among NFL runners. This year, it's a different story. The big ex-Michigan fullback is fifth in the NFL in rushing yardage. Only Jim Brown, Jim Taylor, John David Crow, and J.D. Smith (of San Francisco) are ahead of him. What's more, Peaks has only one fumble—his big bugaboo in past seasons.

Peaks may have tough cruising against the Steelers. Pittsburgh is the toughest team in the NFL to run against. In six games, they have yielded only 3.2 yards per carry to opponents, holding even the mighty Browns to 132 rushing yards. However, Cleveland quarterback Milt Plum switched to an aerial attack to beat the Steelers, throwing 10 completions in 14 attempts for 296 yards.

The success of the Browns' air attack prompts the Eagles to look skyward in strategizing for the Steelers. Van Brocklin has been averaging about 26 passes per game, a figure inflated by the 30 tosses he needed in vainly playing catch-up in the Cleveland opener. Amazingly, none of the Eagle receivers are included in the league's top five. Thus far, Tommy McDonald has caught only 12 passes, while league leader Ray Berry has snared 32.

On November 6, 1960, faith flows back to Philly, as 58,324 fans—the largest crowd since 1950—herd into Franklin Field. This time, the Eagles dominate. The hometowners win their fifth straight, their longest string of victories since 1950. The Eagles, as they do all year long, flabbergast all analysis by rolling up 167 yards on the ground. Peaks, with 78 yards, leads the Philly pack. The maligned Eagles' running backs gain more ground yardage against the Steelers than both Cleveland and Green Bay. In fact, the Eagles pile up more yards rushing than Pittsburgh has surrendered all year. Philadelphia's offensive line is sensational, opening holes for runners and providing Van Brocklin ample time to pass. The defense is equally awesome, foiling the Steelers at every turn. The Texas folk hero Bobby Layne is pressured into one of the worst days of his entire career. He completes only 2 of 16 passes for an anemic total of 23 aerial yards. The Eagles' lightly regarded defense also harnesses the Steelers' excellent backfield of future Hall of Famer, John Henry Johnson, and Tom "the Bomb" Tracey.

The Eagles build a 14-0 lead in the first quarter, which grows to 17-0 at the half. In the first half, the Eagles run 52 plays to the Steelers' 29, outgaining Pittsburgh 252 yards to 34 in the process. Pittsburgh doesn't even score till the fourth quarter—and they do so only after Philadelphia has rolled up 27 unanswered points.

Van Brocklin enjoys another banner day, connecting on 19 of 30 passes for 295 yards, for his best performance of the campaign. For the first time all year, Dutch does not throw an interception. Tommy McDonald scintillates as well, hauling in eight passes for 141 yards, including three touchdowns. The little flanker credits his new shoes for the big day.

Rookie Bill Lapham from Iowa makes his first start at center, as Concrete Charley relinquishes his center position and continues at linebacker. The injured Nocera returns and sees some linebacking action as well, but Shaw opts to plant Bednarik, with his experience, leadership, and intensity in the linebacking corps. Lapham performs well as he halts the charges of future Hall of Famer, Ernie Stautner.

After the game, Steeler coach Buddy Parker fumes: "Ours was a great team effort. We stank both ways. No team I ever coached played a worse game." In the same interview, Parker recalls another team that "stank," "When the 49ers first came into the NFL and played me at Detroit, I busted Buck Shaw 48-7. That's the worst I've seen a pro team look until I saw my own club today."

~ Buddy's Bye-Bye ~

Stan Campbell, offensive guard for the '60 Eagles, recalls the bizarre way that Buddy Parker, his coach at Detroit, exited the Lions:

STAN CAMPBELL: "Buddy was a good coach. He was big on bringing in guys from Texas. We had quite a few of them on the Lions—Yale Lary, Bobby Layne, Doak Walker, Cloyce Box, Keith Flowers—guys like that. Buddy was also big on practicing that two-minute drill. We ran it every day at practice. It paid off. Bobby Layne could really move a team down the field at the end of a game. I think he did it better than any quarterback I ever saw. But the thing I'll never forget about Buddy was what he did at a banquet, right before the '57 season was about to start. We were all at a banquet—the whole Lions team. Buddy got up at the podium, right there at the banquet, and said he was quitting as coach. He left the podium and walked out on the team, right then and there at the banquet—and never came back! He went over to Pittsburgh, took the head coaching job there, and brought Bobby Layne over with him to the Steelers. George Wilson took over at Detroit, and we went on to win the '57 championship—even after a start like that!"

As for Buck Shaw, he calls the Eagle victory the best game a Philadelphia team has played since he came to town. "I reminded the boys between halves about the Redskin game last year, when we had Washington down 30-9 at half-time, and then went to sleep and needed a goal-line stand late in the game to win. Today, our lads didn't coast. This club seems to have a fever now. Beating Cleveland really lit the fire."

Norm Van Brocklin assesses his team's intensity in a Philadelphia *Bulletin* interview: "We've got a whiff of the loot ahead. There's probably $5,000 apiece in it for us, if we can win the big cigar. There's nothing quite so inspiring as that cool, green stuff."

In the locker room, the Birds find out that in the biggest match-up of the day, the Giants defeat the Browns, 17-14 at Yankee Stadium. The Giants' Front Four of Katcavage, Modzelewski, Grier, and Robustelli hold Jimmy Brown to 29 yards on 11 carries, and Mitchell to 14 yards in nine carries. When Milt Plum's lost yardage on sacks is included in the rushing totals, the Browns net only six rushing yards on the day. Plum tacks on a mere 89 yards in passing yardage. The Browns' loss gives sole possession of first place to the Eagles, who are followed by the Giants at 4-1-1, and the Browns at 4-2.

Philly fever officially hits. Receipts for the Steeler game surpass $60,000, blowing away the previous mark of $35,000 for a Steeler-game gate. Fans crowd the aisles, and vendors complain they can't hawk their wares. The fans get a little too exuberant. Nine spectators are hauled off in an ambulance. Three suffer fractures leaping from the wall around the field to the cinder track surface below. For the next game, the Eagles hire 40 additional security guards because Philadelphia police are restricted from the premises, according to contemporary newspaper accounts. The University of Pennsylvania has barred Philly's police force from the inside of Franklin Field since 1946, when mounted policemen charged a little too aggressively into a group of Penn and Princeton students who were tearing down the goal posts at the end of the game.

Without sufficient security, fans pour onto the field after the game. The goal posts are torn down and the padding is ripped off. Later, the Eagle brass bemoans the $320 they'll have to spend to replace them.

REDSKIN RED DOG

The first-place Eagles take on the Washington Redskins next. Washington is generally acknowledged as the weakest team in the East. Thus, the Eagles are hefty 13-point favorites.

Washington quarterback Ralph Guglielmi will be healthy for the contest. The ex-Notre Dame star missed the preseason game against the Eagles. Eagle Day started that one for the Skins. However, with the arrival of Cardinal transplant M.C. Reynolds, Day has dropped all the way down to number three on the QB depth chart.

The Skins' lone victory thus far has come against the Cowboys, who are currently saddled with an 0-7 record. The Cowboys are the "swing" team on the NFL's 1960 schedule. The swing team plays each of the other 12 teams in the NFL once. Consequently, Dallas, thus far, has managed to lose to seven *different* opponents. Dallas will end the campaign with losses to *11* different teams, which may be a record for futility.

This Washington squad is the last all-white team in the NFL. George Preston Marshall, owner since the franchise entered the NFL in 1932 as the Boston Braves, contemplates integrating the squad. Marshall is said to have been influenced by the positive reception the Redskin fans accorded Clarence Peaks, Ted Dean, and Timmy Brown when the two clubs clashed in the preseason at Richmond, Virginia. Without question, Marshall's restrictive hiring practices are making his team less competitive.

On game day, 39,361 fans bustle into Franklin Field, anticipating a laugher. Bill McPeak, the '60 Redskin defensive coach, makes it a nail biter rather than a laugher. McPeak's defensive unit blitzes Van Brocklin relentlessly. The strategy succeeds. The Dutchman fires a pathetic 9 for 24, while coughing up three interceptions.

"Nobody has been blitzing Norm Van Brocklin all season, figuring he would just take the teeth out of the red dog (as a blitz was called in '60) with swings and screens," McPeak explains after the game. "With our record (1-4-2), we had nothing to lose. So, we stunted and blitzed just about the whole game, putting on most of the rush from the weak side. We kept him from getting set."

The Eagles, despite an unimpressive offensive showing, manage to hang on for a victory. Again, they start off in the hole, as Washington scores first on a Bob Khayat field goal in the first period. Bob, a Redskin rookie, is the "little" brother of Eagle defensive lineman Ed Khayat. The week before, Bob had set a Redskin record with a 50-yard field goal. In the second period, Eagle kicker Walston knots the affair at 3 with his own 22-yard boot.

Four minutes into the third quarter, the Eagles surge ahead with a McDonald TD catch. However, Walston misses the extra point. Near the end of the third period, the Skins drive 66 yards for a score, and take the lead when Bob Khayat converts the PAT. Khayat adds another field goal as Washington increases its lead to 13-9, 17 seconds into the final stanza.

With 7:10 left in the game, Buck Shaw makes a crucial fourth-down decision. Instead of taking the field goal, which would make the score 13-12 in favor of the Redskins, Shaw orders a fourth and 10 pass from the 29. It was a gutsy call. At that point, Van Brocklin had missed six straight passes—three on the Eagles' previous possession, and three since the Eagles took possession on the Washington 28-yard line. Dutch doesn't miss this time, however. He lofts one Walston's way. Bobby cradles it in his arms, and, with the help of an excellent block from Retzlaff, scores.

On the next Redskin series, Maxie Baughan intercepts a Guglielmi pass. The Eagles drive to the Washington goal line. However, on third and goal, Dutch bobbles the snap. Fortunately, he recovers the ball. This time, on fourth down, Shaw settles for a field goal, which means the Eagles can be beaten by a touchdown. Walston connects for a 19-13 Eagle advantage. The Eagles' defense comes on in the ensuing series and slams the door on Washington when Chuck Weber intercepts a Guglielmi pass.

Walston is a hero once more, accounting for 13 of the Birds' 19 points. Coach Charley Gauer, after the game, praises the guy they call Cheewah: "When the chips were down, old pro Walston came through by catching the winning touchdown and booting the three-point clincher."

As for Van Brocklin, Dutch never really does get untracked all day. He is discombobulated by the relentless Redskin "red dog."

The Eagle defense comes up stellar to save the day. Shaw chirps: "Bobby Walston played a wonderful game. But if it weren't for the wonderful defensive game turned in by those other two old pros, Marion Campbell and Jesse Richardson, Bobby wouldn't have had the opportunity to win that game. I'll bet Jesse made 20 tackles today (he made 17, eight of them unassisted)."

Big Jesse, a Philadelphia native from the Roxborough section of the city, played his college ball at Alabama. He and Marion Campbell set the pace in the trenches. Maxie Baughan again plays great, snagging his first pro interception on a ball that bounces off the hands of Tom Brookshier. The bad news for the day is that Clarence Peaks, who suffers an oblique fracture of the fibula, is lost for the rest of the season. Peaks entered the game as the fifth-ranked rusher in all of football, flashing a 5.4 yard per carry average. Peaks has also chipped in with three touchdowns. Since the ex-Michigan Stater is also an excellent blocker and a good receiver coming out of the backfield, the loss is devastating.

~ *The Professor*

"Just tell them this about Clarence Peaks: 'He wants to know.'"

That's what Clarence Peaks has to say. These days, he eschews the spotlight, preferring the solitude of an esoteric book to the clamor of a football crowd. But in 1960, that clamor reverberated around Franklin Field toward Clarence Peaks. Peaks was in the midst of his most productive season. He had suddenly become a star, a vital cog on a train that was rolling toward a title. And then, in one painful moment, his season, his ankle, and his career took a cruel twist.

"I was the first African American that the Eagles ever drafted in the first round," the Professor, as he was nicknamed, points out. "After a couple of slow years, I got going pretty well in 1960. I was just learning the important things about my position when I got hurt in that Washington game. It was disappointing 'cause the same thing had happened to me back in college. I got hurt against Illinois in '56 and didn't play the last five games."

In an interview that Clarence gave back in 1960, he explained that his emergence as a premier NFL running back was no fluke. It was the result of a premeditated plan, a conscious change of style:

"I was counting too much on power. I'd been taught at Michigan State not to get too cute, not to juke around with the ball. With the Eagles, I'd been running sort of stupidly, just barging straight ahead. I decided to cut more and look for the holes."

That's the Professor in him coming out. Peaks executed his plan to a "t"—a plan that required one difficult piece of discipline: he had to stop eating. He needed more speed to transform himself into the type of runner he foresaw, so he reported to Hershey in 1960 trimmer and faster. And it paid off. When Clarence got hurt in that seventh game, he had already piled up 465 yards in 86 carries, for a glittery 5.4 average. Unfortunately, after the injury, Clarence never regained those same lofty peaks, at least not as an Eagle. The Professor looks back analytically:

CLARENCE PEAKS: "When I went to Pittsburgh in 1964 and 1965, I found out I would have had a Hall of Fame career if I'd have had a big blocking back to clear the way for me throughout my career. Nothing against our backs on the Eagles, but they weren't big guys. They weren't real effective blockers on sweeps and running plays. At Pittsburgh, I was back there with John Henry Johnson, and each of us could block well for the another. I remember one game we played, where John Henry got about 205 yards and I got 127."

Today, the Professor prefers to be left alone. He is a talented person, with multiple and varied interests. Clarence has played the guitar for years, he sings well—he was in a group in college—and he's even a good cook.

CLARENCE PEAKS: "My dad was actually the great cook. He had restaurants in Michigan, and, way back in 1961, I brought him here to Philadelphia to start a restaurant. We ran it for awhile. It was called "Peaks' Place.""

Clarence carries some painful memories of those years. Sometimes, these shadows are harder to get past than any defensive line he ever faced. Clarence played in a past where insensitivity toward people who were not white could cripple the spirit far more profoundly than a hard tackle could bruise the body. The Professor does not wish to dwell on those wounds. He prefers to dwell on healing and moving forward. Today, he devotes himself to gaining knowledge and truth. These days, Clarence Peaks wants to know.

The Eagles gain no ground on either the Giants or the Browns. Cleveland hangs on for a 28-27 win over St. Louis, while the Giants scratch and claw their way to a 27-24 win over the—with due respect to Ed Kiely and Buddy Parker—luckless Steelers.

The football world is unconvinced by the first-place team's credentials. With the New York press at the vanguard, everyone awaits the bursting of the Eagle bubble. The stage is set for the season's critical show-down: back-to-back games against the Giants. And now, at the most inopportune time, the Eagles are hammered by an injury. To a large extent, they're on top because they have avoided injuries to key personnel. Clarence Peaks falls into that category: key personnel. Given the anemic ground game they have mustered aside from Peaks, his loss could be crippling. Even with Peaks in there, the Birds are ranked dead last on the NFL's team rushing chart. Clarence's spot will be filled by Ted Dean, an untested rookie, who finds himself thrown into the pressure-cooker of a title fray. Fortunately, Ted Dean believes in himself. So do his teammates. They believe in each other, those '60 Eagles. But, above all, they believe in their quarterback.

Ten Ten Ten **Ten** Ten Ten Ten Ten

Dutch

"*Much has been written and said about my father. Some of it is more true than others. I knew him as a father. He was as complex as he was simple. He could be mean spirited and cruel at times, and sometimes so gentle and understanding. He was a passionate soul, who could not understand everyone not sharing his need to drink up life. I can say he was fairminded, honest, often to a fault, firm of handshake, eager to love, and be loved. And I will forever love this man I called 'Daddy One-One' (his jersey number was 11).*"—Kirby (Van Brocklin) Vanderyt, from her personal memoirs.

The search for the real Norm Van Brocklin stalls in a house of mirrors. The reflections of the myth distort and confuse the essence of the man. Van Brocklin's images are ying and yang: the sarcastic, barbed-tongue assassin versus the loyal, trusted buddy; the impatient, growling intimidator versus the patient, understanding listener; the long-sighted, masterminding strategist versus the short-sighted, improvising manipulator; the introverted, stubborn individualist versus the extroverted, generous sidekick. And these are but a few images. There are others not widely known to a public that paints its heroes in primary colors and wants to understand all its stars via short, uncomplicated sound bytes. To Van Brocklin's children, "Daddy One-One" was a caring, compassionate father, big-hearted and loyal to his many brothers, sisters, and relatives. To the friends he trusted, he was a generous soul with a big heart. To reporters and others he disdained, he was one ornery son of a bitch.

Van Brocklin was as extraordinary as he was enigmatic. He read people crisply, like he read defenses on gridirons. But he did not read flawlessly. He was delightfully human—a quarterback and a person with a quick release, too quick sometimes. His split-second judgments sometimes yielded spectacular, sometimes disastrous, results. What made him extraordinary—and he was extraordinary—was his ability to lead others, particularly his ability to lead a group back from disaster. The 1960 Eagles came back in nine of their 11 wins. The team credits that ability

The enigmatic Van Brocklin was an extraordinary natural leader.

to a belief in Norm Van Brocklin. Through Van Brocklin, and because of Van Brocklin, they believed in themselves. They believed they were winners, and in believing, they acted the part. Abraham Lincoln once said: "A leader is someone who can take people where they want to go. A great leader takes them where they need to go." Norm Van Brocklin could take a football squad where it needed to go.

"Sometimes, Dutch would call plays that didn't seem to make sense," Sonny Jurgensen recalls. "I'd question him about some of his calls when he got to the sideline, and he always had good tactical reasons for them. Maybe it was the way the defense was reacting to a certain play, maybe he wanted to set them up for something on the next series of downs. Whatever the reason, he was always setting the opponent up. He was out a few steps ahead of them. Usually, he was right. I got an education just watching him."

The lingering image of the Dutchman is that of a grizzled veteran, growling his charges into submission. His style was more intricate than that. Contrast what four of his 1960 offensive linemen say about him. It's obvious that the Dutchman had more than one style in his playbook.

Gerry Huth, an offensive guard who came to the Eagles in 1959 from the Giants says: "Oh, yeah, Dutch was tough, all right. If he thought you weren't doing your job, he'd walk you right over to the sideline. He'd tell the coaches: 'Get this guy out of there, and get me someone who can block.' Dutch got down on me one time in New York, and I'll tell you, he let me know about it right away."

J. D. Smith, the starting offensive tackle on the 1960 squad, is now a successful Texas businessman in the energy field. J. D. comments on the Dutchman's storied nastiness: "A lot of people say Van Brocklin was a real butt-kicking kind of guy, but I'll tell you, I don't remember him ever chewing us out. I thought Dutch was one of the nicest guys around, a real gentleman."

Jim McCusker, another starting offensive tackle who left the Eagle fold in 1959 remembers: "Norm Van Brocklin never left anything unsaid. If he was unhappy with you, you knew right away, and he didn't mince any words. He could get you mad, but you got over it quick."

Stan Campbell, a lineman who, prior to coming to Philadelphia, spent his Sundays keeping tacklers off Bobby Layne, recalls: "Layne was more pushy than Van Brocklin. He would cuss and scream and yell. Not Van Brocklin. You know what Dutch used to do. He would eye you—just give you that eye. He never said a harsh word to me. He would just give me that eye, and then I knew. I knew he was unhappy with me."

The Dutchman was flexible in his dealings with his teammates, selectively provoking, cajoling, attacking, praising, commiserating—according to his read. Call it a leadership style, for want of a better term. Van Brocklin relied on instinct, charisma, and a mishmash of other techniques. Today's corporations spend millions trying to *develop* leaders, trying to identify the key elements of leadership, seeking to catalog, study, define, and refine them. The quest is an art, not a science. It's the alchemy for a new millennium. In the Middle Ages, alchemists attempted to transform ordinary elements into gold. Today, perhaps just as blindly, corporations try to transform ordinary people into leaders. But ordinary elements can't be thrown into a cauldron and transformed into gold, and ordinary guys can't follow a mechanical, 12-step process and emerge a leader—at least not the kind of extraordinary leader that Van Brocklin was in 1960.

It's tempting to diminish the man's leadership as circumstantial. Van Brocklin played quarterback, the expected leadership position on any football team. He was a 34-

Forty years later, his teammates still credit Van Brocklin for the 1960 championship.

year-old veteran surrounded by green, young guns in the follow-*any*-leader stage of their personal football life-cycles. Here, in Van Brocklin, they saw an old soldier who had starred in NFL championship games. They saw a national figure who appeared in Vitalis commercials on TV. They saw a guy who had withstood the searing spotlight of '50s Hollywood when he was embroiled in the Rams' Waterfield

- Van Brocklin starting quarterback controversy (Waterfield was married to glamorous, voluptuous Jane Russell at the time). Finally, they saw the guy, Norm Van Brocklin, who was heir apparent to the team's head coaching job. With all those circumstances on his side, it's reasonable that the 20-somethings on the Eagle roster needed direction, and circumstance alone placed Van Brocklin in the spot to provide it.

But, that's not the way it was. What is compelling about the depth of Van Brocklin's role on that team is that, 40 years after that championship season, his teammates *still* credit his leadership for the title. Those 20-somethings have matured into 60-somethings. In the current millennium, Van Brocklin certainly holds no Svengali sway over a group of football neophytes and innocents. The 1960 Eagle alumni are seasoned and successful. They've held head coaching jobs, anchored national broadcasts, shaped young minds, secured key business positions, and served in government. They've watched their sport and society change under their feet. They are leaders themselves—excellent leaders. Yet, 40 years hence, in the eyes of these men, the central figure on the championship team remains Norm Van Brocklin. One by one, the '60 Eagles speak of Van Brocklin as a larger-than-life leader—far from a deity, but a flesh-and-blood guy who had an extraordinary gift to unite, inspire, and lead.

The 1960 Eagles were, and remain, Norm Van Brocklin's team. Dutch was the man who led that team to where they needed to be in order to beat more talented competitors. He melded a roster of disparate elements: blacks and whites, southerners and mid-westerners, west coasters and east coasters, into football's most successful force. He found a way to make the whole greater than the sum of its parts. That's alchemy. Today's corporations would call it *achieving synergy*. Dutch didn't call it anything. He just did it. He rallied the team, brought them together, using Donoghue's as his conference room. Today's corporations would call his get-togethers a *bonding exercise*. I imagine Dutch called it drinking, having a good time, and giving teammates shit about bad plays. They laughed about yesterday and planned for next Sunday. They dropped the bad stuff and dwelled on the good stuff. I guarantee Dutch would not call Mondays at Donoghue's *an exercise*. It was too natural and uncontrived. Sometimes surly and churlish, even hurtful, Van Brocklin nonetheless brought out the best in his teammates. He never did it better than 1960. He had an extraordinary season.

Norman Mack Van Brocklin was the eighth of nine children, the youngest of four sons, born to Ethel and Mack Van Brocklin in Parade, South Dakota. His family fell victim to the Dust Bowl of the '20s, so they packed up and headed their Model T Ford west. They eventually pulled up in Walnut Creek, California, near San Francisco. Times were tough. Young Norm, like every other family member, pitched in to help his struggling family make ends meet. He picked whatever crops were in season, washed dishes, cleaned out spittoons, delivered newspapers, and did assorted odd jobs. Van Brocklin was a star high school athlete at Acalanes

High School, lettering in basketball, baseball, and football. He was a mediocre tailback, but a punishing tackler from his linebacker position. Though not a distinguished student, he took a fancy to math and history, particularly Civil War history. At 17, he enlisted for World War II by forging his mother's name at the Navy recruiting office.

When the war ended, Van Brocklin attended the University of Oregon on a football scholarship and the GI Bill. He details why he went to college in his 1961 book: *Norm Van Brocklin's Football Book: Passing, Punting, and Quarterbacking*:

"When I was a youngster playing high school football, I never gave a thought to football as a career. … Pro football players at that time were held in low repute on the West Coast, probably because there weren't any National Football League teams west of Chicago. Actually, I didn't even have any intention of going on to college and playing football after I graduated from high school and joined the Navy.

"In the Navy, I was just another swabbie with a mop, a bucket, and a pair of dungarees. But it was then that I began noticing things that shaped my whole future life. While we swabbies slept in three-high bunks, washed our own clothes, and ate food that must have been cooked by a guy who was a grave digger in civilian life, the officers had their own individual quarters, ate special food, got deferential salutes, and could change from wet clothes to a dry martini with impunity.

"The only apparent qualification of many of these officers, or so it seemed to a mind that was still maturing, was that they had a college education and I didn't. I said to myself that if a caste system in the Navy was predicated on a college degree, there must be quite a lot of the same in civilian life. So, after I had spent three years swabbing the deck and also the head—I had firmly decided to get into college by hook or by crook."

Van Brocklin attended summer classes and earned a degree in Physical Education from Oregon in a three-year period. In his senior year, he was an All-American quarterback for the Ducks, and was drafted in the fourth round by the Los Angeles Rams. He described his college years, in a 1960 interview in the Philadelphia *Inquirer*, as "the best years of my life," espousing that "every kid should go to college." His wife, Gloria, was a major reason for those happy college years.

Dutch's daughter, Kirby, visited the Oregon campus after her father's death. She was accompanied by her two sisters and her mother. Kirby writes of the visit:

"You think after all the years that you know your parents, there are no secrets or surprises! I can remember asking my mother how she and daddy had met. She told me, 'It was love at first sight.' I accepted that at face value, and never thought to ask the particulars. It was so touching for her to be standing under this huge tree (on the campus at the University of Oregon), telling all of us how dad had literally run into her, and in his usual abrupt manner wanted to know, 'Where the hell is Deedy Hall?' We all laughed. It sounded just like dad! Mother said she told him she was going that way, and, as a matter of fact, was teaching a class in that building. Guess who became her student? Mother had kept that report card from her lab class and there was dad's name, with straight Cs across the ledger!"

On the gridiron, Van Brocklin was far from an instant sensation at Oregon. He was the seventh of seven tailbacks on the squad. The future Daddy One-One threw only 11 passes (perhaps the number was an omen, although his Oregon jersey number was 25) his freshman year in 1946. In 1947, Oregon switched to a T formation, and Van Brocklin took over at quarterback. In 1948, Van led the Ducks to a sparkling 9-1 record; however, the Ducks lost to Southern Methodist in the Cotton Bowl. Dutch ended his Oregon career with 144 completions out of 316 attempts for 1,949 yards and 16 TD's. He was voted into the College Hall of Fame in 1966.

Dutch came of age at Oregon. No longer a swabbie, he assumed the role of leader. Some of his ex-Duck teammates, in interviews given back in the '60s, stated that Van Brocklin drove Oregon's young coach, Jim Aiken, crazy. Dutch wouldn't pay attention to the coach's plays. He ran his own, making up his own pass patterns in the huddle. If anyone ever blew a block, his mates said you could "hear *Stubby* at the top of the stadium giving him hell."

Stubby? That was Norm Van Brocklin's nickname at Oregon, because of his stubby fingers. Her father, daughter Kirby laughs, was the ultimate nicknamer. He dreamed up a special handle for everyone:

"Daddy supposedly gave 'Crazy Legs' Hirsch his nickname, but then, he had a nickname for *everyone*. He called Tommy McDonald 'Motormouth' and 'Squeaky' (McDonald was 'Shoo Fly' at Oklahoma). Tommy was my favorite when I was a kid. Each of us 'Van Brocklin girls' had our own favorite Eagle. Lynne's was Pete Retzlaff, and Judy's was Tommy Brookshier. Daddy had nicknames for us, too. I was Gumdrop, because all my baby teeth fell out at once. Judy was Pill cause she was always getting into trouble, and Lynne was Dixie cause she talked like a southerner when she first began to talk."

Van Brocklin stormed into the NFL, leading the league in passing as a rookie, while sharing quarterbacking duties with Bob Waterfield—a situation that made for stormy years. The two Hall of Famers alternated duties till 1952, when Waterfield retired. The Waterfield monkey off his back, Van Brocklin led the Rams to a division title again in 1955, only to lose 38-14 to Cleveland, in Otto Graham's farewell appearance. By 1956, Dutch was smack dab in the middle of another quarterback controversy with Billy Wade. Van Brocklin demanded a trade to any city but Philadelphia or Pittsburgh. Naturally, the Rams dealt him to Philadelphia. Disappointed at first, he grew to love the city and its people. So did his family.

Dutch debuted in Philly in 1958 with a 2-9-1 season. Teamed with Buck Shaw, the new QB picked proven commodities—vets like Don Burroughs and Jerry Reichow whom Dutch knew would shape Philly's young squad the right way. For all intents and purposes, Van Brocklin was a coach. He worked full-time in the off-season for the Eagles' staff. Van Brocklin, Shaw, and GM Vince McNally teamed in a race against Father Time, before time ran out on the 62-year-old Shaw and the 34-year-old Van Brocklin. The triumvirate catapulted the Eagles from the bottom of the heap to the top in three seasons. Sadly, the fairy tale ended abruptly in January, 1961.

"Daddy was expecting to get the head coaching job after the championship," recalls Lynne Clarke, Dutch's middle daughter. "But management reneged. They insisted that he play one more year as player-coach. That's not the understanding that my dad had originally. Unfortunately, he had nothing on paper. Dad always made agreements on handshakes. He was far too trusting."

Daughters Lynne and Kirby loved their days in Philadelphia, when Van Brocklin's three girls attended Philadelphia's Friends Central School. Kirby has vivid recollections not only of the move from Philly, but of all the other moves the family had to make—as well as some of the pain those moves brought the family:

"My dad was furious (at not getting the Eagle head coaching job)*! We didn't want to leave our new home, and new-found friends, but there was no negotiating. Dad was offered the new head coaching job in Minnesota, and that's where we moved. In the dead of the winter, we packed and moved to yet another motel room in search of yet another home and neighborhood. We may have moved closer to California, but it was a whole lot colder in Minnesota than Philly! I can still remember sitting in our train cabin watching our neighbors, the Hickeys, and as we waved goodbye, crying. Their five sons ran alongside the train waving their good-byes. It has been a life of saying good-byes. One of the saddest things my mother said to me, years later, after taking her for her chemotherapy treatment, was that 'it was no use making new friends anymore, because all I've ever done in my life is make new friends only to say good-bye.' That really stung. It is no accident that, when my husband, who had a similar childhood experience, and I started a family, that we decided to set down roots, and stay put."*

Dutch's life after Philadelphia was stormy. He coached for several years in the pros. Unfortunately, he did not enjoy the same success as a sideline commander that he had as field general. Dutch spent six years in Minnesota, followed by seven years in Atlanta. Overall, his coaching log was 66-100-7. Kirby writes:

"He enjoyed brief moments of glory, endured front-office intrigue, and tried to survive an emotional roller coaster ride with an alcoholic owner. In 1974, he was again fired, never to coach in the NFL again. He coached briefly at Georgia Tech as an assistant quarterback coach. Dad was still recovering from brain surgery, and not totally with it. I will remember that period with special fondness, because those young players gave him a reason to live again."

Van Brocklin loved children. He loved kids so much he adopted three—two boys and a girl—to boost the number of children in his family to six. The sensitive side of Norm Van Brocklin is not well known or publicized. He was unselfish to friends and those in need. Jim Gallagher, of the Eagles' front office, recalls the time Dutch offered him $5,000 (a staggering sum in those days) for a down payment on Jimmy's new home. Bill Campbell, inducted into the Broadcaster's Hall of

Fame for his 52 distinguished years behind the microphone, tells a story that is typically Van Brocklin:

"Dutch comes over to my house with the Eagles' coaches one Sunday night after a home game in 1960. He's talking to my daughter, Chrissie, who was four at the time. 'How come you don't have a dog?' I hear Dutch asking her. 'Every kid needs a dog. Look, you're going to have a dog for your birthday.' I'm listening, aghast. After Chrissie went to bed, I told Dutch he shouldn't have gotten her hopes up like that. I told him she was going to take everything to heart and then have her little heart broken. Dutch snaps back: 'Who the hell are you? Dr. Spock? Stay out of it and don't worry about it.' I forgot about the whole thing, till her birthday came around seven months later. On July 24, we hear a knock on the door at 8 a.m. It's Dutch with a puppy! Chrissie was never more excited in her life. She fell in love with that puppy. We all did. Chrissie's a lawyer now. You know, to this day, Norm Van Brocklin is the *only* football player in the world to her. She thought he was wonderful."

Campbell continues, recounting Van Brocklin's thoughtfulness.

"I got a call early one morning. It was Dutch, who told me that Dr. Dowd had died. Dowd was the Eagles' team physician at the time. Dutch was real close to him, so when he died, Dutch hurried down to the Dowd's house right away. He made it his business to take care of the Doctor's family after Doc was gone. He felt so bad for those kids. He took their son with him up to training camp at Minnesota the next year. He personally finished painting their house. Dr. Dowd had just started painting the house when he passed away. People who didn't know the Dutchman would never realize how generous and loyal he was as a friend."

So many of Van Brocklin's virtues are unknown to the public. Unfortunately, his football legacy is fading as well. Playing in a run-dominated era of 12-game schedules, Van Brocklin's statistics have lost some glitter to those that have been rung up by ensuing generations of gunslinging quarterbacks. Dutch still ranks first in the history of the NFL in yards gained per pass attempt. Van Brocklin's average of 8.16 yards per pass attempt is the only such average in NFL history to exceed eight yards. He ranks 37th in touchdown passes thrown, and he ranks 13th in career punting average. Lost in the telling of his quarterbacking and leadership skills is the fact that he was an artful punter. He was a virtuoso in accuracy as well as hang time.

In most other all-time categories for passers, Dutch has dropped out of the top 50. What's more unfair is that the Van Brocklin name, once revered, is seldom brought up nowadays when the names of the "greatest" quarterbacks are bandied about. Former teammate Dick Bielski, who spent 29 years in the NFL as a coach and player, offers this view, "Van Brocklin would never put up the statistics a lot of those other guys put up. What he did was the same thing I thought (Fran) Tarkenton did. Dutch played superbly under pressure. He was the most intelligent quarterback under pressure that I've ever seen."

Pat Summerall has seen them all, from Otto Graham to Peyton Manning. Summerall was never a teammate of the Dutchman, only an adversary. Summerall played on the '60 Giants and got to observe Van Brocklin from a different vantage point than Dutch's Eagle teammates. The long-time broadcaster pays Van Brocklin a glowing tribute:

"Van Brocklin was far ahead of his time in knowing how to read defenses. As for passing, he could throw the ball as well as any quarterback before or since."

Fellow sportscaster Bill Campbell agrees on both counts. "Van Brocklin was an awesome pure passer. But I think his greatest attribute, besides leadership, was in-depth knowledge of the game. In my 52 years of covering this game, I learned more about football by listening to Dutch than everyone else put together. The two of us did a radio show together in 1960. We'd watch game films from the week before and comment on them. The show was pre-taped, and Dutch would tell me off camera, 'You don't know anything about this game.' Then he'd explain the finer points to me. He'd point out different blocking techniques, and expound on how to read defensive keys. He had such an impressive grasp of the game."

~ Ted Dean Remembers ~

It was Tom Brookshier's voice on my answering machine. "You know, I don't know if I made a strong enough point the other day about Ted Dean's role on that championship team. We talked about so many people and things. But I want to make sure you give Ted the credit he earned that year, because we couldn't have won it if Ted hadn't stepped in as fabulously as he did after Clarence Peaks went down. Ted kicked for us, caught the ball, ran the ball, returned punts, kickoffs. He was so valuable. He was a super talent, and if he hadn't been injured in Minnesota, he would have been one of the true greats in the history of this league."

Ted Dean was a softspoken, intelligent rookie who joined the Eagle flock in 1960. Ted tells of the mutual respect he and Dutch developed:

"I liked Dutch. We got along well and respected each other a lot. When I came into camp, they were making the rookies get up on the table and dance. I told them no, I was here to play football, not to dance. I think I gained Dutch's respect when I said that. He was like a brother to me. We saw things eye to eye. And the guy was such a great passer! So accurate. He hit me in the hands with a pass in the Giant game—that ball came to me so hard, it just kind of stuck in my hands. Then, he brought me up to Minnesota, later on, to play for him up there. He talked to me about becoming an end. I told him that was fine with me. I only wanted to play football. I'd play anywhere. I loved the game. Unfortunately, I had a car accident, and my career was over. Dutch was really upset when he saw me in the hospital. He called me every name in the book after that accident. Then he cried. He cried 'cause he knew it was the end of my career, and he felt genuinely bad about that."

Ted Dean was born and raised in a suburb of Philadelphia called Radnor, which also claims Hall of Famer Emlen Tunnel as a native son.

~ Dutch and the Duke ~

Perhaps Sonny Jurgensen, whom Norm Van Brocklin nicknamed "Duke," passes the greatest tribute of anyone to Norm Van Brocklin. Van Brocklin had spent his early years on the same roster with another Hall of Fame quarterback, Bob Waterfield. In his final years, he appeared on the same roster as Christian Adolph Jurgensen III. Sonny blitzed into the league in 1957, behind Bobby Thomason, the incumbent Eagle quarterback who retired after Sonny's rookie season. Sonny started only four games that year, but the Eagles won three of them. In the off-season, however, the Eagles acquired Norm Van Brocklin. Over the next two years behind Van Brocklin, Jurgensen played a total of 46 minutes. In the opening game of his fourth season, 1960, Sonny Jurgensen witnessed Norm Van Brocklin's three interceptions pave the way to a 41 - 24 trouncing at the hands of the Cleveland Browns. What does this future Hall of Famer and proud athlete have to say about his limited role on the 1960 Eagles? After all, in 1961, Jurgensen replaced Van Brocklin and was selected as the All - Pro quarterback. Sonny almost led the Birds to a second championship. A fiery competitor, one of the headiest field generals in history, Sonny was the NFL's top-rated passer in the decade of the '60s. Many of his teammates, like Billy Barnes and Jimmy Carr, feel that Sonny had the best arm of any passer in the game's history. Sonny's comments follow.

"Quarterback's an easy position to play when it's not yours! It's a lot easier to come in as a replacement than to own the job. I found that out the next year, in 1961, when the Eagles became 'my team.' When the team is yours, relying on you, and stamped as 'your team,' it's tough. In 1960, the Eagles were Dutch's team. I felt that he should have started, not me. I learned a lot from him in those years. I'm not sure that I was even ready that year. I found out I still had a lot to learn in 1961 when I did take over! But I watched and learned from Van Brocklin the whole time he was here. He was a great one. I give him a lot of credit for my own development. Sure, he could be tough. He was always tough on me. He'd come up behind me at practice and scream and holler at me. That was just Dutch's way. But we got along well. We even roomed together.

"Dutch was exceptional in his knowledge of the game. He'd improvise plays in the huddle. That doesn't happen nowadays. It's a coach's game now. They draw up all the plays themselves. It wasn't that way in those days. I interviewed Sammy Baugh a few years ago—talked with him for three hours. It was great! Baugh said the greatest part of the game for him was out-thinking the opposition. The quarterback doesn't do that now. You know, in Baugh's day, it used to be a penalty for the coach to talk to the guys on the sidelines? I really think that quarterback is the worst-coached position in football. Why? Because they have too many guys coaching it who never stood back there themselves."

Eleven

Toppling Giants

The Eagles had a number of small-town kids on that 1960 squad. John Wilcox grew up in a small town of 1200 people in Oregon. These days, he lives on an apple orchard near the Walla Walla River in Oregon. John Wittenborn hailed from a small town in Illinois. Wittenborn is retired now, living in a small town only 12 miles from where he grew up. Both are comfortable where they live. At home.

Of course, the rest of the NFL teams had small-town kids too. NFL rosters were peppered with small-town kids far from home. Small-town kids, big-city kids —like Jesse Richardson from Philadelphia—and kids from every size town in between. Of course, from the stands, the fans couldn't tell where those anonymous hulks in that sea of green came from. It really didn't matter. The fans see the machine—the offensive unit, the defensive unit, the bomb squad. They don't see how the people who form that machine have been jettisoned into sometimes unfamiliar, if not menacing, surroundings. For a young John Wittenborn, could nature's most violent thunderclaps howling through the plains of Indiana prepare him for the hostile din of Yankee Stadium? Or, did the mountain peaks of Oregon prepare 22-year-old John Wilcox for the jagged steel skyline of New York city? Sure, some small-town guys played to big crowds in college. But, when football becomes your livelihood, when all that is dear and familiar to you is half a country away, and when your buddies are suddenly 30-year old men, rather than 18-year-old students, life changes dramatically. The whole scene is a lot to throw at a 22-year-old.

John Wittenborn can reconstruct the cultural shock that awaited him when he arrived in the pros.

JOHN WITTENBORN: "I was a farm boy. That's how I grew up. When I got drafted and went to San Francisco, it was quite a change! The city was so big, and there were so many places to go, and so many things to do. You could really get distracted from football in the big cities. Then I got traded to Philadelphia, and it was the same thing there. I was living right in the middle of that huge, old city without knowing anyone. Veterans can really help those young kids, or they can hurt them. They direct the young guys at a critical time. If they do a good job, they can get a guy started in the right direction, and keep him pointed in the right direction."

Leadership is the central nervous system (CNS) of a football team. It's the invisible life-sustainer that feeds every fiber of a squad. When the CNS malfunctions, the body withers. So does a football team when leadership goes awry. Leadership doesn't show on a roster or a stat sheet. Yet, without strong leadership, teams don't assimilate their new players productively, and they don't develop their young players properly. New players and rookies on the 1960 Eagles got acclimated seamlessly. In the corporate world, they call it "getting up to speed quickly." In a 12-game season, there's no time for a long process. Rookies on the Eagles became contributors quickly, thanks to the leadership skills of the veterans. Bill Lapham, from Des Moines, Iowa, talks about what it was like for a rookie to play on the road.

Small-town boy John Wittenborn became a big-time guard for the Philadelphia squad.

BILL LAPHAM: "Rookies were humble when they came into the league in those days. On a lot of other teams around the league, the veterans resented everyone who was new. They figured anyone new was just trying to take their jobs. They wouldn't talk to anyone but the other vets on the club. That wasn't the atmosphere on the Eagles. The veterans helped us new guys and showed us around. You know, when you're just a kid and you play your first away game, you don't know anyone in the town. When we got to those towns, the Eagle veterans had been there before. They knew people, and they helped the new guys get their bearings. It didn't work that way on most teams. But the Eagles counted on the veterans for that role. We only had four coaches. When I played college football at Iowa, they had a big football program. We had more coaches there than the Eagles! The guys here joked about the club being cheap, but at Iowa they must have had a bigger budget. We changed pads daily, changed shoes—we basically got whatever we needed. It wasn't like that on the Eagles in those years. It's different now in the pro game. They have coaches and staff people to help kids adjust, but back then, that kind of leadership and guidance came from the players themselves. So,

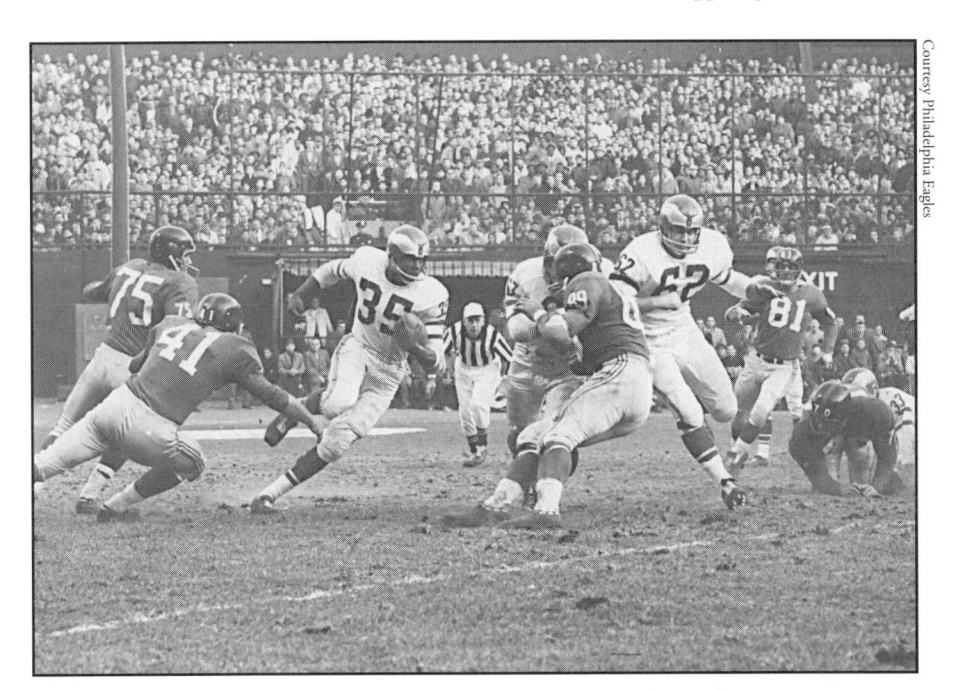

Dean (#35) with ball outmaneuvers Giants Lindon Crow (#41) and Jim Katcavage (#75).

I think the way those veteran leaders steered the new guys and the young guys contributed a lot to our success that year."

Ted Dean, the brilliant rookie running back and kicker, feels that leadership at the peer level fostered a winning attitude:

TED DEAN: "Our success was due to leadership and team chemistry. It's hard to put a finger on it, but we had great team chemistry and what I would call a blue-collar work ethic. Everyone came to play and win, through pain, through adversity, through anything. We simply expected to win. The guys on that sideline spread that feeling and never lost it."

Eagle leadership spanned the gamut in style. Buck Shaw set the tone as the quiet, reserved chief—somewhat like a latter-day Connie Mack when it came to dignity and unflappability. Van Brocklin was the focal point of the team, the man who "could take them there," with his impenetrable blend of intimidation and friendliness. Bednarik inspired his peers by his stolid, unmitigated power. Brookshier was the most vocal, sprinkling humor, comic relief, and mischief into the leadership mix. Retzlaff motivated others by dint of his own perfectionism, Peaks, with his placid self-confidence, Barnes with his brashness, Khayat with his openness, Marion Campbell with his tenacity, Chuck Weber with his toughness—and the other vets added their own distinct ingredients. For some reason that year, all those random traits aligned and created an atmosphere that was encouraging, forgiving, and constructive. As John Wittenborn expresses it:

November 20, 1960—Eagles vs. Giants at Yankee Stadium. Despite the efforts of Chuck Weber (#51) and Maxie Baughan (#55), the Giants (including Mel Triplett shown here) rolled around end.

JOHN WITTENBORN: "Yeah, everyone on that team will tell you the same thing: we had great team chemistry. If one guy got in trouble, the whole team got behind him, on and off the field. There was no running anybody else down, no looking for scapegoats. Our team used to jack guys up, not down."

It all sounds simple—so simple that it hasn't occurred again in the last 41 years in Philadelphia.

OLD GRUDGES

The Eagles must prepare for the make-or-break part of their schedule: back-to-back games against the New York Giants. The Giants are awakening. New York is 5-1-1 and poised to make their run for the title. In the Giants' triumph the previous week over the Steelers, Pat Summerall broke out of a season-long kicking slump with a 42-yard field goal that sparked a furious Giant second-half comeback. With 30 seconds left in the game, Summerall booted a 37-yarder to seal a New York victory. Frank Gifford also starred, grabbing two TD passes from quarterback Charley Conerly, who was injured in the game and is listed as 50-50 to play against the Eagles.

New York is used to having it their way when Philadelphia visits. In fact, the Eagles-Giants series has been practically all New York. The rivalry started way back in 1933, when New York drubbed the Eagles, 56-0, in the latter's NFL debut. By 1960, the Giants dominate the series 33-18-1. Not since 1952 has Philadelphia toppled New York on Giant turf. The score in 1952 was only 14-10, but the Eagles laid a tough physical pounding on the New Yorkers in the process.

~ Rough Loss for Giants ~

Charley Conerly, Kyle Rote, and Frank Gifford are the only Giants on the 1960 squad who were there, but the Giants were simply manhandled by the Eagles when the two teams squared off in 1952 at the Polo Grounds.

Immediately preceding that game in 1952, the once-proud Eagles had been swamped two weeks in a row—first by the Giants 31-7, and next by the Browns, 49-7. To bolster their beleaguered defense, Philadelphia scrambled their entire line-up. Norm (Wild Man) Willey returned to defensive end from offensive guard. Wayne Robinson shifted from center to linebacker. Hall of Famer Pete Pihos moved from offensive end to defensive end, and offensive halfbacks Jim Parmer and Ebert Van Buren were reinserted into the defensive backfield. When the Eagles met the Giants in the rematch at the Polo Grounds, the Eagles' defense manhandled them, particularly the quarterbacks, Charley Conerly and Fred Benners. Willey and company threw Conerly and Benners for 127 yards worth of losses. In one sequence, Willey dumped Conerly for a 15-yard loss on first down. On second down, Pihos dropped fullback Eddie Price for a 5-yard loss, and then, on third down, Willey nailed Price so deep behind the line of scrimmage that the Giants faced fourth and 37.

The Eagles flaunted a reputation in the '40s and '50s as a bruising, physical team. Jim McCusker, Eagle lineman, recalls their reputation.

JIM McCUSKER: "When I was coming up with the Cardinals, you knew you were going to feel sore after you played the Eagles. Back then, the Lions, Steelers, and Eagles were the most physical teams in football. You might beat them, but they'd beat you up pretty good. You'd be sore the rest of that week."

Pat Summerall, national broadcaster and member of the Giants' '60 team, adds:

PAT SUMMERALL: "I'd have to agree that the Eagles were physical, though I'd say that Pittsburgh in the '50s was the most physical team. You knew you were going to be banged up when they came to town. But there was something more important about the Giants and the Eagles. I'd have to say those two teams did not like each other in 1960 and they didn't like each other before 1960. I don't really know what the reason was. It went way back, I think. But there wasn't a lot of love between them."

THE JIG AND THE JABBER

The Eagles enter the hostile confines of Yankee Stadium on November 20 as underdogs. A partisan crowd of 63,571 watches their Giants jump out to a 7-0 lead in the first quarter. At the start of the second quarter, New York embarrasses the Eagles, when punter Don Chandler fakes a punt and carries the pigskin from Giant territory all the way down to the Eagles' 15. The Birds tighten up at that point, forcing a Summerall field goal from the 26-yard line. After another Eagles' drive is foiled, Van Brocklin punts again. The Giants drive from their own 38-yard line to the Eagles' 6-inch line. With the half winding down, the Giants go for six points on fourth down. Eagle defensive back Gene Johnson, however, sticks Frank Gifford at the line of scrimmage, and New York comes up empty.

"Looking back, that's the play that killed us," moans Jim Lee Howell after the game.

At the end of the half, the Giants have a ten-point advantage, which, given the lop-sided nature of the contest, is daunting to a Philadelphia offense that has failed to get untracked. The Giants have rolled for 208 first-half yards, compared to 31 for the Eagles. The Giants shut down the Birds' offense with the same tactic that Washington used the week before. They blitz Van Brocklin relentlessly. Under a savage pass rush, Dutch completes just one of six first-half passes, while losing 31 yards on sacks. As Giant linebacker, Sam Huff, observes at the end of the game: "We've never blitzed anyone like that since I've been with the team. We knew we had to belt him, or he'd kill us with passes."

The Eagles retreat to the locker room at half time, where the House that Ruth Built feels more like the House of Usher. New York is an intimidating place. John Wilcox recalls this trip—his first—to the Big Apple.

JOHN WILCOX: "I was in awe of Yankee Stadium and the whole city. I was a 22-year-old kid, in that big stadium for the first time. And the city was so huge. It was sort of intimidating, I guess. I remember walking down to Times Square, looking around, and just being awed at the sight."

Riley Gunnels, a big, good-natured lineman from Georgia, talks about his memories of Yankee Stadium.

RILEY GUNNELS: "I think it took the young guys a half to get settled down that day. It was such a big game, and it was my first trip to Yankee Stadium. I remember we were in the Yankees' locker room. I don't remember why we were on the Yankees' side, but we were. All I remember is that I had Roger Maris' locker! Wow! I'm sitting in front of Maris' locker with all those screaming people outside, throwing bottles and things. Fortunately, we had guys like Chuck and Dutch who had been through things like this before. The veterans settled the whole team down, and got us all focused, 'cause it was a whole new thing for us young guys."

John Wittenborn remembers that the Eagles weren't panicked by their first-half futility. He recalls how Van Brocklin and Bednarik got their heads together in the locker room at half time.

JOHN WITTENBORN: "The linemen were all resting in the locker room at halftime, kind of sitting around together. I remember seeing Dutch and Chuck over in the corner with Charlie Gauer and Buck Shaw drawing up plays. Those guys figured out how to beat that blitz. Of course, Dutch always figured a defense out. You couldn't stop him for a whole game."

The second half is a different game. Just as he had done in the second Cleveland game, Concrete Charley Bednarik comes on to play both ways. To try to halt the relentless Giants blitz, Buck Shaw inserts Bednarik at center, replacing starter Bill Lapham. As Sam Huff puts it after the game: "They put that Bednarik in at center. First thing off, he says to me, 'Well, boy, the fun's over—the veterans are taking over.' He was sort of right."

Bill Lapham recalls what happened.

BILL LAPHAM: "The center called a lot of the offensive sets on our team. That's why Nick Skorich wanted Bednarik in the game. Chuck had the experience that I lacked. He certainly did a great job, but my pride was a little hurt when he came in. I had played a good game the week before against the Steelers. But I understood. Chuck got the results."

At the start of the second half, the Eagles' offense falters, and they are forced to hand the ball back to the Giants. When New York's drive falls short, Summerall misses a 26-yard field-goal attempt. The Eagles take the ensuing kickoff, and drive the length of the field on a variety of quick-release passes and draw plays. The Dutchman starts calling numerous audibles, and the Giant defense begins to unravel. "It got to be a guessing game between Van Brocklin and Huff," Bednarik snickers after the game. "Huff lost."

Rookie Bill Lapham made his first start at center against the Steelers on November 6, 1960.

Van Brocklin caps off the drive with a 25-yard pass to McDonald, who makes a circus catch on the one-yard line before flopping into the end zone. McDonald laments after the game that his parents did not see his momentum-shifting catch: "My parents drove here all the way from New Mexico to see the game, but they couldn't get a ticket to get in."

Eagles vs. Giants November 20, 1960—Van Brocklin lofts a pass. Bill Lapham (#54) comes over to block.

    McDonald's acrobatics bring the Eagles within three points. The Giants counter with a mild drive to the Eagle 39, but Summerall misses another field-goal attempt, this time from 46 yards out. The Eagles respond with a drive from their own 20 to the Giants' 10, which proves futile when Walston's field-goal attempt from 17 yards out is blocked. The Giants march up the field, but again come up pointless when Summerall misses another shot at three points from 46 yards out. Given new life, the Eagles ramble downfield on a succession of short passes until the drive stalls at the 10, where Walston successfully boots the tying field goal.

    From this point on, Chuck Bednarik creates some choice footage for football's perpetual archives. On New York's next possession, Mel Triplett, their bruising fullback, pops into the line on third-and-inches. Bednarik hammers him. The ball flips up into the air (much like the Miracle at the Meadowlands some years later), Jimmy Carr grabs it, and gambols 38 yards for a Philadelphia lead. Triplett shakes his head after the game: "It was a slant play. I never really got the ball. It bounced off my fingers. I was so intent on making that first down, and next thing I know, there goes Carr down the sideline with it. First time I ever blew a game."

    As the clock winds down, the Giants launch a desperation drive, setting the stage for one of the most famous plays in football history. Frank Gifford catches a short pass from quarterback George Shaw, playing for the injured Charley Conerly. Gifford glances downfield, preparing to juke Eagle safety, Don Burroughs. Gifford

Toppling Giants 149

Eagles vs. Giants November 20, 1960—The Giants' Frank Gifford (#16) runs free before Bednarik's hit.

Eagles vs. Giants November 20, 1960—The famous Chuck Bednarik (#60) tackle ("The Jig") that sidelined Frank Gifford. Kyle Rote (#44) looks on. Ed Khayat (#73) walks off. Chuck Weber (#51 on the ground) cradles the ball.

does not see Bednarik bearing down on him with a full head of steam. Bednarik pulverizes Gifford, separating ball from carrier, and knocking the Giant receiver unconscious. As the Eagles' Chuck Weber recovers the fumble, ensuring an Eagle victory, Bednarik pops his clenched fist into the steel gray New York sky.

~ "Pop-Pop" You're on TV ~

Knute Rockne used to say: "You don't have to see a good tackle. You can hear it." Chuck Bednarik's hit was a good, clean hit. Frank Gifford, the guy on the receiving end, never disputed that. Number 60's tackle would have made Knute Rockne beam—then wince. Everyone on the field heard the clash, which Eagle Riley Gunnels describes in grisly terms: "It sounded like a rifle shot." Contrary to what many believe, the collision did not end Frank Gifford's playing career. It ended his season. It ended the next season as well. But Gifford came back strong two years later. In 1962, he caught 39 passes for a personal high of 796 receiving yards. He averaged 20.4 yards per catch, another personal high, and he tallied seven touchdowns, yet another personal high. His triumphant return was a testament to his courage.

Over the years, the photograph of Bednarik and Gifford in the aftershock of their collision has burrowed deep into the game's consciousness, starkly illuminating the side of a sport that can be brutal and dangerous. In one of football's undying moments, two immortals collided. In a team sport that pits 11 against 11, two of the game's superstars waged one-on-one war. The irresistible force, indeed, met the immovable object, and as the song promises, "Somethin's gotta give." It did. A fallen athlete lay in stillness on the turf, while, above and around him, his adversary whooped the cries of victory. The scene is part of the game's perpetual gallery. The contrast gives us pause. But, while the incident makes Gifford a victim, it does not make Bednarik a villain. Gifford succumbed to a football fundamental, executed to its most elemental and frighteningly powerful level. Gifford was tackled the way Rockne said runners should be tackled. Bednarik did nothing illegal or extraneous or cheap or despicable. He simply executed a punishing tackle. His tackle was classic because it didn't have to be seen. It could be heard. It was immortal because it can still be felt.

The poignant lesson of the incident is not what can be seen in the photo, but what cannot be seen. Two years after the incident, Frank Gifford returned to the field of battle, eager to face anew the inherent perils of a game he loved—perils he had felt firsthand. Gifford's courage in getting back up and carrying the ball again, better than ever, is his legacy, his testament on how to wage combat on any of life's fields.

The Chuck Bednarik hit on Frank Gifford has been replayed hundreds of times over the years. Both men have been interviewed and questioned *ad infinitum* about that single moment in time. Their stock reply never waivers. It was a good, clean hit—simply a part of the game. They've dealt with the question for so many years now that nowadays, they add spice the story. Chuck Bednarik tells about the time he and Frank Gifford were both speaking at the same engagement. When Chuck's turn rolled around, he ambled to the podium, and faced the audience to speak. Suddenly, the house lights went off, as Bednarik had prearranged, throwing the hall into pitch darkness for several seconds. When the lights came back up, Chuck turned to Frank, and said: "Hey, Frank, remember that?"

There was another Chuck in the picture besides Bednarik. The other Chuck—Chuck Weber—is the guy who recovered Gifford's fumble. Weber admits, "I get to benefit from the notoriety of that play, too. Whenever they run it on TV, I'm in it, too, recovering the fumble. Last year, I was out visiting my daughter and her family in San Diego over the holidays. My 5-year old grandson was watching TV in another room, when all of a sudden, he got up and came running into the room where the adults were. He was all excited, yelling: 'They're saying Pop-Pop's name on TV. Come on in and see.' We went in, and, sure enough, that's what he was watching. They were showing the clip of that Gifford fumble."

As this game passes into the history books, the Eagles again find themselves on the short end of the game's statistics. The Birds gain a scant 61 yards on the ground, compared to the Giants' 144. The Eagle offense is held to one touchdown. In the final analysis, the game is decided by Summerall's three missed field goals. After the game, the opposition pours profuse praise all over Van Brocklin. New York assistant coach Allie Sherman (who takes over as head coach for the New Yorkers the following year, and keeps the job till 1968, compiling a 57-51-4 record), gushes: "I've never seen a finer performance by a quarterback. There is nobody like Van Brocklin. Shaw (the Giants' quarterback who filled in for starter Charley Conerly) pitched a magnificent game for us, but Van Brocklin is a genius. He just picked us apart in the second half. No team can contain him for a full game."

Van Brocklin himself endures another tough day physically. Like Washington, New York pounds him incessantly with their blitzes. At game's end, Dutch returns to the Yankee Stadium locker room, his muddy uniform tattered and spattered. Ex-Eagle mate, Lee Riley, who saunters over to visit his ex-mates after the game, needles Van Brocklin: "I see you got dirty today." "I see you didn't," Dutch zings Riley back, in reference to the meager playing time that Riley is getting on his new team.

The Van Brocklin jab at Lee Riley is one of the opening salvos in a week of jabber between the two teams and cities. The New York press, along with Giant QB Charley Conerly, condemns Bednarik for his "cheap shot." In contrast, New York coach, Jim Lee Howell, clears Bednarik: "He didn't do any illegal headhunting." Nevertheless, Howell grouses daily that Philly used dirty tactics to win. The Giant

Giant quarterback George Shaw looks downfield as Joe Robb (#66) charges at Yankee Stadium.

coach promises retaliation if the Birds rough up his placekicker, Pat Summerall: "If they want to waste three blockers to get our placekicker, it's perfectly legal, although not too smart. But then they must remember that Van Brocklin kicks, too."

The Philly press portrays the Giants as being embarrassed at the defeat. New York not only lost on the scoreboard, but they also lost two of their biggest stars for the season. Besides Frank Gifford, defensive end Jim Katcavage also went out with an injury. Howell bristles: "We don't want any vendetta, but we're not going to be had. It just doesn't make sense to let the Eagles eat up our ballplayers. Our guys know what's going on, and I don't have to tell them to retaliate."

Down the Jersey turnpike in Philly, Buck Shaw is incredulous at the jabber he's hearing. "Some of Howell's allegations are ridiculous. The things we did were perfectly legal. You can rush the kickoff man with your entire team if you want to. Look at how they rushed Van Brocklin. On punts, they had as many as eight men rushing. Why, they were penalized once for roughing the kicker, weren't they?"

~ *Get Some or All of Him* ~

New York tempers and passions were running high after the Giants lost the first game in the back-to-back series with Philadelphia. The contemporary newspaper accounts were filled with talk of New York retaliation for Philadelphia's

Former gridiron rivals Pat Summerall and Tom Brookshier later became broadcasting buddies for CBS.

cheap shots. The Eagles, led by Buck Shaw, showed righteous indignation at the accusations, never owning up to any intentional roughing. According to Giant coach Jim Lee Howell, the Eagles were out to get some or all of his place-kicker on the opening kickoff. Forty years later, Pat Summerall sets the record straight:

PAT SUMERALL: "Oh, yeah, they were after me, all right. On the opening kickoff, about three Eagles came after me and practically mugged me out of bounds for five yards or so. I remember coming over to the bench, and Howell asking me if I wanted a policeman stationed out there for protection."

John Wittenborn, Eagle lineman, was on the bomb squad that day. Forty years after that opening kickoff in Yankee Stadium, he admits what his assignment was.

JOHN WITTENBORN: "To tell you the truth, we *were* after Summerall. Charlie Gauer was behind it. He told us to go get Summerall on the kick-off, so Howard Keyes, Gerry Huth, and I all went after him. Pat's right. We were still pushing him after we were way out of bounds. We got him pretty good."

But why Pat Summerall, of all people? Gerry Huth, himself an ex-Giant, unveils the thinking underlying the plot:

GERRY HUTH: "The Giants had a great defense in those days, with Robustelli and Grier and Lynch and Patton and the rest. They won so many close games by kicking a field goal at the end of the game that Charley (Gauer) figured Summerall was a key guy who might beat us. Since Summerall could hurt us, we wanted to make him a little nervous in case he had to kick at the end of the game."

Just think, if Eagle draft choice John Madden had not gotten injured at Hershey training camp, he would have heartily joined in the Summerall mugging mission. Had there been an All-Madden team in 1960, Summerall might have earned a spot because of his grit against that Eagle hit team. Unfortunately, there was no

All-Madden team back then. But there is now, and maybe Pat Summerall will finally make it. But not as a kicker. Given John Madden's exuberance and animation, Summerall was probably safer with Eagles stalking him than he is in a small broadcasting booth with Madden flailing his arms. Does the All-Madden team have a spot for broadcaster?

Amidst the war of words, Chuck Bednarik, the epicenter of the controversy, sends a basket of fruit to St. Elizabeth's Hospital in New York where Gifford is convalescing. Bednarik's get-well card reads: "Sorry that you're in the hospital, and I hope you get out soon enough to play your usual great game on Sunday."

Violence happens to be topical this week in the NFL, particularly in the wake of television's airing of "The Violent World of Sam Huff." Over in Chicago, the Lions and Bears have a big brawl. Commissioner Rozelle fines every member of both teams $25. Now Rozelle, his interest piqued at all the talk about retaliation by the Giants, arranges to attend the Eagles-Giants rematch in person.

The New York press introduces another theme that ruffles the Birds. The Giants, according to some columnists, had looked past the Eagles. Philadelphia won simply because they caught New York napping. Bill Lapham disagrees:

BILL LAPHAM: "Don't let anyone tell you the Giants eased up. They were playing their asses off out there. Like it or not, we just beat them. I was just a rookie and I could see that. They were a great team, with a roster full of veteran players. The Giants had the big-name stars at the time. Everyone knew the New York players because they had played on television in the championship game for the past two years. But they were out there to win."

~ The View from the New York Side ~

Pat Summerall rates the 1960 Eagles as a good team. He doesn't feel that the Giants had underestimated or looked past the Eagles. But the Eagles were definitely not the Giants' main focus or threat.

PAT SUMMERALL: "We didn't think the Eagles were our rivals. We thought the Browns were the team that would push us for the championship. The Eagles had a bunch of characters on that '60 team. They had a charismatic leader in Van Brocklin, and several guys who had career years. Everything came together for them that year. But I have to admit, those Eagles did have a tremendous sense of togetherness and camaraderie. One year, in the late '50s, some of the guys from the Giants and Eagles got together and went out after we had played against each other, even though our two teams weren't too fond of each other. Those Eagles kept us out late, and several Giants wound up missing a plane connection the next day as a result of being out late the night before. Leave it to the Eagles to get the Giants in trouble!"

Pat Summerall launched his ten-year NFL career with Detroit in 1952, coming into the pros in the same rookie class as Stan Campbell. Summerall played offensive and defensive end, but he made his biggest mark as a placekicker. He connected on 100 out of 212 field-goal attempts in his career. In his best year, 1958, Summerall led the league in field goals with 20, and field-goal percentage, with an accuracy of 69 percent. Pat is aptly named. He finished out his career with three consecutive seasons where he was perfect in Points After Touchdowns (PAT's).

Statistically, after the first Giants' contest, the Eagles continue to pale, compared to their competition. The Baltimore Colts, still acknowledged as football's finest team, lead the NFL in points scored, as well as in fewest points given up. That's a pretty powerful one-two punch. Cleveland boasts the top rusher, Jim Brown, as well as the top passer, Milt Plum. Norm Van Brocklin, Philadelphia's marquee player, ranks a distant third among NFL passers, trailing both Plum and Unitas. Furthermore, Van Brocklin has coughed up 13 interceptions, compared to zero for Plum.

Pete Retzlaff is the top Eagle receiver, yet he is only ranked eighth among his peers. Bobby Walston is second in points scored with 79. As a team, the Eagles lead the NFL in only one category: pass defense. The Birds have allowed only 94 completions in 204 attempts.

~ *"We May be Slow, but at Least We're Big"* ~

The big-play Eagles were tied for second in the NFL in interceptions in 1960. The linebackers got into the act as well as the defensive backfield. Pat Summerall's assessment about "several Eagles having career years" is on target. Three of the Eagles' defensive backs—Gene Johnson, Bobby Freeman, and Don Burroughs—had more interceptions in 1960 than in any other year of their careers. Of the five linebackers, Chuck Weber nabbed 60 percent of his *career* interceptions in that one season. In fact, Weber grabbed 30 percent of his career interceptions in the Dallas game alone. Maxie Baughan intercepted three in 1960, one short of his career high; while Chuck Bednarik filched two in limited action at linebacker.

The Eagles' penchant for the big play was their hallmark. They ranked near the top in team interceptions, but their defensive backfield also stopped the run as well as any other backfield in football. Gene Johnson stopped Frank Gifford in a pivotal goal-line stand at Yankee Stadium. Jimmy Carr was instrumental in bottling up Bobby Mitchell in the second game against the Browns. In fact, Carr and Brookshier were feared as tacklers as much as any two cornerbacks in football. And, though two members of the defensive backfield—Burroughs and Freeman—were late arrivals to the unit, the group was cohesive, again a tribute to the team's leadership and togetherness. Bobby Freeman remembers how tight-knit the backfield group was.

BOBBY FREEMAN: "Brookie was a tremendous leader in that defensive backfield. Jimmy Carr kept us loose. All of us were good friends, and we played like a unit. At practice, when it got cold, the defensive backfield guys would all hang around together right behind those big linemen. Of course, that wasn't togetherness as much as the fact that we were using those big guys as windbreakers to stay warm. Our backfield wasn't dumb! As for all the big plays we came up with, all I can say is that we covered for each other. We kind of knew what everyone else was doing and where they'd be. We had a big defensive backfield for that era. In fact, that was our slogan: 'We may be slow but at least we're big!' Still, we were faster than people gave us credit for. Most important, we had an intelligent group that could get to the place the ball was being thrown. A lot of times we got there before the guy they were throwing to could."

~ The Interceptors ~

	# of Int. in 1960	Best Year for Int.	# of Int. in best year	# of Career Int.
Defensive Backs				
Gene Johnson	3	'60	3	4
Tom Brookshier	1	'53	8	20
Bobby Freeman	4	'60	4	15
Bobby Jackson	0	'60	0	0
Don Burroughs	9	'60, '55	9	50
Linebackers				
Chuck Bednarik	2	'53	6	20
Maxie Baughan	3	'67, '68	4	18
Chuck Weber	5	'60	6	10
John Nocera	0	'62	1	1
Bob Pellegrini	0	'58, '62	4	13

A DRIBBLER AND DUTCH'S DUPE

The Eagles' victory at Yankee Stadium locks them solidly in first place, since the Browns are tripped up by the Steelers the same weekend. Coming back to Franklin Field for the rematch against the Giants, the Eagles' lead has ballooned to one-and-a-half games.

Other than Clarence Peaks, who is lost for the season, Philadelphia is at full strength. And, although the loss of Peaks hurts, Ted Dean filled in well for him in the first New York game. The Giants, in contrast, have been ravaged by injuries. Gifford is out for the season, as is Katcavage, who has a broken collar bone. Kyle Rote has a bad hand, Charley Conerly is still hobbled and listed as doubtful, and Mel Triplett has a bad foot.

It's a big weekend all around the Philly sport scene. Philadelphia is hosting three high-profile events. On Saturday, pro basketball will be focused on Wilt Chamberlain's Philadelphia Warriors who battle Bill Russell's Boston Celtics in Philadelphia's Convention Hall. Also on Saturday, the Army-Navy game will take place at Municipal Stadium, or Philly's "White Elephant," as it is known at the time. The mammoth structure, which is used in the '60s for little else than the annual Army-Navy game and the annual Police Thrill Show, is fated to be torn down in the '90s. As for the Army-Navy game itself, both service teams rank in college football's top echelon in 1960. Navy is ranked number eight, and their running back, Joe Bellino, who stars in the Navy victory, goes on to win the Heisman Trophy at season's end.

The final big event of the weekend is the Eagles-Giants tilt. Scalpers, according to contemporary accounts, are selling tickets for $75 a pair. The Birds have not swept the Giants since 1949. A win over New York on Sunday would stretch the Eagle win streak to eight in a row—another feat they have not accomplished since 1949.

In his office, Buck Shaw is looking ahead with trepidation. The Eagles' final three games are on the road. The seasoned skipper fears that a Giant win could halt the Birds' momentum just as they vacate the friendly confines of Franklin Field. Shaw holds secret practice sessions and bars all outsiders the week before the game.

On game day, November 27, 1960, 60,547 fans squeeze into Franklin Field. On the first play from scrimmage, Giant quarterback George Shaw tosses a 71-yard bomb to Kyle Rote. After the game, Brookshier fingers crowd noise, not Bobby Freeman, who was covering Rote, as the culprit: "The Giants caught us in a zone defense. When I saw the play developing, I yelled, 'Switch,' meaning change defensive patterns, but the crowd was yelling so loudly, Bobby Freeman didn't hear me. That's how Rote got behind us. After that, I thought we had their passing offense fairly under control." Freeman looks back on that play, and offers another insight.

BOBBY FREEMAN: "It was loud out there. But crowd noise wasn't the only problem. Gifford and Rote were a great duo, very cagey. They knew our backfield relied on those verbal signals, so they'd run out into the backfield and yell, 'Switch' to mess us up. You had to learn to recognize voices to know who was yelling."

The Eagles go nowhere on their first possession and punt to the Giants, who march 83 yards in only eight plays for a second touchdown. On the Eagles' next

158 **1960** *Philadelphia Eagles:* **Nothing but a Championship**

possession, Van Brocklin throws an interception to Harland Svare at midfield. Svare returns it to the Eagle 18. Giant end Bob Schnelker drops a sure touchdown in the end zone, and the Giants settle for a Pat Summerall field goal, and a seemingly insurmountable 17-0 lead after only one quarter.

Things don't improve as the Eagles' next drive also stalls. Van Brocklin is forced to punt, and the Giants again start to march. Philadelphia turns the tide swiftly, going the big-play route in the nick of time. This time, Bobby Freeman picks off a George Shaw pass at the Eagle 44, and returns it all the way to the Giants' 9. Eagle coach Jerry Williams later calls the play, "the turning point of the game."

According to coach Jerry Williams, Bobby Freeman's (#41) interception was the turning point of the win over the Giants.

McDonald catches what appears to be a TD in the end zone. However, he is ruled out of bounds, and Philadelphia settles for a Walston field goal. On New York's next possession, Baughan picks another Shaw pass, and returns it to the Giant 27. This time, Van Brocklin connects with Dean for a 25-yard touchdown catch and scamper.

On New York's next possession, Don Burroughs pinches a third Shaw pass, and returns it to the Giant 33. The Birds advance to the 6-yard line. Billy Ray Barnes drives to the one-yard line, where he coughs up the ball. Two fleet Giant defensive backs, Dick Lynch and Jim Patton, and one lumbering Eagle lineman. J.

Above: Eagles vs. Giants November 27, 1960—Eagles' Ted Dean (#35) outruns Jimmy Patton (#20) to score the winning touchdown.

Left: Ted Dean scores the winning TD while being pursued by the Giants' Jimmy Patton (#20). Bobby Walston (# 83) trails.

D. Smith, follow the bouncing ball. Smith comes up with it and scores his first touchdown since he "did some fullbackin' back in high school." It's the first and last touchdown of his pro career. And it couldn't have come at a more crucial time. Instead of a touchback making the score 19-10, the game is knotted at 17. The Eagles have successfully erased the 17-0 deficit they faced after the first quarter. After

160   **1960** *Philadelphia Eagles:* **Nothing but a Championship**

Above and below: Eagles vs. Giants November 27, 1960—A pile up ensues after a fumble by the Eagles' Barnes. The Eagles' J.D. Smith (#76) recovers it.

the game, Barnes tells the press: "Yeah, we practice that dribble play a lot in practice."

Forty years later, Billy sticks to his guns:

BILLY RAY BARNES: "Sure we practiced that play. I gave that ball up purposely so J. D. could get himself a touchdown."

Billy Ray is as consistent as he is insistent.

~ Following the Bouncing Ball ~

"Those defensive backs couldn't believe I beat them to the ball!" J. D. Smith says, with characteristic reserve. Smith's fumble recovery was a monster play in a season of big plays. "The Giants and I all got there the same time, actually, but I got my body in good position, and I was determined to get that ball."

Drafted in the second round in 1959, J.D. Smith never truly had the opportunity to apprentice in the pros. In his first exhibition game, he was thrown quickly into combat and was never again removed.

Eagles vs. Giants November 27, 1960—J.D. Smith (#76) pulls off one of the season's biggest plays—recovering Barnes' fumble for a touchdown.

"We played Baltimore in a '59 exhibition game. Their defense was really beating up on one of our linemen, so they put me in against Gino Marchetti (the Colts' Hall of Fame defensive end, who later opened a chain of fast-food restaurants called 'Gino's'). I was totally green and I had to rely totally on strength. But I didn't do bad. I was strong, but it took awhile to get smart."

Smith played in Philadelphia through 1963, and typified the toughness of the entire '60 bunch.

"It was a different era then. We didn't have the facilities they have nowadays. One game, I got my hand stomped on and needed stitches afterwards. They gave me a shot of whiskey and sewed it back up right there in the locker room. We didn't make the money back then, either. I actually made more money on my off-season job, selling harvesting equipment."

After five great years in Philly, J. D. was shipped off to Detroit in 1964.

"It wasn't the same there. I never experienced anything like Philadelphia in '60. That was such a tight-knit team. We'd all get together on Mondays at Donoghue's Bar, and all the guys went places and hung around together off the field. I don't know how to explain it, but it always seemed like that '60 group could give extra when it was needed. That was probably the key to our success. In Detroit, there were too many different groups of individuals. Everyone didn't act like they wanted to be part of the team. I'd even include the front office as part of the team in Philly. They were nice guys. The whole organization was more like a family."

J. D., who was selected for the Pro Bowl in 1962, had to quit in 1966 when bad knees, a problem that first beset him in college, hobbled him out of the game. After football, he went on to a long and successful career in the energy field in his home state of Texas.

As the half ends, the Giants surge back to regain the lead, 20-17, on Pat Summerall's 31-yard field goal.

The Eagles begin the second half with a feeble three-and-out series. The rejuvenated New Yorkers push to the Birds' 7 before sputtering and settling for another Summerall field goal. Again, the Eagle offense goes nowhere and Van Brocklin is forced to punt. Once again, the defensive backfield comes to the rescue. Burroughs intercepts, and Philly takes over at the New York 49. On the first play, the Dutchman finds Ted Dean at the 15-yard line. The rookie running back gets an assist from a crisp Retzlaff block and lopes into the end zone, giving the Eagles their first lead of the day. They never relinquish it.

Chuck Bednarik beams about Van Brocklin's play callng in the locker room after the game: "Sam Huff was reading our 21 trap audible. Van told us in the huddle, I'll call it, but ignore it. Huff was duped. His zone was open."

November 27, 1960, Don Burroughs' interception sets up the game-winning pass to Ted Dean. Bobby Freeman (#41) assists in the coverage.

On the next Giant series, Joe Robb, who plays a marvelous game at defensive end, jars the ball loose from running back Joe Morrison. Jimmy Carr recovers on the Giant 30, and the Eagle offense converts the New York mistake into seven points when Van Brocklin locates Barnes in the end zone for a score.

~ The 21-Trap Audible ~

The New York games were the pinnacle of Van Brocklin's 1960 season. Dutch was acclaimed as the headiest player of his time because of the way he picked the Giants apart. The acclaim came from every direction—from his own team, from the Giants, and even from the New York press. As Chuck Bednarik said after the first New York game, Van Brocklin and Giant linebacker Sam Huff engaged in a chess match, and Van Brocklin won. Dutch put checkmate on Huff when he improvised a ruse on the Eagles' 21-trap play. Bobby Jackson remembers where Dutch first plotted his strategy:

BOBBY JACKSON: "After that first game in New York, Dutch got an idea on how to set Sam Huff up. In that first game, the Giants had figured out our 21-trap audible. They stopped it 'cause they had it smelled out after awhile. Instead of changing the audible, Dutch figured he would keep calling it the same way until he really needed a big play. Then he'd call the audible the same way, but Dean would go downfield deep instead of faking into the line. See, Dutch noticed that Huff was overcommitting and vacating that zone. So Dutch diagrammed out what he wanted everyone to do and where he wanted Ted Dean to run. You know where he drew that play up? In the parking lot, while we were all waiting for the bus to

Murphy Field. Dutch drew it up there, and stationed everyone where he wanted them. Then he walked everyone through the play right there in the parking lot. Well, Dutch did save that trick for a crucial time, and it worked. He came up big, 'cause the Giants were totally fooled, and Ted Dean got that big touchdown."

In contrast to the choreographed perfection of the modern game, quarterbacks like Van Brocklin improvised in the huddle and flouted the playbook. Dutch would frequently ad lib plays and diagram them on the turf in the huddle, based on feedback from the offensive unit. As 1960 Eagle coach Nick Skorich explains:

NICK SKORICH: "Dutch would take what the defense gave him. If he thought something would work that wasn't in the play book, he'd draw it up in the huddle. He wasn't afraid to take chances that way. But if a receiver came back to the huddle and told him he could get free on a certain pattern or beat somebody deep —or if a lineman said he could trap somebody or drive them back, they'd better be right. Or they'd hear about it right away. Dutch wanted to make the calls. It was his game."

With time running out and the Eagles at a 31-23 advantage, the Giants lose the ball on downs. The Birds go on to run the clock out for their second consecutive win over the Giants.

The Eagles put on another great show, and characteristically, there's an enormous cast of heroes and supporting actors. First and foremost on the hero list is Chuck Bednarik, who again answers the call of his team. An hour before game time, Buck Shaw had tapped Chuck on the shoulder, and, according to reports, said apologetically: "Sorry, Chuck, I'm going to need you both ways again." Chuck plays 55 minutes, four minutes less than he had played against Cleveland. Again, Concrete Charley stabilizes the offense, thwarting the deadly Giant pass rush, while on defense, Number 60 is all over the field.

Burroughs intercepts two passes at key points. Bobby Freeman comes up with the big interception and long runback in the first half that prevents the Giants from putting the game out of reach. And J. D. Smith, normally an anonymous behemoth on the offensive line, pulls off one of the season's sterling plays.

The New York press jumps on the Smith touchdown as irrefutable proof that the Eagles are lucky. Ex-Eagle Lee Riley is quoted in a contemporary interview: "The Eagles aren't a bit better than they were in 1959, but this year the ball is bouncing their way every time. They've gotten every break in the book." New York pouts about the J. D. Smith fumble recovery, because the outcome would have been completely different if it had happened on fourth down rather than third.

Had the same play occurred on fourth down, the Giants would have been awarded the ball at the point of the fumble. As NFL official Jack Glascott rattles off in a post-game interview: "The play is covered in rule 7, Section 4, Article 2(2). If there is a fourth-down fumble (unintentional) on or inside B's (the defensive team) 10-yard line during a play from scrimmage, and the fumbling player recovers before touching by B, he only may advance—hand off and/or pass ball (backward or forward) as prescribed by rule. Otherwise, if recovery is by another player, spot of next snap is spot of fumble, unless spot of recovery is behind such spot, in which case it is spot of recovery." Translation: had Barnes fumbled on fourth down, it would have been the Giants' ball on downs at the one-yard line. It would not have mattered that Smith recovered in the end zone.

The Eagles' victory over the Giants is their final home game of the regular season. Although they're tantalizingly close to a title with an 8-1 record, the Birds have not clinched the Eastern Conference. They now must clinch on the road, which, as Shaw points out, is always an iffy prospect. The Eagles play best at home. The Eagles lost four of six games on the road in '59. Regardless, the Philadelphia fans have faith in their team. Requests for championship game tickets had started piling up on the desk of Eagle Executive Vice President Joe Donoghue even before the second Giants game. The Eagles' brass is cautious. The club announces it will take no action until the title is clinched.

Twelve

Clinching and Cloud Eight

Eight straight wins. Momentum is a powerful engine, especially when it's fueled by high-octane confidence. Philadelphia's team confidence operated in a safe zone, far removed from arrogance or self-doubt. Nor was their confidence choked by smugness or self-delusion. By acknowledging their own limitations, they chugged beyond the knocks and pings that destroy lesser engines. Their confidence purred along throughout the regular season and opened full throttle in the championship game. As J.D. Smith affirms, nothing succeeds like success:

J.D. SMITH: "I believed we had a good team back in my rookie year in 1959. But then, several new guys came to the club in 1960—guys like the Blade, Bobby Freeman, Ted Dean, Maxie Baughan, and others. When we started winning week after week, I realized these new guys were players too. They were real Eagles who fit right in. The momentum we built during that win streak and the confidence we gained were powerful. It didn't matter that the papers said we couldn't do it. We believed in each other because we *were* doing it."

Nick Skorich observed that same pulsating dynamic growing ever stronger each week of the win skein.

NICK SKORICH: "Each week the whole team seemed to bear down more. You could see each guy pushing the other guys harder and harder. That's how that team's great camaraderie played into our success. Our guys didn't get tense and tight. They didn't let the pressure get to them. Too many guys on that team kept everybody loose. The Eagles got tougher every week."

Pro football is an instinctive sport. The great quarterbacks can "feel" pressure from the defense. They can "feel" when a receiver is breaking clear. The great backs know instinctively whether to zig or zag, whether to cut back or break to the sideline. The guys out there in the pads feel the ebb and flow of momentum in a game, and in a season. Marion Campbell shares some insight into what the competition was feeling in 1960.

MARION CAMPBELL: "At the Pro Bowl that year, many of the players from other teams told me they could see that something special was happening in Philadelphia just by watching our films. They said they gained respect for the Eagles because of our confidence. They knew we were for real."

Reviewing films in preparation for the big game.

Philadelphia confidence captured on film—shades of Rocky I. Just as Apollo Creed's manager saw danger in TV clips of Rocky Balboa pummeling meat carcasses, Philadelphia's competition saw something deadly in the Eagles. Siskel and Ebert weren't the only ones who picked up on those kinds of intangibles, or vibes, as the '60s would name them later in the decade. The Eagles were putting out serious vibes.

Team confidence was their heaviest vibe. Time and again, the Eagles dipped into their reserve of confidence to fuel an exciting victory that somehow equated "come from behind" with "never a doubt." They never bankrupted that reserve, not even in the championship game. The opposition scored first in all but four games that championship season. Against the defending Eastern Conference champion Giants, the Eagles fell behind in two straight contests—spotting New York 10 points in the first match and 17 in the second. Both times Philadelphia roared back to win.

JOHN WITTENBORN: "We never thought we'd lose a game that entire season. We felt like if we could stay within three touchdowns, we'd come back and win. We always figured that Dutch would think of a way to come back. That's what Van Brocklin gave to this team—self-belief."

Of course, most Eagles don't deny that some good luck came their way during that win streak.

SONNY JURGENSEN: "Hell, yeah, we were lucky! Wouldn't you rather be lucky than good! A lot of our luck, though, was that we stayed healthy. And sure, we had some luck and some good breaks, but we took advantage of them."

GENE GOSSAGE: "I define luck like my coach, Ara Parseghian, at Northwestern, did. Luck is where preparation meets opportunity. We knew what to do with the breaks that came our way. Breaks don't mean anything if you don't take advantage of them."

Teaming momentum, confidence, and opportunism into a mighty triumvirate, the Eagles trekked that tricky terrain that separates talent from success. To this day, many of their rivals can find no reason why the Eagles bested them. They dismiss the 1960 Eagles as lucky. They're wrong. They're looking for luck in all the wrong places.

VICTORY, VITALIS, AND VINDICATION

The Eagles are out to clinch the East as soon as possible. They face another determined foe in the St. Louis Cardinals. The Redbirds feel the same as every other Eastern Division team. With the right bounces, they, rather than the Eagles, could be number one. As it is, St. Louis, with its 5-4-1 mark, is battling for second-place money, approximately $800 a man, and a berth in the newly instituted Runner-Up Bowl in Miami. Coach Pop Ivy holds practices behind closed doors, adding new wrinkles and gimmicks to his already complicated double-wing offense. St. Louis wants this game badly. So does Buck Shaw. In Philadelphia, Shaw closes off Murphy Field, stationing private policemen at the gate, while a few more security police screen off the view of the field from the expressway.

The Cards flash more impressive statistics than the Eagles, but that's been the drill all year. John David Crow is closing in on his greatest season. Crow is second in the NFL in rushing yardage, behind Jim Brown. But Crow isn't the only threat. Mel Hammack, the Cards' second-leading rusher with 347 rushing yards in '60, Joe Childress, and Bobby Joe Conrad are dangerous runners as well. Whereas Eagle backs have averaged only 110 yards rushing in nine games, the Cardinals average more than 200. The Birds rush for 3.5 yards per carry, versus the Cards' glitzy 4.9. Sonny Randle, the Cards' talented rookie receiver, is second in the NFL in number of pass receptions. He leads the circuit in touchdowns with 12. By season's end, Randle will have caught 15 TD passes, the most in the NFL since Cloyce Box's 15 in 1952. In comparison, *none* of the Eagle receivers rank in football's top ten. One Eagle-Cardinal comparison is compelling. St. Louis has given up a whopping 44 interceptions in ten games. That's an average of 4.4 interceptions per game. The Eagles lead the league with 24 interceptions, or an average of 2.6 a game. In other words, in each game the Cardinals fling away almost two interceptions more than the Eagles—tops in intercepting—pick off! The previous week,

Cards' QB, John Roach, tossed away five passes to the Cleveland Browns. St. Louis still managed to tie the Browns, a tribute to the potency of their running attack.

Shaw plans only one major line-up change for the game. Chuck Bednarik will play only on offense. He'll be reinstalled at center, with Bob Pellegrini assuming the left linebacker assignment. Shaw wants Bednarik at full strength against the Cardinals in order to bolster the Eagles' running attack, which was stymied in both Giant games.

The Cardinals line up the same squad they did the first time the two rivals met in October. The only difference is at defensive tackle, where ex-Eagle Don Owens has replaced Frank Fuller, who is out with a broken leg. Fuller is generally considered one of football's finest defensive linemen. Owens, a native of St. Louis, has played well for his home-town team, and Shaw does not diminish the power of revenge as a motivator.

In an interview before the game, Marion Campbell expounds on the peculiar challenges that Pop Ivy's offense presents. "If you overcommit yourself on their shallow reverse, you find them behind you while you're out chasing rainbows. The reverse is designed so the ball carrier can go wide or cut off tackle. And all the Cardinal backs, especially John David Crow, are good at cutting. The ball is hard to follow. It's hard to play 'keys' against them."

The Eagles defense has matured since the teams' first encounter. In that one, line coach Jerry Williams had his defensive line stunting, trying to jumble up the blocking assignments for the Cardinal linemen. The Eagles employed a three-man line in that first Cardinal game. Afterwards they scrapped that approach and switched to a four-man line. They've had success ever since.

The Swamp Fox, sounding like the coach in training that he is, outlines the preparation problems posed by the Cardinals: "One of the major difficulties in going against the Cardinal offense is that you have to junk almost everything on defense that you used in the ten other games. This doesn't give us, or the rest of the Cardinals' opposition, for that matter, enough time to spend in practice defensing them. In my opinion, that's the reason the Cardinals are leading the league in total offense."

On game day, a sparse crowd of 21,358 shows up at Busch Stadium. The Eagles are slight favorites, more in deference to their first-place ranking than to respect. The Cardinals start the game off aggressively after receiving the opening kick-off. They mount a ground assault and drive 41 yards on four straight carries by John David Crow. Mel Hammock and Joe Childress tack on 17 more. However, the Redbird drive runs out of steam at that point, mainly because quarterback John Roach is reluctant to throw the ball against the Eagle defensive backfield in the wake of his five interceptions the previous week. Gerald Perry, the St. Louis kicker, fails on a 47-yard field goal attempt. After the game, Bob Pellegrini says: "We knew we could contain them at that point. They didn't look like they could throw. And if they were going to stay on the ground, we knew we'd stop them."

Again, the Eagle big-play bug leads to a score. Burroughs intercepts a Roach pass and runs it back 46 yards, setting up an Eagle field goal and a 3-0 lead. Shortly into the second period, Van Brocklin hits Dean on a swing pass for a 36-yard gain. He follows with what appears to be a touchdown toss to Walston. However, a McDonald offensive interference penalty nullifies it. In quick succession, Dutch finds Retzlaff for 16 yards, gets sacked for a 13-yard loss, and throws a 22-yard touchdown to the Baron, which brings the score to 10-0.

The Eagles lengthen their lead to 13-0 before St. Louis puts some points on the scoreboard. Jerry Norton, the ex-Eagle who leads the circuit in interceptions, pulls down a Van Brocklin pass on the 39, and returns it to the 25-yard line. The Cardinals smash their way down to the goal line. After a few unsuccessful plunges, Mel Hammock rams it in. Bobby Joe Conrad, however, misses the extra point. Hammock's score is the Cardinals' last hurrah. They never mount another serious threat. Their quarterbacks complete only four passes for 30 yards. Halfback John David Crow adds another 15 aerial yards on two completed halfback passes. Of five Cardinal passes that do not hit the ground, three go to Cardinals, and two to the Eagles.

Philadelphia pretty much has its own way in clinching the title. Their defense peaks, thwarting St. Louis on the ground and in the air. On the ground, Crow grinds out 74 yards in 15 carries, but in the same number of tries, Hammock manages only 30 yards. In the air, Roach does not complete a pass in the entire first half. In the press box, Assistant Cardinal coach Charlie Drulis observes, "Roach looks like he's afraid to throw the ball."

Following the game, season-long Eagle basher Pop Ivy rescinds his "lucky" label and reassesses the maligned Philly bunch: "We thought we could beat the Eagles with our ground game. After all, we were leading the league in total offense and rushing. But they threw the best defense at us we have seen all season. They are not a lucky team. They are a solid, well-balanced outfit."

The harassed Card QB, John Roach, after the game, observes: "They're twice as good as when we played them last month."

Middle linebacker Chuck Weber credits coach Jerry Williams with his unit's stultifying defense.

"We stunted them dizzy. All during the game, Baughan, Pellegrini, and myself were jumping into the gaps. Give the credit to Jerry Williams. He had their offense all figured out for us."

At the end of the game, with the pressure now off, the Eagles' first regular-season skirmish breaks out. Stan Campbell and Cardinal defensive halfback Jimmy Hill square off. All season long Shaw preached pacifism, not for idealistic reasons, but to avoid costly penalties. As hard-hitting a bunch as they are, the Eagles have remained remarkably disciplined all season in avoiding personal fouls and other penalties of passion. In a post-game interview, Stan Campbell insists he was merely defending himself: "Hill came up swinging. I didn't do anything to provoke him."

Against the Cardinals, it's Pete Retzlaff's turn to shine. The Baron grabs five passes for 133 yards. Two of them are impossible catches. The McDonald—Retzlaff duo each contributes a touchdown. The "other" receiver, Bobby Walston, does not cross the end zone by foot. "Mumbles" splits the uprights in the first quarter and sets the club record, 13, for most field goals in a season, eclipsing the mark of 12 that he established in 1953.

~ The Kickers ~

Bobby Walston turned in perhaps his greatest season in 1960. He finished second in the NFL in scoring, behind Green Bay's Paul Hornung, who set an NFL record that still stands for points scored in one year (176). The former Golden Boy's record has been threatened a few times, but has withstood every challenge for 40 years. In fact, given the way the pro game has changed, the Hornung single-season point record may be football's "most unbreakable" mark, similar to DiMaggio's 56-consecutive game hit streak in baseball.

Since Hornung's time, kickers have evolved into specialists. Hornung, in contrast, was arguably the sport's finest generalist. If not the finest, he was the last of the great generalists. Hornung racked up points every which way: by kicking, running, passing, and catching. His mark of 176 points is formidable for any non-kicker. Emmitt Smith's 25 rushing touchdowns in 1995 set the single season standard for rushing. However, Emmitt's mark falls 26 points short of Hornung's. For receivers, Jerry Rice tops the list, with the 22 touchdowns he caught in 1987. Rice's point total falls 44 points short of Hornung's. For anyone to challenge the record exclusively via touchdowns, 30 touchdowns would be required. Although not impossible, that's an average of almost two touchdowns per game over a 16-game season—a daunting pace in any era. In 1961, Hornung came close to reprising his

End Bobby Walston specialized in big plays in 1960.

1960 season when he tallied 146 points, which rates seventh on the all-time list for points scored in a single season. Despite these two awesome seasons, Hornung barely cracks the NFL's top 50 for points scored in a career.

That's not the case with Bobby Walston. His 881 career points place him 31st on the all-time scoring list—far ahead of his Green Bay adversary. At season's end in 1960, Walston, with his 736 points, had ascended to third on the list, trailing leader Don Hutson (823) by 87 points, and Lou Groza (742), by a mere eight points.

Groza had retired in 1960. However, Lou the Toe came out of retirement the next year and tacked on seven more productive years, during which he widened the gap between himself and Walston. Groza ended up with 1,349 career points; Walston with 881.

Interestingly, Sam Baker, the man who wedged in-between Groza and Walston on the all-time scoring list in the '60s, replaced each of them on their respective teams. Baker took over for Groza on Cleveland after the Toe had retired in 1960. However, when Groza returned in 1961 and resumed his place-kicking duties, Baker was relegated to punting (Baker's lifetime 42.6 yards-per-punt average ranks in the all-time top 15 for that statistic). In 1962, Baker was traded to Dallas, where he stayed till 1964. After Walston retired, Baker assumed Mumbles' vacated kicking spot. Baker spent the rest of his career with the Birds. While on the Eagles, he zoomed past Walston into the second spot on the all-time scoring list.

These three greats of the '50s-'60s era—Groza, Baker, and Walston—are the only performers from the '50s and '60s who still claim a spot in the top 35 on the NFL's all-time scoring list. No one else whose career ended before 1970 remains in that select group.

Most of the post-game laurels from the St. Louis side are thrown Van Brocklin's way. Ex-Eagle Jerry Norton, in a locker-room interview after the game, tells the press that Dutch should be awarded 38 shares of the championship money (meaning Van Brocklin should be given *all* of it, since there are only 38 men on the roster). Don Owens, dealt ingloriously to the Redbirds earlier in the '60 season, volunteers: "What can you do? We swarmed Van Brocklin from all directions, but the Dutchman completes passes while he's standing on his head."

Van Brocklin calls his decision to come to Philly the best decision he's ever made. "I've been on one championship team and two teams that won the division, but this was the most satisfying of all. When I first came here, I didn't know a soul and we wound up with a 2-9-1 mark. Two years later, we win the title. I wasn't sure at first that I was making the right move coming to Philadelphia, but, as things turned out, it was really the best move I ever made."

Three weeks before Christmas, the Eagles have brought the City of Brotherly Love a basket of Yuletide cheer. The national press scrounges for reasons for the Eagles' victory. They land on Van Brocklin. The Dutchman is praised coast-to-coast for his leadership.

Van Brocklin's 1960 statistics, while respectable, are hardly formidable by today's standards. He ranks third among NFL passers in 1960. However, the six interceptions he threw in the first two games almost buried his team. The Dutchman has completed 50 percent or more of his passes in only six of the ten games played thus far in 1960. Only six times in 10 games has he passed for more than 200 yards. In three different games, he handed over three interceptions. Twice he threw two interceptions in a game. In fact, in only two games of ten, has he *not* thrown an interception. Yet he leads his team past all obstacles. Like their leader, the Eagles never let adversity dim the quest or lust for victory.

~ Greasy Kids Stuff ~

"I'll never forget the plane ride home after the clincher," muses Bill Campbell, who did the Eagles' play-by-play in 1960. "All the guys were partying—the whole plane. Dutch had a commercial on TV in those days for Vitalis Hair Cream. The commercial had a pretty well-known tag line that went: 'Stop using that greasy kids stuff.' Anyway, the guys got me to walk up to Dutch's seat with a glass of beer. I poured the beer all over his head, saying, 'Stop using that greasy kid's stuff.' The guys didn't have the nerve to do it themselves. They were sort of intimidated by Dutch. So, there's Dutch, with beer dripping down all over his face and head, and he says to me, 'You be at Donoghue's tomorrow at quarter to twelve.' I knew I had to show up, but I wasn't too thrilled about it. I had no idea what he had planned, but I knew he'd get even. I was driving down the street, looking for a parking spot, when I saw Billy Barnes and Bobby Walston and a few others milling around outside. They greeted me as I was walking down the sidewalk, and kind of ushered me in, positioning me under the transom. Then, they peeled off. Dutch looked over, and next thing I know, a whole bucket of beer that they had put up there on the transom was tumbling down on me. Dutch was vindicated.

"That Donoghue's get-together every Monday was a team ritual. I became a part of it myself that day. You know I've been broadcasting for 52 years, and, I have to admit, that the '60 Eagles team was the beacon of my career. I really liked that team. You couldn't help liking them. They had a real cast of characters. I've been saddled over the years with lots of losing teams. I announced for the '64 Phillies, who blew that big lead with 10 games to go, and the '72-'73 '76ers, who went 9-73 for the season, so it was refreshing to be with a winner in 1960. But, it was more than that. In all my years around professional teams, those 1960 Eagles were the closest-knit team I ever saw. They were truly an outstanding bunch. They had spirit, great camaraderie, and they just loved to have fun."

SNOW SLIDING

The front office sets about planning its first NFL championship game in 11 years. The game is set for a noon start on December 26, provided the western conference is decided by then. In the West, there's a real dog fight. The Colts appear to be faltering. On November 13, Baltimore wins what turns out to be its last game of the season. On November 20, as the Eagles are beating the Giants in the first of their back-to-back bouts, the Colts, with their record at 6-2, have a bye. Baltimore is the odds-on favorite to repeat. However, one month after Baltimore's bye week, as the Eagles, with the Eastern title in hand, prepare for Pittsburgh, the Western Conference race has turned into a free for all. Baltimore has collapsed. From a 6-2 record on November 13, Baltimore has slipped to 6-4.

While Baltimore scrambles for survival, Philadelphia plans the big dance. The Eagles are giving some thought to changing the location of the title game. However, they nix the idea of vacating Franklin Field for Municipal Stadium, out of consideration for their season-ticket holders. There's no way to correlate the seats between the two vastly different venues. Some, or many, season-ticket holders would be upset. The Eagles arrange to expand Franklin Field's seating capacity by 6,000 seats. A total of 67,504 seats will be available for the championship: 2,138 seats sell for $10 per ticket; the rest, for $8. The 17,000-plus season-ticket holders will be given first crack at championship tickets. Season-ticket holders must respond—and pay—by December 16. After that date, tickets will be available to the general public.

Eagles treasurer Joe Donoghue gloats over the anticipated windfall. "If the game is a sellout, it could be the greatest gross (over $500,000) in the history of the National Football League. The TV rights have been sold to NBC for $200,000, and the radio rights have been offered to sponsors here and in whatever city wins the Western Conference title."

The finances for the 1960 championship battle look more promising than the purse for the Giants and Colts in 1959. The '59 title match was played at Baltimore's Municipal Stadium, which has 10,000 fewer seats than Franklin Field. The winning Colts received $4,674.44 per man; the losing Giants $3,083.27. Preliminary figures indicate that the winning team's share in 1960 might top $5,000 per player.

It benefits Philadelphia fans if the Packers or 49ers win the 1960 Western Conference, because more tickets will be available for local fans. As treasurer Donoghue explains: "There will be a seating problem for local fans if Baltimore wins the Western crown. We'll have to give them 20 percent of the tickets. If the Green Bay Packers or the San Francisco 49ers win, there won't be a problem. Green Bay has only 52,000 people in the whole city, and there won't be many who will make the trip from the West Coast if San Francisco wins." Of course, that all translates into more tickets for the hometown folks.

Two games remain in the regular season. For the first game, the Eagles trek to the western part of Pennsylvania to battle the Pittsburgh Steelers, a disappointed bunch that also views the Eagles as pretenders. Philadelphia is the team that knocked Pittsburgh out of contention in their October encounter. The Steelers' coach, Buddy Parker, has called the Eagles "lucky" all year. In a well-publicized interview a few weeks earlier, Parker had picked the Giants to beat Philadelphia in the game at Yankee Stadium. Parker and Pitt publicist Ed Kiely are vocal in asserting that Pittsburgh and Philadelphia are equals. Riley Gunnels disagrees:

RILEY GUNNELS: "I played both places. I know Buddy and Ed were saying those things that year, but, believe me, I played in both cities, and they weren't the same. The Steelers didn't seem as serious as we were with Buck Shaw. And the atmosphere with the front office here was friendlier. The Philadelphia front office was more down to earth. The whole organization here seemed closer."

Going into the game, the Eagles hold a 31-19 advantage in the overall series. However, Pittsburgh walloped the Birds, 31-0, the year before at Pittsburgh.

A sparse crowd of 22,101 slaloms into Forbes Field. For the second year in succession, the field is blanketed in snow and the game is played in a heavy snowstorm. The game follows the same script as 1959, at least for three quarters. Pittsburgh's 13-0 first-quarter lead inflates to 27-0 by the end of the first half. Steelers' running backs mangle Philadelphia's defense. The veteran and future Hall of Famer, John Henry Johnson, rolls up 182 yards on only 19 carries. His 87-yard touchdown jaunt is the NFL's longest run from scrimmage in 1960. Bill Lapham recalls it:

BILL LAPHAM: "You couldn't even see the field markers or the sidelines that day. The snow was coming down that hard. On John Henry's run, I was standing on the sideline, well out of bounds. I swear that John Henry ran alongside our bench on that score. Everyone that was standing there thought the same thing. He had to be five yards out of bounds, but the referees had no idea where the sidelines were."

Pittsburgh outrushes the Eagles by a whopping 238 yards, rolling up 275 rushing yards to the Eagles' 37 yards. The opposition has gained more rushing yardage than the Birds nine times out of eleven tries.

Riley Gunnels shuttled in and out frequently on the defensive line.

And, in one of the two games the Eagles outrushed the opponent, the margin was eight yards.

Van Brocklin stutters through a miserable first half before yielding the reins to Sonny Jurgensen later in the second half. The Eagles enter the final stanza facing a 27-0 deficit. Then things flip around, fueled once again by big plays by the defensive backfield. Don Burroughs intercepts a Bobby Layne pass at the Philadelphia 20-yard line and returns it to the 29. Jurgensen completes a 19-yard toss to Retzlaff, before finding Timmy Brown over the middle on a short pass, which Brown converts into a 52-yard TD. A few minutes later, Jurgensen again finds Brown for a 9-yard touchdown, closing the gap to 27-14. Shortly afterward, Bobby Freeman pries the ball out of the arms of Steeler end Bobby Orr, and the Birds drive for a third quick touchdown. The pivotal play of the drive is the 61-yard catch and run by Tim Brown, setting up a 19-yard Jurgensen-to-McDonald score. Philadelphia's fourth-quarter rally falls short, however. Time runs out with the score 27-21. As opposing quarterback Bobby Layne elaborated so often in his illustrious career: the Eagles didn't lose, they just ran out of time.

Shaw and his staff are distressed by their team's performance, particularly the play of the defensive line. If Green Bay should win the West, Shaw faces a huge problem. The Packers live by the run, and if the Steelers can blast the Birds' line for 275 yards, what will the Packers do? Shaw's other worry is the weather, or rather, how well his franchise quarterback handles cold weather. Van Brocklin has toiled long years under the California sun, and it was apparent that the 27-degree Pittsburgh temperature did not agree with him. Buddy Parker quips: "Tell Van Brocklin I hope the weather is warm for the championship playoff. He certainly didn't look like an Arctic explorer out there."

Sonny Jurgensen recalls Van Brocklin's aversion to the cold:

SONNY JURGENSEN: "Dutch didn't want to be out there that day! We had already won the Division, and it was cold and messy on that field. He came over to the bench and told Buck Shaw: 'Put the kid in.' That was me, the kid—Duke, as Dutch called me. So, Buck put me in."

The Steelers played the game with a lot of fire. Gerry Huth remembers the line play that day:

GERRY HUTH: "Ernie Stautner had a cast on his hand. Now Ernie was a great player. He wasn't a dirty player, or a cheap-shot guy. But, he had this cast on his hand. Now, I was always taught that if a guy is slapping your helmet, let him do it, 'cause he'll just hurt his hand. I don't know what got into Ernie, but he hauled off and slugged me with that cast. I was dazed, and there's Dutch yelling at me to get back into the huddle."

Gene Gossage recalls that Big Daddy Lipscomb was charged up as well.

GENE GOSSAGE: "Timmy Brown had a big day. Of course, Timmy was always capable of a big day. But, after his second big run that day, Big Daddy jumped offside. You know, we were always yapping at each other down there on that scrimmage line, so Howard Keyes said something to Big Daddy, like: 'What's the matter? Can't you count?' and Big Daddy nailed him!"

Shaw did not want his charges simply to go through the motions because the Eastern Conference had been wrapped up. The Bird mentor feared that his squad's momentum would fizzle prematurely. John Wittenborn recalls:

JOHN WITTENBORN: "Buck was upset with the way we played that day. As a matter of fact, he really gave it to us in the locker room at half time. That's the only time I ever heard him cuss."

The Eagles did manage to leave the Smoky City with a good head of steam, thanks to their second-half blitzkrieg. They also had a preview of two upcoming superstars: Sonny Jurgensen and Timmy Brown. Both were sensational. Finally, the Eagles did not leave without at least one small victory, as Jerry Reichow points out:

JERRY REICHOW: "The best part of that Pittsburgh trip was that we won the snowball fight with the Steelers before the ball game."

COMING HOME

The blizzard that invaded Pittsburgh finds its way to Philly, and the Eagles postpone their return trip. Tom Brookshier looks back:

TOM BROOKSHIER: "The blizzard was so bad we couldn't leave, so we stayed over in Pittsburgh and had quite a party. When we got back to Philly at 30th Street Station at about 8:00 a.m., the whole city was immobilized with the snow. It was so bad, the whole team stayed in a hotel in Philly, and we celebrated again, except for Bobby Walston. Bobby trudged all the way back to Maple Shade, New Jersey in the snow. You've really got to know Bobby to realize how unusual that was. Walston was always looking for a party. What made him decide to go out walking in all that, I'll never know, especially with a party going on!"

Like Walston, Shaw and Bednarik brave the elements and head home. They take the train to North Philadelphia, and, from there, ride the subway to the end of the line. Then, Chuck flags a car down. The intrepid motorist picks up the Eagle coach and linebacker, and the trio rides home behind a snowplow.

Shaw cancels Tuesday's practice, complaining: "Because of the storm, I figured we couldn't get hold of half the squad anyway. And if we had, most of them wouldn't be able to make it because of traveling conditions." The Eagles hold their remaining practices that week indoors, in the armory at 32nd and Lancaster, despite an offer from nearby Swarthmore College to use its dirt-floor field house. The squad is loose preparing for the finale against lowly Washington.

The day before the Redskins game, the Western Conference is sorted out. Green Bay takes the flag, besting Los Angeles, 35-21, in front of 53,445 spectators in the City of Angels. The Pack is favored by 10-1/2 points in this nationally televised game. However, Green Bay does not take the game lightly, since the

Rams whipped them, 33-31, in an earlier meeting. This time around, the Rams are decimated by injuries and illness. First-string quarterback Frank Ryan and All-Pro end Del Shofner are on the injured inactive list. Starting defensive ends Lou Michaels and Gene Brito do not start, and several other Rams are injured or ill.

Had the Rams won, the Western Conference would have been turned topsy-turvy. The Baltimore Colts, San Francisco 49ers, and Detroit Lions would have ended in a three-way tie for first. The championship game would have been pushed back till January 8, 1961, forcing the title match into the next calendar year—something that had never occurred in the NFL's 40-year history. The fledgling AFL ignores that tradition. Their 1960 championship is played on New Year's Day, 1961, to avoid going head-to-head with the NFL for the TV market.

As the Eagles prepare for the Washington game, all 67,242 seats for the December 26 championship game have been sold. Joe Donoghue, the Eagles treasurer, laments: "Right now, there are $300,000 worth of checks and money orders that have to be sent back to their owners. And still the mail brings in more."

Shaw reveals his strategy for the game: "We have to get up to Cloud Eight for this game against Washington." Cloud Nine is too high for now. Shaw doesn't want his Eagles to soar that high till the day after Christmas.

In the finale, the Eagles regain their stride, whipping Washington 38-28 in front of 25,558 fans at Griffith Stadium. Van Brocklin turns in a good performance, completing 8 of 15 passes for 190 yards. Twice in the first half he finds Tommy McDonald for touchdowns. McDonald finishes the 1960 campaign with 12 touchdowns, eclipsing Pete Pihos' Eagle record for touchdown catches in a season. McDonald catches 39 passes—12 of which are touchdowns.

For the second straight week, the backup duo of Sonny Jurgensen and Tim Brown is superb. "Duke" completes 9 of 11 for a hefty 196 yards. Tim Brown leads all Eagle receivers with 128 yards on five receptions. Timmy also leads all Philadelphia rushers, with 25 yards on six lugs. Three Eagle receivers exceed 100 yards in receiving for the day. Brown tallies 128; McDonald adds 111 yards on only two catches; and Retzlaff

Timmy Brown starred in the snow against Pittsburgh. He was also superb in the finale at Washington.

chips in with 110. On the down side of the ledger, the Birds rush for a measly 39 yards. Washington backs, in contrast, slash through the Philadelphia line with alarming ease. A band of Redskin backs, led by Don Bosseler (86 yards) and Dick James (35 yards), total a worrisome 192 yards.

~ Tim Brown ~

His whole life, Timmy Brown has picked his way through adversity with the same style and pluck he showed running back kickoffs. The Eagles' popular running back with the jersey number 22 was raised at the Indiana Soldier's and Sailors Children's Home near Richmond, Indiana. He also lived with a family that served as his guardians in a home near the school. "My guardians were good to me," Timmy says quietly. "They gave me good advice and steered me toward college." Timmy wound up at Ball State Teacher's college in the mid-'50s. He was one of only 16 African Americans at the school. Timmy's college days did not mirror Rickie Nelson's. He had to wash dishes and do other odd jobs for hours on end to make ends meet. He didn't have much money, so on holidays he'd sometimes be forced to stay in the basement at the school. Sometimes he walked and ran home on weekends—a 40-mile trip back to Richmond. Despite such hardships, Timmy looks back fondly on those days. "I've always made games out of any drudgery I was forced to do," Timmy explains. "No matter what I'm faced with, I can always get past it, just by singing or making a contest out of it. Even when I ran home from school, I'd try to beat my best time each time I set out. I kind of had fun that way."

It wasn't all drudgery at Ball State. Timmy had a singing group in college, called "Timmy Brown and the Thunderbirds." Later on in the '60s, he cut a couple of records like "I Got Nothing But Time," that enjoyed moderate success, particularly in the Philly marketplace. His heroes growing up were Hugh McIlhenney, Johnny Bright, and Steve Van Buren. "But I really didn't think much about playing football for a living," Timmy adds. Timmy wound up getting drafted by Green Bay in the 27th round of the '59 draft. He was also drafted by the NBA's Philadelphia Warriors. Green Bay Coach Vince Lombardi released him later that season, reportedly because he considered Brown a fumbler. "Actually, they weren't really ready for me in Green Bay at that point," Timmy reflects. "I was too irreverent, I think, too disruptive to the kind of atmosphere that Lombardi demands."

When Timmy Brown was released, he was picked up by Philadelphia. He didn't play much in 1960, except for punts, kickoffs, and taxi squad work. He slowly gained acceptance by the coaching staff. In 1961, he only carried the ball 50 times, but he averaged 6.8 yards a pop. Timmy was discouraged and credits continuing his career to the kind words of encouragement of the people he was living with in Philadelphia, Ernestine and Al Greiss. In 1962, Tim emerged as a premier all-around offensive star, rushing for 545 yards, catching 52 passes, averaging 13.5

yards per punt return, and returning kickoffs for 831 yards.

When Timmy retired in 1968, he was fourth on the all-time list in total yards gained. The only thing he didn't do offensively was kick the ball. Otherwise, he was remarkably versatile. As a running back, Timmy twice surpassed 800 rushing yards for a season. Twice he caught 50 passes from the set back position. Twice he averaged more than 13.5 yards on punt returns for a season, and his career average for 184 kickoff returns was 26 yards.

He's probably best remembered as an electrifying kick-off return man. Timmy ranks in the top 20, all-time, in both kick-off return yards and number of kick-offs returned.

When Tim Brown retired in 1968, he was fourth on the all-time list for total yards gained.

He once returned two kick-offs for touchdowns in the same game. In the long history of the game, only Ollie Matson, Travis Williams, and Gale Sayers have done that.

Handsome and svelte, Timmy was a model for the Jantzen Sport Club line in the '60s. Howard Cosell wooed him for a slot on the Monday Night Football team in the early '70s, but Tim was focusing on an acting career at the time and declined. He appeared in 14 movies, including Robert Altman's "Nashville." His TV credits include "M*A*S*H," "Gimme A Break," and the soap opera, "Capitol."

~ Duke Dupes Dutch ~

The Eagles demonstrated their bench strength in 1960 once they had clinched the Eastern Conference. In the games against Pittsburgh and Washington, Timmy Brown and Sonny Jurgensen came up big. Both continued to come up big for most of the decade. Jurgensen didn't call it quits till 1974 at age 40. By that time he was a superstar. Only Unitas had thrown more completions and amassed more yardage. Almost 40 years after retirement, Sonny is still among football's top 20, all-time, in each category. He remains in the all-time top ten in yards per attempt. Statistically, Sonny was the top quarterback of the '60s, leading everyone in yardage and number of completions. He was selected to the All-Pro team in 1961, 1964, 1966, 1967, and 1969.

"I had some great receivers," Jurgensen reminisces. "I had Bobby Mitchell in Washington, and, of course, I had Retzlaff and McDonald here. McDonald was so quick and had such great concentration. He used to turn his back to me, and I'd throw tennis balls over his shoulder and he'd catch them. He just had great reactions. And, of course, Tommy was up for anything. When we were all living at the Walnut Park Plaza, Dutch and Lum Snyder, one of the old Eagle coaches, were cooking steaks on their balcony. Tommy and I climbed up the back and stole them. They were furious, really ticked. But we never told them what we did. Steaks tasted good, too. They cooked them just the way I liked them."

The finale is a bruising battle, as Tom Brookshier recounts:

TOM BROOKSHIER: "I was the captain that day. I went out there for the coin toss, and Bob Toneff was their sole captain. It was the last day of the season. Washington had a horrible record, but they had some talent on that team. It was the last game they played in Griffith Stadium. Before the game, those Washington guys acted like all they wanted to do was to get the game over with and get off the field. I went over to the sidelines after the coin toss and said to McNally it was going to be an easy game. Was I wrong! Washington hit like hell out there! We won, but what a physical pounding we took."

A more physical game is coming. Over in the West, Vince Lombardi's Green Bay Packers are running over anyone who gets in their way. They're running for daylight—and they're scaring the daylights out of Buck Shaw and his staff.

Thirteen

The Opposition

Run for Daylight is the title of Vince Lombardi's book from the '60s. The title gallops right to the bottom line of Lombardi's theory on offensive football. The Lombardi philosophy changed the way offensive linemen went about their business. In the past, offensive linemen were assigned specific defenders to block. Lombardi's scheme shifted that paradigm. Lombardi's linemen didn't block designated defenders. They sealed off areas. Linemen drove whatever defenders ventured into their area in the same direction as their pursuit. The ballcarrier's responsibility was to "read" the lineman's block and react to it by cutting in one direction or another in order to break into the open field. In a nutshell, the ballcarrier's job was to run for daylight.

The 1960 Packers have mastered Lombardi's art. Their runs for daylight have led them into the national spotlight, nudging the Eagles into the penumbra. Philadelphia is considered lackluster. They're the "other" team in the championship bout. Sure, the Birds have pulled off the same miraculous, two-year, last-place to first-place dash as Green Bay, but the Packers have managed to catch the nation's fancy in the process. The Packers, fronted by the powerful personality of Vince Lombardi, already have image, which, as every new-millenium child knows, is everything. The Packers are hailed as the next super team. Philadelphia is dismissed as an enigma. They're a team that can neither be explained nor explained away.

The '60 Eagles were not accorded a champion's due in their heyday. The press dubbed them with unflattering nicknames like the Cheese Champs and the Team with Nothing But a Title. Such was their reputation. Such is their legacy. In football history, the Philadelphia Eagles are a blip on the time line between two eminent eras—the Colts of the '50s and the Packers of the '60s.

Forty years after the hoopla of a world championship, the members of the '60 Eagles don't seem overly upset about their legacy, or lack thereof. They shrug off the snubs of history. Practically every member of the team avers that, personnel-wise, position-by-position, the '60 Eagles fell short of their top competitors. Yet, not a one concedes that there was a better *team* than Philadelphia in 1960. As Riley Gunnels puts it:

RILEY GUNNELS: "People don't understand that football is a team sport. Position by position, we may not have had the best personnel, but it's a 'whole-team concept' out there on the field. That's what wins. What matters is how well each guy covers for the next guy, and how well a team plays together as a unit. There wasn't a team around that could compare to the Eagles as a whole team."

Eddie Khayat echoes Gunnels' feelings:

EDDIE KHAYAT: "There's never been a champion where, when you went down their roster player by player, grading each guy, like: 'He's an A guy, he's an A+ guy, he's a B guy, etc.,' that you came out with lower grades individually, on a man-by-man basis. We didn't have the big stars that some other teams had, but collectively we couldn't be beaten. We proved that. We had different heroes every week. Everyone played an important role, and everyone contributed. Very few teams can say that. They rely on a few guys, and if those guys don't come through, the team is done."

Bobby Freeman chimes in with the same argument:

BOB FREEMAN: "The '60 Eagles were relics from a bygone era. We had a bunch of misfits, young guys, old guys, African American guys, Southern guys, Northern guys—you mix them together, and a team personality comes out. Sometimes it works and sometimes it just doesn't click. It worked with the Eagles. We had an outstanding team personality. I played for Green Bay and Washington, and, I'll tell you, it was a different atmosphere at each of those places than on that Eagle team. The Redskins were less zany, you could say. The Eagles were always set for a laugh, but we were always set for a scrap, too. We were loose, but we had, let's say, sort of a deadly sense of seriousness when it counted."

When the members of the '60 Eagles look back on that season 40 years ago, it quickly becomes clear that this team cared more about its people than its X's and O's. Separated by time and miles, the members of the squad still view one another, and speak of one another as mates, as friends—not as detached, disconnected, or forgotten colleagues, and certainly not as lifeless names on a long-ago roster. For members of the '60 squad, the most vivid and significant memories of that championship season concerned people, not events or achievements or awards or things, but people.

But, what about those people as football players? How true is it that the Eagles' competition was superior?

In 1960, the Eagles placed three members—Van Brocklin, Bednarik, and Brookshier—on the first-team UPI All-Pro team. That's one more than any other team in their conference. Cleveland landed two on the All-Pro team: Jimmy Brown and lineman Jim Ray Smith, as did New York, whose Rosey Brown and defensive back Jim Patton were honored. Two Western Conference teams placed four each on the first team All-Pro. Baltimore's Ray Berry, Jim Parker, Lenny Moore, and Gino Marchetti all earned slots, as did Green Bay's Ringo, Hornung, Henry Jordan, and Bill Forester. Two Eagles, Tommy McDonald and Jesse Richardson, were selected to the second team, while four Packers made the second team: Forrest Gregg, Jerry Kramer, Jim Taylor, and Jesse Whittenton. Cleveland had four representatives on the second team: Mike McCormack, Bobby Mitchell, defensive tackle, Bob Gain, and linebacker Lou Michaels, while the Giants had two: Sam Huff and Andy Robustelli.

So if the focus is narrowed to 1960 alone, the Eagles held their own against the competition on the All-Pro lists. Green Bay was dominant, but the Eagles weren't far behind. Of course, a whopping nine Packers who started in the 1960 championship game later made the Hall of Fame. But aside from the Packers, the Eagles match the Giants and Colts of their era in Hall of Fame representation. Five of the '60 Colts are enshrined (Berry, Marchetti, Moore, Jim Parker, and Unitas), as well as four of the '60 Giants (Rosey Brown, Gifford, Huff, and Robustelli). The '60 Eagles also boast four Hall of Famers. And don't forget that Maxie Baughan, with his nine Pro Bowl appearances, along with Pete Retzlaff, eventually could—and should—up that total to six. Doing the math indicates that, if the '60 squad eventually claims six Hall of Famers, an impressive 15% of the entire squad, and 27% of the starting lineup, would be enshrined. Clearly, the '60 Philadelphia Eagles had more than a title.

The 1960 Eagles drew from some undeniable, yet undervalued strengths. In an era in which a second-place team like the St. Louis Cardinals was fielding quarterbacks who tossed an average of 4 $1/2$-plus interceptions per game, Philadelphia

FIGURE 1

EAGLES	Catches	Yards	COLTS	Catches	Yards
McDonald	495	8,410	Moore	363	6,039
Retzlaff	452	7,412	Berry	631	9,275
Walston	311	5,363	Mutscheller	220	3,684
TOTALS	1,258	21,185	TOTALS	1,214	18,998
PACKERS	Catches	Yards	GIANTS	Catches	Yards
Dowler	474	7,270	Rote	300	4,797
McGee	345	6,346	Gifford	367	5,434
Kramer	229	3,272	Schnelker	211	3,667
TOTALS	1,048	16,888	TOTALS	878	13,898

featured two Hall of Fame quarterbacks on the same squad. As for receivers, only the Colts rivaled Philadelphia. In fact, Philadelphia places first in a career statistical comparison of the four top receiving corps of the era (see Figure 1).

But the Eagles had more than just quarterbacks and receivers. Other talent on their roster rates with the sport's finest. Don Burroughs is tied for 14th on the all-time list for career interceptions, sharing his spot with Hall of Famer Yale Lary and Deron Cherry. The Blade's backfield mate, Tom Brookshier, rumbled through multiple Pro-Bowl and All-Pro campaigns, as did Jesse Richardson and Marion Campbell. Unfortunately, Brookshier was actively compiling a Hall of Fame portfolio when injury terminated his career. Brookie was a tenacious cover man. However, it was as a tackler and team leader that he was unparalleled. The Birds' lightly regarded running game featured a host of gamers whose credentials were marred by bad breaks—an irony, since everything that touched the Eagles was tainted as lucky. Billy Ray Barnes made the Pro Bowl his first three seasons before injuries led to his demise. Clarence Peaks had come into his own in 1960, advancing, game by game, into the ranks of elite running backs, when an injury knocked him off stride. Fate never allowed him to regain that stride. Ted Dean, as Tom Brookshier affirms, was ticketed for greatness, but injuries slowed him down, and an accident ultimately snuffed out his career. Timmy Brown had a marvelous career, though he was underfired throughout most of it. There's no telling how many miles of turf Timmy Brown would have churned up had the ball been put in his hands 25 times or more a game.

Gene Gossage was one of a cadre of linemen who moved in and out on offense and defense.

Philadelphia had hidden talent on the bench. An entire cadre of linemen, like Riley Gunnels, John Wittenborn, Gene Gossage, and Howard Keyes was constantly shuttled in and out on both offense and defense. Guys like Jerry Reichow performed fabulously, though inconspicuously, on special teams. No one returned a punt or kickoff for a score against the Birds all season. As a position player, Reichow was primarily an end, but he didn't catch a pass all season in 1960. Given his chance, in 1961 with the Vikings, Reichow caught 50 passes. He finished the season by playing in the All-Pro game against his former mates, McDonald and Retzlaff. Another receiver, Dick Lucas, caught only three passes in 1960. In 1961, he zoomed up to a McDonald-like campaign, nabbing five touchdowns on only eight catches.

The Eagles tapped into their vast reserve of versatility in 1960, just as Shaw had envisioned they would. Bednarik is the most obvious example. In 1960 and 1961, at ages 35 and 36, Number 60 was selected to *both* the offensive *and* defensive All-Pro teams in at least one of the major polls. His praises are well sung. But Bob Pellegrini also started on offense and defense at various times in response to crises and needs. Gene Gossage, likewise, logged a lot of time on both offensive and defensive units. Tim Brown was a gifted offensive weapon. He could run, catch, and even pass. He was also one of the surest tacklers on the bomb squad. Ted Dean kicked off, ran, caught the ball, and could punt if called upon. Jim McCusker, the starting offensive tackle, was often inserted on defense for goalline stands. And, in case one or both of those Hall of Fame quarterbacks flopped or floundered, Jerry Reichow was available for signal-calling duty. In general, wherever and whenever a fissure propagated, fractures did not follow. Buck Shaw could look to his own bench for a quality player to plug any gap.

Yet, many of the '60 Eagles still tell you that other teams had more talent. In the same breath, they'll tell you they're firmly convinced that the best *team* won in 1960. They don't have a problem with the apparent breach of logic. They simply did not, and do not, delve too deeply into reasons why. Like the single-minded chargers of the Light Brigade (not the ones from San Diego), to reason why was not what the '60 Eagles were about. What they were about was squeezing every drop of talent from a versatile football squad. When they were done squeezing, their bucket was as full as anyone's in football.

A LITTLE GREEN BAY HISTORY

Green Bay had always been one of the NFL's glory franchises, fielding great clubs from the NFL's early years well into the late '40s. When the Pack took a nosedive in the '50s, football forgot Green Bay and its splendid legacy. The Colts became football's new glory boys. Johnny Unitas, Lenny Moore, Gino Marchetti, and the rest of the Colts stampeded across TV tubes nationwide, trampling the memory of bygone Packer dynasties. By 1960, the great Green Bay Packer teams of the '30s and '40s were history. Young fans didn't know or care about the exploits of Don Hutson or Curly Lambeau or Johnny Blood, even if those guys had cooler names. They cared about now, not then. The Happening Generation was starting to happen.

Suddenly, late in 1960, the Packers reawaken. In a matter of a few short weeks, Baltimore topples over. The Packers surge to a Western Conference crown and the litany of Colts' superheroes becomes yesterday's news, replaced by the soon-to-be-lionized likes of Taylor, Hornung, Nietschke, and Starr. Vince Lombardi, Green

Bay's coach, redefines smash-mouth football, pumping it up with a hefty dose of space-age precision.

The Eagles' opponent is a little bit dangerous. The Packers belong to Green Bay in a more personal, gutsy way than any other team belongs to its city. The Packers are the rough, tough symbol of a proud blue-collar town, the garish buckle on Green Bay's Midwest belt. Green Bay alone survived pro football's inevitable migration from tiny, nascent Midwest towns to big eastern citadels. Whereas Massillon, Canton, Muncie, Toledo, and other small-town teams withered and disappeared long before World War II, Green Bay is still vying for NFL titles after the last sputnik has dropped earthward.

The Green Bay Packers were born in 1919. Curly Lambeau, formerly a local high school football star, approached his employer, the Indian Packing Company, to finance a football team. The company gave Lambeau $500, and out of gratitude, Lambeau gave his team the name of its benefactor, the Packers.

Lambeau's fledgling Packers got out of the blocks fast, putting together what has to be one of the finest first-season records in the history of sport. In their first game, they breezed to a 53-0 victory over the Menominee North End Athletic Club. Green Bay shut out their first four opponents, racking up 255 unanswered points in the process. Not until game five did one of their foes, Racine, score on them. Racine scored six; Green Bay 76. The Packers did lose one game that year. The Beloit Professionals squeaked by them, 6-0. At season's end, the Packers sported a 10-1 record, scoring a sensational 565 points (an average of over *55 points* a game) while surrendering a scant 12 (an average of *one point* per game).

In the franchise's pioneer period, a bond developed between team and city. Today's "Lambeau Leap" is nothing more than a manifestation of that bond. The 1919 Packers played at Hagemeister Park, which was a mere vacant lot with a gridiron laid out on top of it. There were no fences or gates. On game days, ropes were stretched around the playing field. Spectators seated atop cars rimming the field cheered their boys on for the honor of Green Bay. A swarm of fans shadowed the action more closely, walking up and down the field along the sidelines. Sometimes the crowd spilled over onto the field of play, encircling the players themselves. The team and fans spent half-time together. The Packers, wrapped in blankets, plotted second-half strategy in the end zone, with interactive participation from the loyal gentry.

In 1920, the American Professional Football Association (APFA), which would rename itself the National Football League, or NFL, two years later, was created. The 1920 Packers hadn't been around long enough to prove themselves worthy of admission, but, by 1921, their status had zoomed, and the Packers were welcomed into the fold—only to be unceremoniously drummed out at the end of the same campaign. The APFA's president, Joe Carr, had prohibited the signing of collegians until they graduated from college. The 1921 Packers violated the rule. Their roster was tainted with several college players performing under fictitious names.

When Carr got wind of Green Bay's little scam, he ejected them from the league.

The city immediately rallied. Curly Lambeau resurrected the team, and applied for a new franchise, which Carr and the AFPA granted. In 1922, Green Bay once more fielded a professional team. This time around, the team was called the Green Bay Blues, perhaps to put some distance between the new entry and the club that was ousted. At about the same time, the American Professional Football League also switched names, becoming the National Football League—a name it kept forevermore. The town of Green Bay wouldn't let go of the Packer name either, so Lambeau dumped the name, Blues, and Green Bay became known, forevermore, as the Packers.

In their first year in the NFL, 1922, bad weather on game days almost bankrupted Lambeau's franchise. In order to stay afloat, the player/ coach/ owner Curly Lambeau created a nonprofit organization in 1923. The local citizenry made Lambeau's scheme pay off. Their funding saved the club, which, in this millenium, remains the only publicly held franchise in the NFL.

From the first, the Packers were a force in the NFL. They debuted by ticking off 12 consecutive winning seasons. In 1929, 1930, and 1931, the Packers became the first NFL franchise to win three consecutive titles (Meanwhile in Philly, during that same three-year period, the A's were running off three consecutive American League pennants, and two Major League titles—falling one championship short of becoming the first baseball franchise to win three consecutive World Series.)

There was no championship game in that era. The entire NFL was lumped in one jumbo league. The NFL title was conferred solely on the basis of won-lost percentage. It wasn't until 1933 that the first National Football League championship game was played, when the Chicago Bears eked out a win over the New York Giants, 23-21, in front of 26,000 onlookers.

The Packer's '30s-era championship teams were headlined by mythical gridiron greats like Johnny (Blood) McNally and Cal Hubbard, both of whom were charter members of the Pro Football Hall of Fame. Another Packer star, Mike Michalske (who had played for the New York Yankees against the Philadelphia Quakers in Red Grange's ill-fated AFL of 1926) was inducted into Canton's second Hall of Fame class.

In 1933, the Green Bay franchise hit rocky financial times. Again, the local community rushed to the rescue, raising $15,000 to restructure the corporation. Six hundred shares of stock, which paid no dividends, were sold. The stockholders would gain nothing should the club be sold—the proceeds would go to a local nonprofit organization. The Packers are a franchise of the people, by the people, and for the people of Green Bay.

After the glory years of the early '30s, the Packers hit a brief skid, recording their first losing records in 1933 and 1934. Then, in 1935, Don Hutson, fresh from a sterling career at Alabama, donned a Packer uniform to become, for all intents and purposes, the NFL's first superstar. Hutson led the NFL in pass receptions in eight of his 11 seasons, a record that exists to this day. The slim receiver paired with Clarke Hinkle to herald a second era of Packer supremacy. Hinkle, another enshrinee in football's second Hall of Fame class, starred for Green Bay from 1932 until 1941, when he left for military service and ended his career. The former Bucknell back left the pro game as the NFL's leading all-time rusher with 3,860 yards. His standards were eclipsed by Philadelphia's Steve Van Buren.

In 1936, the Pack won its first world championship tilt, 21-6, against the Boston Redskins (who were later to become the Washington Redskins). After slipping to second place in 1937, Green Bay won consecutive Western Division titles in 1938 and 1939, splitting victories with the New York Giants in the two championship games. In 1941, the Packers tied the Chicago Bears for the Western Division title, losing in the tie-breaker 33-14. A few years later, in 1944, Green Bay again took the Western Division crown, besting its old nemesis, the New York Giants, in the title match.

When Hutson quit in 1945, the Packer powerhouse started to falter. They managed two more winning seasons without him. However, 1948 brought a halt to a string of 14 consecutive winning seasons. By the time founder Curly Lambeau relinquished the reigns in 1950, the Packers had come undone, losing their heart, soul, and direction. Green Bay floundered in the second division throughout the '50s. John Wittenborn recalls:

JOHN WITTENBORN: "I remember in the '50s when Green Bay was the only sure win of the season (John was with San Francisco in the '50s. The Eagles, on the other hand, lost all four games they played at Green Bay in the '50s. It wasn't exactly a golden age for Philly football, either). It was so cold up there! One time, we were standing on the sideline in the bitter cold, when these two drunks came down to our bench from the stands. These guys went over to our water bucket and poured whiskey in it. The players saw that and we started hitting it pretty good. The coaches couldn't understand why everyone was all of a sudden drinking so much water on such a bitter, cold day!"

Things changed in 1959. The Packers transformed an abysmal 1-10-1 record in 1958 into a 7-5 log in 1959.

The amazing Packer turnaround was brought about by their new coach, Vince Lombardi, who succeeded Ray "Scooter" McLean in 1959. Lombardi had gotten his start on the gridiron as one of Fordham University's Seven Blocks of Granite in the late '30s. He never played pro football. Instead, he coached under Earl (Red) Blaik at West Point, before gaining fame as a Giants' assistant coach for five years in the mid-'50s. Nick Skorich, an Eagle coach in 1960, was on Scooter McLean's 1958 Green Bay coaching staff when Lombardi was named head coach. Apparently, Nick Skorich was destined to be on the sidelines, one way or another, in the '60 championship game:

NICK SKORICH: "Before Lombardi moved over to Green Bay, Vince McNally had already contacted me and asked me if I would come to Philadelphia to be part of Buck Shaw's staff. I accepted. After I had already accepted, Lombardi called me and asked me to stay on in Green Bay with him. Lombardi was coming in as General Manager and coach. I couldn't take Lombardi's offer, only because I had already said yes to McNally. That's how I wound up in Philadelphia."

Green Bay's blue-collar ethic suited Lombardi, despite his big-city, Brooklyn roots. As a rookie coach in 1959, Vince Lombardi was a unanimous choice for Coach of the Year. He took an underachieving 1-10-1 team in 1958 and started shaping them into one of the most relentless machines in the annals of sport. In Lombardi's rookie year, the Packers were inconsistent and streaky, lacking the confidence and steadiness of proven winners. They had started the 1959 season afire, winning three consecutive games. They came untracked after that and lost five straight. Lombardi regrouped his troupes at that juncture, and set them back on track. The recharged Pack responded by closing out the season with four consecutive wins.

Lombardi's rebuilding program was swift and disarmingly simple. A nucleus of young stars was already in place when he walked in the door. Future Hall of Famers Paul Hornung, Jim Taylor, Bart Starr, Forrest Gregg, Ray Nitschke, and Jim Ringo had all suffered through that disastrous 1-10-1 season. Lombardi built his dynasty around that nucleus, sorting out the old-line Packers, keeping only the few with the right stuff: Bill Forester, Jesse Whittenton, Hank Greminger, Tom Bettis, Gary Knafelc, Bob Skoronski, Max McGee, and John Symank. His first order of business in rebuilding was to beef up his offensive line. He added Fuzzy Thurston, an Eagle reject, who, together with Jerry Kramer, formed perhaps the '60s' best tandem at offensive guard. For his defense, Lombardi plucked Willie Davis and Henry Jordan—two future Hall of Famers who enjoyed long careers with the Packers—away from Cleveland. He also nabbed defensive end Bill Quinlan from the Browns, along with defensive back Em Tunnel from the Giants. Lombardi's magic forged these stars into a tight-knit unit in only two seasons.

When the '60 campaign began, the Packers were upstarts, long shots to dislodge

Two proud gentlemen take the field: Eagles head coach Buck Shaw and Packers' legend Vince Lombardi.

the Colts atop the Western Conference. Green Bay's streaky 1959 season had failed to make believers of the football establishment. The *Philadelphia Bulletin's* Hugh Brown, however, foresaw big things for Green Bay before the '60 season got underway, writing:

"Wellington Mara, boss of the Giants, said after his team lost to the Packers in Jersey City, that the 'surprise Western team of 1959' has come up with a 'marvelous' defense. Well, the Packers already had a good offense built around scoring king Paul Hornung, fullback Jim Taylor, rookie end Boyd Dowler, veteran end Max McGee, and linemen Jim Ringo and Jerry Kramer. They still have these men as well as one of the NFL's finest coaches and organizers, Vince Lombardi. Quarterback Bart Starr is believed to have finally reached stardom, and if he hasn't, he has a good replacement in Lamar McHan. The marvelous defense is spearheaded by linebackers Bill Forrester and Tom Bettis. The Packers look as though they could take the whole package."

But as the 1960 campaign got underway, football luminaries were clustered mostly in Baltimore, New York, and Cleveland. Baltimore quarterback Johnny Unitas was pro football's first national TV hero. His signature high-top black shoes underscored his gridiron gunslinger image. Johnny U had a style that was all his own. His posture and mannerisms were unmistakable. His teammates, Raymond Berry, Lenny Moore, Alan Ameche, Gino Marchetti, and Art Donovan were also household names. The Giants had Sam Huff, Frank Gifford, Roosevelt Brown, and Roosevelt Grier, national figures all. They had the New York press. And Cleveland had Jimmy Brown, after only three years, the biggest-name running back in the history of the game.

Though the Packers started the '60s on football's perimeter, they started the season ablaze, winning all six of their exhibition games. Misfortune almost dealt them a crippling blow as the regular season was about to start. On September 1, a gust of wind toppled a 25-foot tower, which konked middle linebacker, Ray Nitschke, on the head. Fortunately, Nitschke was wearing his helmet at the time (Had the Occupational Safety and Health Administration existed at the time, they would have honored the Packer linebacker). A woozy Nitschke explained afterward: "It was raining a little and it looked like it would rain pretty hard. I didn't want to get my head wet, with this thin hair. So I put my helmet on." The bone-crushing linebacker put his helmet back on in the nick of time, right before the tower fell. One of the bolts in the tower pierced his helmet completely, stopping just short of his skull. Nitschke was shaken and stirred, but uninjured.

The Pack closed out their preseason with a 41-7 thumping of the Washington Redskins in Winston-Salem, North Carolina. Their confidence was starting to gallop. Throughout the preseason, Green Bay alternated quarterbacks. Bart Starr was indecisive with flashes of brilliance. His backup, Lamar McHan, was unspectacular, but steady. Lombardi couldn't decide between the two, so Green Bay entered the regular season with the quarterback spot up for grabs.

In the 1960 regular-season opener, Chicago's Monsters of the Midway invaded Lambeau Field. The two clubs had been rivals since 1921. They waged the bruising kind of war that ultimately earned their conference the nickname, "The Black and Blue Division" one decade later. The Packers, thanks to short touchdown runs by Jim Taylor and Paul Hornung, carried a 14-0 lead into the final quarter. The Bears knotted the contest as time wound down on long touchdown runs by Rick Cesares and Willie Gallimore. On the Packers' final drive, Earl Leggett, a 250-pound tackle intercepted a batted Bart Starr toss, and set up the Bears' winning field goal with 35 ticks left on the clock.

In losing, the Packers blew some critical plays. In the first quarter alone, Hornung missed one field goal and had another one blocked. Also, in the first quarter, a Starr pass was picked off to stifle a serious Packer drive.

After the first week of the season, the Western Conference had aligned much as anticipated. The Colts and Bears shared the top spot after the Colts had topped the Redskins, 20-0, in their opener. As for the Bears, their win over Green Bay extended their victory streak in league competition to eight.

But the natural order was soon to crumble in the West. The Colts annihilated the Bears, 42-7, in week two, while the Packers humbled the Detroit Lions, 28-9. The Pack came back in week three to club the Colts, 35-10. The Packers' defense picked off Unitas four times and recovered two Colt fumbles to bag the win. Lamar McHan replaced Bart Starr at quarterback—Starr's confidence having been shaken by the opening-day loss. In week three, the Bears, Colts, and Packers all shared first place.

By Halloween, the Packers stood alone atop the western conference with a 4-2 mark. However, October's success swiftly unraveled. On November 6, Baltimore beat Green Bay in Baltimore to reclaim first place. Then, after the Packers trounced the punchless Cowboys, 41-7, they bungled back-to-back games, first to the lowly Rams, and then to the Lions on Thanksgiving. The Pack's Turkey Day disaster tumbled them down to third place, and most of the football world wrote them off. However, mimicking their 1959 end-of-the-season surge, Green Bay beat the Bears, 49ers, and Rams to finish with another flourish. Meanwhile, the Colts were collapsing, bowing first to Detroit (despite the fact that the Colts were 13-point favorites), and then to the Rams and the 49ers.

During their late-season rally, Green Bay came of age. From preseason longshots, they emerged from the regular season as monsters. Lombardi's Packer dynasty had begun. By the end of the regular season, football fans everywhere were exalting the Packer end sweep and hailing the Packer's two punishing running backs, Hornung and Taylor, as the game's premier backfield combo. Football forgets. A scant three months earlier, Jim Brown and Bobby Mitchell were so hailed.

Bart Starr shined in the televised Packer finale against Los Angeles. While the Rams contained the vaunted Packer rushing attack to a mere 20 yards in the first half and 38 in the second half, Starr was proving he could direct an aerial attack.

The former Alabama star went the long-distance route against the Rams, pitching touchdown strikes of 57 yards to Max McGee and 91 yards to Boyd Dowler. Scoring champ Paul Hornung added a 40-yard scoring heave to McGee, putting an exclamation point on the Pack's solid 35-21 thrashing of the Rams.

The Packers' triumph signaled the changing of the guard. Football fans would be hearing different names than those they had heard in the two previous championship games. The 1960 title tilt would pit a young, talented, aggressive, physical bunch from Green Bay against a Quaker City squad that the national pundits characterized as a two-man show. Two *old* men. To most fans outside the Quaker City, Van Brocklin and Bednarik *were* the Eagles.

The Packers are picked as favorites. Their fame is destined to skyrocket throughout the decade. In 1964, when the Beatles invade America, one popular—and incorrect—rumor has it that Beatle Ringo Starr drummed up his name from Green Bay's center-quarterback combo: Jim Ringo and Bart Starr. He did not, but, early in 1964, the Green Bay Packers were more popular than the Beatles, who, a few years hence would claim to be more popular than Christ.

In contrast to the Packers' celebrity, the Eagles, by 1964, had slipped into the anonymity that besets a 6-8 team. Their 1960 championship was a distant memory by mid-decade; although the Packers never forgot that 1960 Eagles team. For the '60 Eagles did to the Packers and Vince Lombardi what no other team ever did in ten postseason tries. They beat them.

Fourteen

December 26, 1960

THE WEEK BEFORE

The week leading up to the tilt with the Packers begins on a tragic note. Jesse Richardson, the Philadelphia native who has played his entire career with the Eagles, suffers the loss of his seven-week old son on Monday morning, one week before the title game. Jesse had given the infant his bottle at about 2 a.m. Monday morning. When he and his wife, Dorothy, look in on the child six hours later, he is dead. Doctors at Abington Memorial Hospital later perform an autopsy and say the infant most likely died of pneumonia.

Jesse's tragedy casts a pall over the team at the start of the big week. Jesse gamely composes himself and vows to play in the championship game.

The Eagles try to put the tragedy behind them as the week rolls on. The mood of the team is loose and confident, despite some bad weather that blankets the city with snow. The inclement conditions throw the Eagles' practice sessions out of kilter, but not their rhythm and optimism.

ED KHAYAT: "We didn't get too much practice in before the championship game. Murphy Field, where we usually practiced, was snowed in, so Buck bussed the whole squad over to Municipal Stadium. We stayed there about ten minutes, and then came back. It was too cold for Buck! And he wasn't the only one. Dutch didn't like that cold weather, either. We wound up going to the Palestra (the University of Pennsylvania's basketball facility) once or twice that week, as I recall, and we practiced inside. Buck never held practice on Saturdays, no matter what. Then, Sunday was Christmas, the day before the game on Monday, so we didn't practice on Sunday, either. But we were ready on game day."

Billy Barnes recalls practices with Buck Shaw.

BILLY BARNES: "Yeah, our practice sessions under Buck were great. He would say he didn't want anyone to get hurt if the field was slippery or muddy, so he'd call practice off if it rained. But we all figured he just didn't want to get his hair wet. Buck would call practice off if he felt a single raindrop!"

Ed Khayat details the typical Eagle practice day.

ED KHAYAT: "Once the season was over, we didn't practice in pads or helmets. On practice days, we'd bus over to the field about noon. We'd be finished with everything by three—that included film, bus, shower, everything. Buck was a great believer in having a team ready and at full strength for Sunday. Buck Shaw teams never left their best out on the practice field. His teams peaked on Sunday. They always brought their best into the stadium."

Bobby Freeman recalls that the Eagles didn't show any signs of pressure the week before the big title game.

BOBBY FREEMAN: We played more basketball than football that week! We were holding our practices at the Palestra, and wound up playing basketball and having some fun. We had some guys who could really play hoops on that team. Sonny Jurgensen—what an athlete that guy was! He could shoot your eyes out from the outside! Anyway, the team was so loose and confident the whole week—I just figured we couldn't lose to the Packers. We really felt great going into that game."

Of course, not everyone on the squad felt pressure-free. Gerry Huth, for one, recalls that, for him, the entire week of preparation was intense, thanks to his coach.

GERRY HUTH: "That championship week was a bad week, probably the worst week of my wife's life. I was miserable to live with! I worried about Henry Jordan the whole week, 'cause that's all I heard about. Skorich kept saying to me: 'He's real quick.' That's all he'd say. 'You'd better be ready, 'cause this guy is quick.' That was the only guy, all year, that Nick talked about like that. Then, when we watched the films, Chuck Bednarik was very impressed with Jordan, too. Chuck kept saying: 'Huth, watch this guy—are you watching? He's quick, real quick.' I never went into a game so determined. Nick fired the whole line up that way. He showed the offensive line a press clipping. All he said was: 'Here's what Green Bay thinks of you.' The article said that Green Bay felt that they'd beat us easily as long as they stopped our passing game. They said the Eagles offensive line couldn't block for the run. That little article really pumped up the whole offensive line. We wound up having our best running game of the year against Green Bay, and I think we had such a good game because the

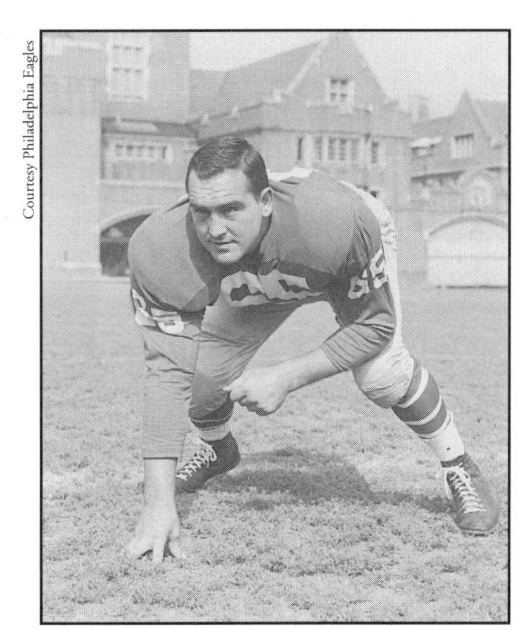

Gerry Huth fretted all week about facing Green Bay's Henry Jordan.

offensive line had something to prove. Playing at home was also a great motivator. I don't know how that played into the whole thing, but I know it meant a lot to us. We didn't want to be embarrassed in front of the home crowd. Philly people were great to us all year. I wound up playing the best game of my life that day. I really think I did. I figured I had something to prove, and the offensive line had something to prove."

Jim McCusker addresses Green Bay's charge that the Eagle offensive line couldn't block for the run.

JIM McCUSKER: "Oh, we could run-block fine. It's just that we never practiced run blocking! All we practiced was pass-blocking. When we set our minds to run-blocking, we did well, but our offense was built on throwing the ball. So, yes, we had something to prove that game, and, when the title was on the line, we proved we could block and move the ball on the ground as well as anyone."

The defensive line has something to prove as well. Buck Shaw and his staff are apprehensive about stopping the Green Bay running attack. Lowly Washington ended the regular season by zipping through the Eagles on the ground. Riley Gunnels explains why the Eagles' defensive line was confident they could stop Green Bay even with the specter of the Washington game hanging over them.

RILEY GUNNELS: "Washington's running attack was a lot different than Green Bay's. Washington 'pop-blocked' us. Green Bay pulled the guards all the time, so, comparing Washington and Green Bay was like comparing apples and oranges. Green Bay could hurt you by getting you out of position with false traps and the like. You had to stay in your lanes better and be better disciplined. But that was our strength. We were a smart, disciplined team that played well as a unit, and we figured we wouldn't overreact."

Physically, the Birds are in good shape for the encounter, except for Bob Pellegrini, who tore a ligament in his left knee against Washington. With Pellegrini's injury, Chuck Bednarik must again roll out his 60-minute man routine. Brookshier also has a minor injury, as Bobby Jackson recalls.

BOB JACKSON: "I prayed real hard that week 'cause Brookie had some sort of minor injury. I just wanted him to be all right, so I wouldn't have to fill in for him! I'm only kidding, but, seriously, Tom Brookshier was a key guy on our defense. We needed him for that game."

Green Bay, in contrast to Philadelphia, spends the week practicing outdoors in Wisconsin's near-zero temperatures. Lombardi tells the press, "This intense cold makes it tough to keep the players sharp in practice. But we've got to play Monday regardless how cold it is, and we may as well get used to it."

HIGH NOON

It is not cold on Monday, December 26, 1960 in Philadelphia. At noon, the temperature is over 40 degrees, with a light 10-15 mile per hour wind from the

Cardinal Dougherty High School band marches at the championship game.

southwest. The skies are clear, the weather is fair, with temperatures expected to rise to almost 50 degrees. It's a great day for football. Green Bay enters Franklin Field as three- to six-point favorites. The line on the game is 6-5, Packers. The Eagles are used to being underdogs. They haven't been favored against the top clubs all year.

A packed Franklin Field on championship day.

198   **1960** *Philadelphia Eagles:* **Nothing but a Championship**

Philadelphia is decked out for the spectacle, as 67,325 hopeful fans pack into the University of Pennsylvania's Franklin Field. Mayor Richardson Dilworth is among the throng. He's there to root the city's team on, as well as to ensure law and order. The Mayor vows to the press: "They will not get our goal posts after the game."

The gross receipts tally a colossal $747,876, including the radio and television booty. That's the largest gross gate in NFL history up to that time. When taxes, stadium rental, and the gate operating expenses are subtracted, net receipts total $591,454.98.

All in all, it's a banner day for the NFL.

Philadelphia wins the coin toss and elects to receive. Timmy Brown, the former Packer, who is deep for the Eagles along with Ted Dean, returns Hornung's kickoff 20 yards to the Eagle 22. On the game's first play from scrimmage, Van Brocklin's swing pass is intercepted by Green Bay lineman Bill Quinlan at the 14-yard line. On the Packers' first play, Jimmy Taylor smashes five yards. The Eagles' defense then stiffens and stops Hornung and Taylor for gains of two yards and one yard, respectively. Coach Lombardi, with the ball resting on the Eagle seven, has a decision to make: either kick a field goal or go for the first down. He decides to challenge the Eagles and go for it. Don Burroughs reconstructs the scene.

DON BURROUGHS: 'This was a big play, and we knew it. I guess Green Bay believed all that stuff about being able to run against the Eagles. But we studied Green Bay pretty well in those films. They didn't try to fool you. When they

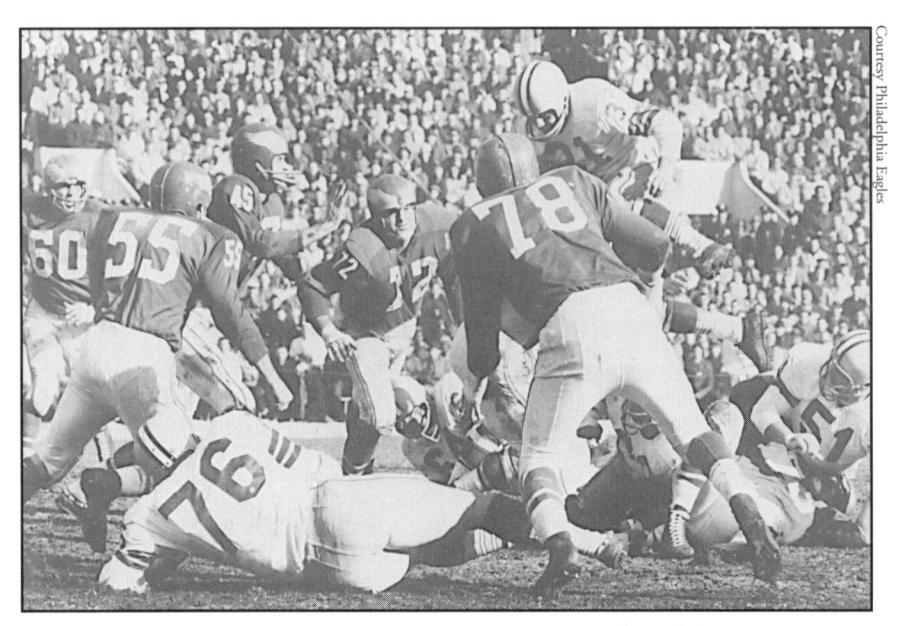

Eagles power including Jess Richardson (#72), Don Burroughs (#45), Marion Campbell (#78) stops Packer Jim Taylor.

decided to go for that first down early in the game, I was watching Lombardi on the sideline. I figured he'd try to run Taylor at us. That's what I told Maxie Baughan in the huddle. I told him that I would read Max McGee's key. If McGee blocked down, I'd crash in. Well, McGee did, and we got in there and threw Taylor for a loss."

Actually, Taylor gained a yard, but still fell far short of a first down.

EDDIE KHAYAT: "That was the game right there, I feel. I knew we had them beat when they missed that first down. It gave our whole team a lift."

The Birds take over at their own five. Barnes runs left for no gain. On the next play, Billy Ray picks up five yards with a slam into the middle. On third down, Ted Dean touches the pigskin for the first time. After slashing forward for 10 yards, Dean fumbles, and Bill Forester recovers for the Packers.

GERRY HUTH: "That was my biggest disappointment of that game. I came close to getting to Ted's fumble before Forester got to it, but I just missed it. That play could have really hurt us, but our defense came up big anyway. In fact, our defense came up big the whole game."

Hornung and Taylor carry twice to crunch out the initial Packer first down of the afternoon. An offside penalty pushes the ball back to the 13-yard line, where Starr throws two incomplete passes. At 6:20 into the game, Hornung kicks a Packer field goal, and for the ninth time in 13 games, an Eagles' opponent has scored first.

When the Eagles' offensive unit takes the field again, Van Brocklin fumbles the first snap but recovers the ball. The Eagles finally get their initial first down via an interference penalty, but three plays later they're forced to punt. The first quarter closes with Green Bay on the move at the Eagles' 29-yard line.

The first quarter has been all Packers. Green Bay ran 21 plays to the Eagles' 14. Furthermore, Philadelphia's offense has been bumbling. In their first five plays from scrimmage, Philadelphia threw one interception and fumbled twice. Van Brocklin's first-quarter ledger shows but one completion—to Bobby Walston, his target on four of five first-quarter passing attempts. The Packers have operated inside the Eagles' 30-yard line on three of their four first-quarter possessions. Despite such lopsided data, the Eagles trail by only three.

As the second quarter gets underway, Green Bay punches down to the Eagles' 14-yard line, where the drive stalls on three successive incomplete passes. The Packers are forced to settle for another Paul Hornung field goal—this time from 23 yards away. Green Bay's advantage climbs to 6-0.

The Eagles' ensuing drive sputters, this time after five plays. One of Van Brocklin's passes is batted back into his own hands. He grabs the swatted football and tosses it a second time. Again it falls incomplete. The play characterizes the Birds' offensive frustration.

The Eagles and Packers exchange punts before the Eagles take over at the Packer 43.

Thus far, the longest drive the Birds have been able to muster is 20 yards. In seven attempts, Van Brocklin has completed only two passes, both to Walston. In fact, five of his seven passes have been flipped Walston's way. Now, the Dutchman looks to McDonald. First, he completes a 22-yarder to Tommy before coming right back with a 35-yard scoring strike to the Eagle flanker. Walston's extra point moments later puts Philadelphia out front, 7-6.

On their next possession, the stunned Packers stall after three downs. McGee punts, and the Birds take over on their own 26. Again, on first down, Dutch fires long, this time to Retzlaff for 41 yards. Van Brocklin follows this toss with a pass to Dean for 22 yards, which moves the ball to the Packer 8. Dutch follows with three successive misfires into the end zone, however, and Philadelphia walks away with a 3-pointer from Walston to extend their lead to 10-6. With little more than three minutes remaining in the first half, the Packers drive 73 yards from their own 20-yard line to the Eagles' 7. On the final play of the half, the Packers suffer a huge letdown as Hornung misses a 13-yard field goal.

Philadelphia leads 10-6 at the end of the first half, despite Green Bay's advantage in practically every statistic. Green Bay has run 48 plays to the Eagles' 30. The Eagles have picked up three first downs, compared to nine for the Pack. The difference in the game has been Van Brocklin's three long completions—two to McDonald and one to Retzlaff—along with obstinate Eagle line play on both sides of the ball and the Packers' inability to convert opportunities into points.

Ted Dean kicks off for Philadelphia to start the second half. The Packers advance from their 32 to their 47 before having to punt. The Eagles receive, only to go three downs and out from their own 15-yard line.

When the Packers get the ball again, they pound the Eagles for two straight first downs. Hornung grinds out 14 yards, followed by a 16-yard Jim Taylor fumble. The Packers stick to the ground for three more plays. Then, on fourth and one at the Philadelphia 25, Lombardi again decides to go for a first down instead of kicking a field goal. Taylor pounds the center of the Eagle line, and again is stopped short. Just as important, however, on the preceding play, Paul Hornung is injured and forced to leave the game. Chuck Bednarik makes the hit—a clean shot—that puts Hornung out of action. As Concrete Charley explains in a postgame interview, "I got Hornung good. I bear hugged him." Hornung describes the injury in a post-game interview: "I was hit on the right shoulder at the base of my neck. My whole right hand, the whole arm, went numb. I couldn't get a good grip on anything with the hand." Hornung leaves the field and sees no further action in the game except for kicking an extra point and kicking off one time.

Juiced up by their second successful, critical fourth-down stand of the contest, the Birds charge back. A third-down, 33-yard pass to McDonald, a couple of runs by Barnes and Dean, and a 25-yard completion to Walston place the ball on the Packer 5-yard line. On second down, however, from the Packer 4-yard line, Philadelphia's hopes deflate when Van Brocklin's pass is picked off by John Symank in the end zone.

The Pack takes over and moves the ball to their 35 before floundering. Max McGee drops back to punt, but instead fakes the boot and bounds downfield. He is stopped 35 yards later by a Ted Dean shoe-string tackle. The embarrassed Birds stiffen up, and Brookshier slams Tom Moore, Hornung's backfield replacement, for a 6-yard loss. Two plays later, however, Starr completes a 17-yard pass for a first down to Gary Knafelc. The Packers are at the Eagle 34 as the third quarter ends.

Again, statistically, the Packers dominate. In the third quarter, Green Bay ran off 19 plays, while the Eagles only managed 13. Uncharacteristically in this quarter, it is Philadelphia who makes the big mistake when they turn the ball over to Green Bay at Green Bay's 4-yard line to come up empty-handed after a nifty 71-yard drive. Van Brocklin completes only two of six passes in the third stanza, which ends with the Eagles still clinging to a precarious 10-6 lead.

The Packers start the fourth quarter with Tom Moore's 12-yard smash for a first down. Taylor and Moore carry successively for another first down, which places the ball at the Eagle 10-yard line. After Taylor's 3-yard spurt, Bart Starr

Hall of Fame running back Paul Hornung set the all-time scoring record during the 1960 season.

finds Max McGee in the end zone for a 7-yard touchdown and a Packer lead. Bobby Jackson recalls the touchdown pass:

BOB JACKSON: "I was in on defense on that touchdown play. We had a mix-up, I guess you'd call it. I was covering the swing man, Tom Moore, and they ran a slant to the free side. We didn't have the proper coverage 'cause Maxie

(Baughan) covered the swing man too. So McGee broke free. That's how they scored."

The Packers burst ahead, 13-10, as Hornung converts the PAT. The stage is set for the key play of the game. Hornung kicks off to Ted Dean, who takes the ball at the 3-yard line and hauls it back 58 yards to the Packer 39. In a postgame interview, Dean, the perfectionist, expresses disappointment with his bolt, saying: "They set up a perfect cup to my left. I was supposed to fake to my right, then hit the lane up the sidelines. With the blocking I had, I should have made it." His teammates today remember his return as a thing of beauty, perhaps the '60 champs' greatest moment. As J. D. Smith puts it:

J. D. SMITH: "When I think of all the big plays we had that year, well, we had so many… But the Walston field goal against Cleveland, and Ted Dean's runback I'd have to say were the biggest. When Bobby made that field goal, I think we all knew we were going to take our conference, and when Ted ran that kick back, we all knew we were going to win the championship game."

Ted Dean credits coach Charley Gauer with exploiting a Green Bay weakness and paving the way for the crucial runback to work.

TED DEAN: "Charley Gauer saw something in Green Bay's films. He was the one who set the run-back up. Charley was a beautiful man. He worked me into the offense that year and really believed in me. When I came to the Eagles, Charley was the one who helped me adjust. Charley came over to my house for dinner and made me feel welcome—he just had a good personal rapport with me and the guys. And Charley was a good football man as well. He proved it that day when he set up that return."

J. D. Smith was the captain of the bomb squad that day.

J. D. SMITH: "We executed so well on that play. Our guys really handled their assignments perfectly. You could feel that play lift the whole team. We weren't going to be stopped on that drive no matter what the Packers did."

After the game, Charley Gauer explains to the press what he had seen in the Packers' last regular-season game: "On their right side on the kick-off, the Packers lined up with two fast men and a slow man, then a fast man and another slow man. We arranged our blockers to take advantage of this alignment so a path could be cleared up our left side. The only flaw was that our center couldn't get to Willie Wood, the fastest man on the Packers. Wood cut back and nailed Dean from behind just as he was breaking into the clear."

When the Eagles take over, Dean and Barnes each gain six for a first down. Van Brocklin is sacked for a seven-yard loss; however, he follows with a 13-yard pass to Barnes. Then, on third and one, Barnes answers with a five-yard, first-down scamper. Bucko Kilroy expounds on Barnes' blasts.

BUCKO KILROY: "When I look back on that season and that championship game, those two first-down runs by Barnes stick out in my mind. To beat the Packers on the ground that way at such a crucial time in the game did something to our team. Billy was such a tough competitor, such a hard-nosed football player! I knew we couldn't lose after that second first down. Those plays characterized our team and our season. We weren't supposed to be able to move on the ground, yet when the game was on the line, we ran extremely well. We weren't supposed to be able to do anything well—until it came time to do it. Then that '60 team always was up to the task and always came up with a big play."

After Barnes' first down, it's Ted Dean's turn. Van Brocklin calls Dean's number for a 4-yard gain, which advances the ball from the 9-yard line to the 5. On second down, Dean sweeps left around end behind Gerry Huth for a score.

GERRY HUTH: "That touchdown was only about the second play we ran to the left (actually, the Eagles ran several plays to the left, but time blurs certain details). That play just went right from the moment the ball was snapped. I wanted to go to the Green Bay locker room after the game and thank Vince Lombardi. When Lombardi and I were both in New York, he made me practice that sweep hundreds of times—me, along with the rest of the offensive line. I wanted to tell Lombardi, 'I ran it just the way you taught me, Coach,' but I didn't think he'd be in the mood to hear it."

~ Ted Dean ~

Ted Dean grew up in Radnor, about 20 minutes west of Franklin Field down the Schuylkill Expressway. As a kid, Ted never gave much thought to playing pro ball. He was too involved in sports himself to think about the distant future.

"I was active in high school," Ted recites matter of factly. "But I've always stayed active. At Radnor High, I played basketball against Wilt Chamberlain, when Wilt was at Overbrook (Overbrook is the West Philadelphia high school where Wilt went to school. Wali Jones, Walt Hazzard, and Wayne Hightower were also Overbrook stars, who played together on the same high school team a few years after Wilt graduated). I also ran track at the Penn Relays. I did pretty well in track, even in college. My coach at Wichita State wanted me to try out for the Olympics in the decathlon because I was a double winner in the discus and shot put in the Missouri Valley Conference championship meet as a freshman."

At 6'2", 210 pounds, Ted Dean had speed and power. He should have been a top-flight high school and college prospect, but inexplicably he was neither. Ted wound up taking a quiet, unballyhooed route to college and the pros.

"I was picked for the All-Suburban team in Philadelphia and the All-American team in my senior year in high school, but wasn't picked for All-State," Dean chuckles, still perplexed after all these years. "Anyway, I wasn't really recruited in high school. My high school coach, Warren Lentz, tried to get me into Penn State, and some other people tried to get me into Villanova, but neither school ever called me. Then one day out of the blue, I wound up with a scholarship to Wichita State. I still don't know how they found out about me out there, but one Saturday a guy drove up to my house in a Cadillac, and offered me a four-year scholarship to Wichita State. Then he drove off. That was it! So I was off to Wichita. It was like an Alice in Wonderland dream."

Ted took advantage of the educational opportunity. He earned a degree in Industrial Arts with a minor in Physical Education. He could have played three sports: basketball, football, and track, but for the most part, he concentrated on football. He wound up as the 40th player selected in the 1960 draft. The Eagles chose him in the fourth round.

"Sure, I was happy to come to Philadelphia. It's my home," Dean says, reconstructing the magic of his rookie season. "It was really a thrill to win that championship, and it was a thrill to run that kickoff back against the Packers and score the winning touchdown. It was such an amazing feeling to be standing on that sideline at the end of that game, knowing that this game was it. I mean, all year long, when a game was winding down, I'd be thinking about that next game, mentally starting to prepare for the next opponent. But, against the Packers, it was so strange, and felt so good, to know that there was no game next week. This game was it. We were champs!"

Ted was beset with injury problems after his promising rookie season. He ended up getting traded a few years later to Minnesota and coach Norm Van Brocklin. It was a chance for new life, and a fresh start at a new position.

"Dutch wanted me to play end, but of course, it never came about," Dean says, retelling the sad episode that ended his career. "One of my teammates, Sandy Stevens, and I were driving in his Bonneville convertible one Sunday after a game. Sandy blacked out at the wheel. The car crashed into a tree. We just missed going into a lake. That Bonneville looked like a Volkswagen when it was all over. Sandy broke some bones, and I had an anterior/posterior dislocation of my hip. They told me I'd need a hip replacement. The Vikings' team doctor told me that night that I'd never play again. Minnesota let me go in 1965. They gave me a medical release. Then Pittsburgh gave me a tryout as a kicker. But then, their coach, Bill Austin, told me I needed to be able to run the ball, too, if they were going to keep me. My running days were over. So was my career. I was through at age 26. I cried many nights about my misfortune, but then I realized I had to turn bad into good."

He did. Ted Dean went back home and taught kids. He taught them for well over 30 years at the Gladwynne School outside Philadelphia.

"It was a rewarding profession, a rewarding life," the Eagles' ex-star confesses. "Getting hugs from those kids, and hearing them say, 'Good morning, Mr. Dean.' It just meant so much to me. I really don't have regrets. And I've got so many other personal interests and hobbies. I play the piano—I have several pianos as a matter of fact—I do needlework, I play some golf, I do some gardening. I'm starting to use the computer more and more. I've enjoyed my life outside of football."

Given the ball in the shadow of the goal line, Ted Dean was not about to let his opportunity pass:

TED DEAN: "I just saw some daylight and put my head down and bulled over. I wasn't going to come up short."

Nor are the Packers willing to come up short. After the Eagles' score, Green Bay starts at their own 30 and crunches out a first down on three rushes. Then Bart Starr finds Max McGee for what should be a 12-yard gain and a first down. But Tom Brookshier jars the ball loose with a big hit, and Chuck Bednarik recovers the fumble on the Eagle 48. The Eagles run three straight times, but Dean is stopped short of a first down, and Van Brocklin has to punt. The Eagles' defense thwarts the Packers, and McGee punts the ball back to the Birds. Again, the Eagles stick to the ground. This time, Billy Barnes is stopped short on a third-and-one plunge. Time is ticking out as Van Brocklin's 48-yard punt is returned six yards to the Packer 35. Battling the clock, Bart Starr completes two passes to his backs, Taylor and Moore. On third down, Taylor rips for a first down, going out of bounds after a nine-yard sprint. Starr sandwiches completions to Knafelc—one for 17 yards, the other for 8—around an incomplete pass intended for Dowler. With only 12 seconds left, Starr flips a pass to Jim Taylor, who catches it and is met first by Bobby Jackson and then by Bednarik. Concrete Charley crunches Taylor to the turf, and then sits on the Packers' frustrated superstar, who lies squirming and struggling to get to his feet. The mini-drama continues, the seconds tick off, and the game ends at the Eagle 9-yard line.

Chuck Bednarik recalls the moment:

CHUCK BEDNARIK: "I saw that clock go to zero and heard the gun, and then I got up. I told Taylor, 'You can get up now. This blankety-blank game is over!'"

As the gun goes off, the final score reads: Eagles 17-Packers 13. Number 60 and Bobby Jackson, number 28, are jumping for joy as Franklin Field erupts. Bobby Jackson describes the scene:

BOBBY JACKSON: "I remember Chuck and me just yelling and having a great time. I said to him: 'You don't know me, Mr. Bednarik, but my name is Bobby Jackson!' I was just joking with him, 'cause I wasn't out there on the field that much—at least not as much as he was. What a great game that guy played! I'll tell you one thing—that Chuck Bednarik is the greatest player I ever played with."

POST GAME AND GOAL POST GAMES

Philadelphia loves their Eagles, and Mayor Dilworth is wrong about the goal posts. As Tom Brookshier laughingly reminisces:

TOM BROOKSHIER: "That stadium went wild after that game! I remember the Mayor saying that no one would get to the goal posts. Well, I was still on the field, when this guy comes up to me with this sliver of wood, and asks me to autograph it for him!"

~ Roswell ~

Many Eagles feel that the championship team died in 1961, the day that Tom Brookshier was injured against the Bears. Philadelphia was 7-1 when Brookshier went down. With their star cornerback out, the Birds went into a tailspin, losing three of their next five. The losing streak cost them their shot at repeating as conference winners.

"Brookie was the most important leader on the defensive unit that year," says Stan Campbell. "I really feel the guy deserves to be in the Hall of Fame. He was as good a hitter as there was in that defensive backfield, a good cover guy, a hard-nosed football player, and Tommy was just a natural born leader—a great asset for any team."

Stan Campbell is not alone in his admiration for Tom Brookshier. Many of his mates share those same sentiments. They feel that Brookshier provided the same level of motivational and inspirational leadership that Norm Van Brocklin had provided in 1960, and that when Dutch left, Brookie took over for him. Brookshier himself downplays his role, saying, "We had lots of leaders on that team, leaders of all kinds—especially on defense. Eddie Khayat, Swampie (Marion Campbell), Chuck Weber, and even Maxie, even though he was just a kid back then. But just as important as the leadership on that club was our camaraderie. That really distinguished the Eagles of that era. We had such unity on that squad. It lifted us above our competition."

Tom Brookshier went on to big things after his playing career was abruptly halted. He has cranked out numerous radio and TV commercials, served as the Sports Director for WCAU radio and television in Philadelphia, and appeared as the football analyst for CBS sports for 15 years. Tom is currently the Senior Vice President for Jackson-Cross Real Estate Company in Philadelphia. With his movie-star looks, he is, presumably, the most recognizable of the Eagles' 1960 crew, having spent several years as Pat Summerall's sidekick broadcasting nationally. He still spends a good deal of time on the airwaves. In recent years, he has been appearing on a Philadelphia cable show, "Eagles Post-Game Live," with a panel that includes Philadelphia's former mayor and astute football fan, Ed Rendell. In numerous discussions exploring the woes of the current flock of Eagles, Brookie advances the notion that team unity, harmony, and togetherness are as important to success as anything in a play book. Brookie sometimes asks the current Eagles who appear as guests on the show if the guys on the team ever socialize or if they get together on their own off the field. The Mayor just smiles and shakes his head, like Brookie is way off the mark (With all due respect, Mr. Mayor, 31 members of your city's last

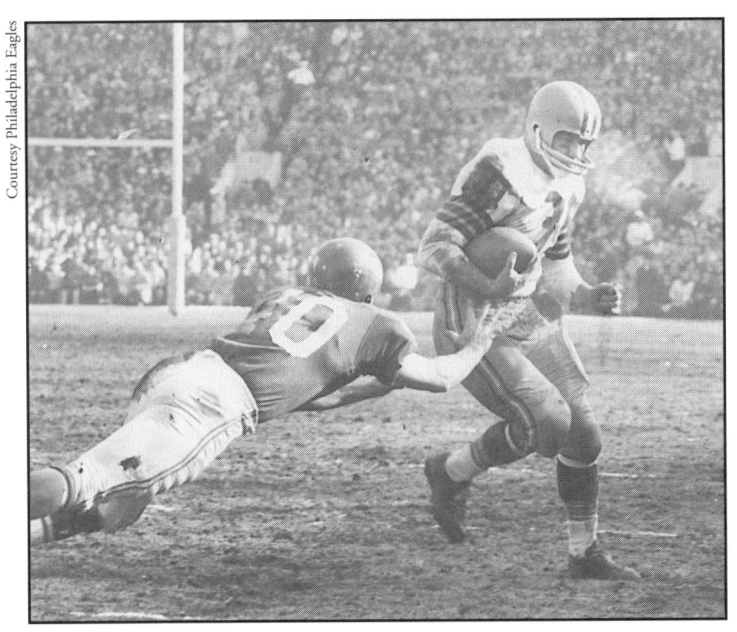

The tenacious Tom Brookshier brings down Packer Jim Taylor (#31).

championship team agree with Tommy Brookshier on this one). The modern players sometimes look at Tom Brookshier as though he were an alien.

They might be on to something there, with that alien thing. Brookie, along with cronies Gummy Carr and Billy Ray Barnes, was the team's leading prankster, action central for practical jokes. Whether Tom was making bogus announcements on airplane PA systems to terrify the acrophobic, or "appropriating" cigar-store Indians to stick in beds in order to buffalo coaches on bed-check rounds at Hershey, Brookshier was at the root of many Eagle shenanigans. Of course, that doesn't make him an alien. What might, however, is the city where Tom Brookshier was born and raised—Roswell, New Mexico. Roswell is allegedly the site where extraterrestrials de-planed, or de-saucered, as the case may be, sometime in the '40s. Granted, that was after Tommy Brookshier was born, but as teammates have pointed out, Brookie could have been one of the advance guard. Some unnamed Eagles observe that aliens might have felt they would blend right in with guys like Tom Brookshier running around Roswell. Perhaps the aliens stopped to refuel at the service station owned by Tom's dad, and when they met Tom at the pumps, they figured they didn't need to phone home. Who knows? In any event, to a man, Brookshier's '60 mates felt that, if anyone on the '60 Eagles could have walked with extraterrestrials, it was Tom Brookshier. So, add another wrinkle to that '60 title. Besides harmony, leadership, intelligence, versatility, big-play offense and defense, etc., the Birds had the—let's call it, the Tom Brookshier-Roswell connection. Maybe some ET force was guiding Walston's kick against Cleveland, or pushing

Jim Taylor back on those unsuccessful fourth-down plunges, or floating all those interceptions the Blade's way. Of course, if you believe that, Tom Brookshier is also a Senior VP in a real estate company, might sell you some choice crater-side property in a distant galaxy.

The fans swarm the field, and the Eagles along with their faithful strut off in victory. It's another great day for the Philadelphia Eagles, and it's another Philadelphia Eagles' victory that flies in the face of statistics. The Packers outgain the Eagles, 401 yards to 296. Green Bay chugs for 14 first downs rushing; the Eagles for five. Green Bay passes for eight first downs; the Eagles for six. Jim Taylor gains 105 yards on 24 carries to spearhead a 223-yard Green Bay rushing assault.

But a season of success has convinced the Eagles that statistics are misleading. They're tired of hearing how good their opponents are. In postgame interviews, Philadelphia's new champions release some pent-up frustration. Van Brocklin says: 'I hope this doesn't sound like sour grapes, but I thought they (the Packers) were going to be a better team than they showed us. Defensively, Green Bay offered no surprises. They red-dogged a couple of times early, and they quit. But, how about us! Everyone said we couldn't run. Our offensive line kept coming back to the huddle saying, 'Let's run on them. We can run on them.' And we could."

Jesse Richardson plows headlong into the tedious topic of being lucky, telling reporters: "So we're supposed to be lucky? This time the other club sure had more opportunities than we did. They're no fantastic superclub. They play good fundamental football, but they don't have the home run, the long ball. We do."

Even the phlegmatic Baron vents mildly: "I can't wait till August to see if those New York writers rate us underdogs against the College All-Stars."

Van Brocklin, voted the game's Most Valuable Player, receives a Chevrolet Corvette. The Dutchman already owns a Ford Thunderbird. He'll be the sportiest "old man" in Philly, at least for a few months—but more on that later.

Dutch is also the guy that Green Bay touts as the Eagles' MVP, although a bit mechanically. Green Bay feels they should have won, and Dutch is the reason they didn't. Years afterward, in 1983, Bart Starr would summarize the championship contest like this: "The game all boiled down to Van Brocklin's leadership and guile. He was a veteran and expert defensive reader."

Statistically, the Dutchman does not have a sparkling day. He throws 9-20, for less than 200 yards. His first pass of the game is picked off. Another one is picked off in the end zone following a 71-yard drive up the field. Yet he is acknowledged by the guys in pads that day as the reason why the Eagles win. Dutch's value to his team and his role as quarterback transcends that of field general. He's like an orchestra conductor, a maestro. Every member of an orchestra, even a virtuoso, takes the lead from the maestro. He sets the tempo, moderates the dynamics, the mix, the flow—everything that powers and harmonizes the ensemble. Even if the maestro is not at his personal best, he finds a way—or ways—for the orchestra to excel. Van Brocklin exercised that kind of control, influence, and ultimately power over his team.

Chuck Bednarik's effort in the game was remarkable, right up to the final play, which is chiseled in Philly folklore.

CHUCK BEDNARIK: "I knew I was going both ways again. I did play both ways, and I was involved in the biggest plays of the game. I felt I had a great game."

Indeed he did. As did Ted Dean. Dean scored the winning touchdown, ran the crucial kick-off back 58 yards, and prevented a touchdown when Max McGee pulled the fake punt.

However, as is characteristic of this team in their championship season, the Eagles boast a full house of heroes. McDonald caught three huge passes. Barnes ran like a man possessed when the chips were down. Brookshier anchored a secondary that not only held the Packers' passing attack in check, but also contained their steamrolling sweep.

Years later, Ray Nitschke, the Packers' great middle linebacker, reflected on the game against the Eagles. It was the only postseason defeat Nitschke or Lombardi's Packers ever endured. Nitschke wrote in his book: *"Philadelphia had an experienced team, a cagey bunch of vets. In a game like that one, there really is a difference between a veteran team and one that's made up of young players. It's not just another afternoon. There's a tremendous amount of pressure built up by all the publicity. All those sportswriters coming from around the country, all those TV interviews, all those people calling you from everywhere—there's a lot of pressure on you as well as on the organization. Players with experience can handle that kind of tension much better than young guys who don't have the self-discipline to control their feelings. I don't think we were prepared to handle the drama of the moment. We were kind of awed by the game and didn't play as well as we could or should have. We played against a real veteran team. Van Brocklin and Bednarik had the capability to make the big play at the right time and they did. I still feel we were the winners, but they won where it counted—on the scoreboard."*

5:30 P.M.

At 5:30 p.m. on the evening of Philadelphia's big victory, the team celebrates with a dinner at the Warwick Hotel. Most of the players don't stay long. The game had been very physical, and both teams emerge banged up from the battle. Mayor Dilworth attends the party. The players work him over, trying to convince him to wave the city wage tax on the championship checks. Unfortunately, the Birds are not as successful against the Mayor as they were against the Packers.

The following day, in an interview in the Philadelphia *Bulletin,* Norm Van Brocklin observes: "It's astonishing what a bunch of young guys can do if they want to win. Desire was this team's story. I remember three years ago when Bert Bell told me, 'The draft is going to equalize the talent in this league so close that the team that wins will be the team that wants the title the most.' I think the Eagles proved Bell was right."

Desire is a facile, incomplete assessment for why this team triumphed in 1960. Somehow, the '60 Eagles assembled a motley group of 38 men who mastered the pitfalls of group dynamics and teamwork. The entire group hit that elusive state of unity that few teams in any profession ever hit, where the total exceeds the sum of its parts. They were a better team than they appeared to be on paper. But even more important, as a unit they were remarkably pragmatic and opportunistic, much like Muhammed Ali in the ring. Ali brandished a full arsenal of weapons, but the Greatest's greatest weapon was an uncanny ability to size up an opponent on the spot and ad lib a style to beat him. He tailored a specific strategy for each rival—different strokes for different blokes. Against one opponent, Ali would stay out of harm's way, avoid getting hit, and throw three punches for every one his adversary threw. In his next fight, he would change everything. He would stand directly in front of his foe, absorb blow after blow, not even responding, until his unerring instincts and sense of timing told him to attack. Both approaches, as different as night and day, netted the same result—a win. The Eagles' leader, Norm Van Brocklin, had the knack to dismantle gridiron opponents in different ways. He could adapt, he could invent, and he could execute, on the spot. Dutch could pass for over 500 yards in a single game, as he did in setting the NFL single-game record in 1951 while still with the Rams. Or, he could march his team exclusively on the ground, as he chose to do against the Packers for the winning score.

As a team leader, Van Brocklin's task had some wrinkles that Ali didn't have to deal with. Van Brocklin had to communicate his ad libs to 37 others. He had to implement his ideas through them. That's what Van Brocklin did so successfully in 1960. He mobilized 38 guys to recognize and capitalize on windows of opportunities. Different heroes emerged every game. A litany of guys outstretched their own limitations and claimed a piece of the team's glory. That was the breadth of control that Van Brocklin brought to his position in 1960. Alex Karras observed in later years: "No one ever played quarterback like Van Brocklin in 1960." Others may have passed better or run better, but few married the position and the role so magnificently.

The group dynamic on the '60 Eagles overrode their other deficiencies. Statistically, they were a 4-9 team. They were outgained week after week, yet they were seldom outplayed. Their faith and self-confidence grew by leaps and bounds, never straying out of bounds into arrogance. Perhaps the national press's lack of respect assisted them, keeping them humble, in a back-door sort of way. Watching opponents parade up and down the field week after week never raised the crippling specter of self-doubt. Nor did it promote dissension between a top-rated offensive unit and a bottom-rated defensive platoon. Their unwavering togetherness is a tribute to the fabric of leadership that intertwined this patchwork quilt of a team. Like a gridiron Ali, the Eagles reinvented themselves for each opponent. They couldn't run, but when they needed a ground game to win, they came up with one, whether it be against the Steelers in the regular season, or the Packers in the title match. When 39 yards stood between them and a championship, they rushed against one of football's stingiest defenses against the rush. In 12 regular-season games, the Eagles hadn't returned a kickoff longer than 40 yards. Yet, with less than six minutes remaining in the '60 campaign, when they really needed a big return, they ad-libbed a 58-yarder, exploiting a weakness Charley Gauer had spotted the week before in the Packers' game films.

The Eagles were not a cautious team that played it safe until opponents beat themselves. They were anything but cautious. They made mistakes—lots of them—mistakes that could have been deadly, would have been deadly for the less resolute. Call it heart, call it guts, call it savvy, call it desire—call it what you will. But don't call the 1960 Eagles a team with nothing but a title.

Celebration!

FifteenFifteen**Fifteen**Fifteen

Aftermath

The story goes that John Wilcox, an Eagle rookie from Oregon, and member of the '60 bomb squad, was a no-show at the Eagle's celebration party at the Warwick Hotel after the title tilt. When the game clock ticked down to zero, his car was packed and revving, ready to bolt. The Eagle rookie was headed south. He had weddings to attend, so when the final gun blasted the game into history, John Wilcox headed out of Philadelphia. He didn't come back. He drove off into a different era. So did his country, his football team, and football itself.

~ *John "Moonlight" Wilcox* ~

"The thing that attracted me to John was how secure he was about himself," Remi Wilcox reflects, still enamored of her husband after almost 40 years of marriage. "John and I were both teaching at the same high school. When I first met John, I didn't even know that he had played professional football. He never talked about it. The only time he ever mentioned his days in the NFL was when the men in the faculty room brought the subject up. Otherwise, John was just a regular person, one of the nicest people I ever met."

John's career contrasts sharply with that of his brother, Dave. John Wilcox played one year of professional football. His team, the Philadelphia Eagles, won the NFL championship that year. Brother Dave toiled 11 years for the San Francisco 49ers. Individually, Dave achieved what every player dreams. He earned a berth in the professional football Hall of Fame. But not once did he play for a champion. The tale of these two brothers is documented in a short film, "Twist of Fate," that was shown on ESPN in 1997.

John Wilcox was drafted by the Eagles in the 17th round of the 1960 draft. "My coach at Oregon, Len Casanova, recommended me to Buck Shaw. I wasn't a big college star, but I played in the East-West Shrine game and did pretty well. Toronto in the Canadian league offered me $9,500 after the game. I thought that was tremendous, till I found out they were Canadian dollars, which was a lot less than $9,500 in U.S. dollars."

John reported to Hershey in 1960 as an unheralded rookie. He shocked himself by making the squad. "Ed Khayat and Brookie and the other veterans took the new guys under their wing. Brookshier set the tone. He was so complimentary—there was no negativity or bad feelings in that group. The year I spent in Philadelphia was one of the best years of my life, one of my happiest times. For a few weeks, I was scared to death I'd get cut. I played as hard as I could every second I was on the field. But again, I got a lot of encouragement to play hard from the veteran linemen, like Marion Campbell. Of course I eventually realized that there was a little something in it for them as well. As long as I played well on that bomb squad, they wouldn't have to race down under those kicks themselves!"

John Wilcox is a rare football story. He accomplished in one year what his brother Dave and a host of greats, ranging from Pittsburgh's Ernie Stautner to Detroit's Barry Saunders, never did. John Wilcox played on a championship team. Then he walked away. John Wilcox vanished from the Eagle roster as mysteriously, and inexplicably as Archibald "Moonlight" Graham dropped off the 1905 New York Giants' pennant-winning baseball roster. The Wilcox saga sounds like the stuff of legends. How could he just walk away? Where did John Wilcox go, and why did he never return?

"You know I really can't say why I didn't return!" John smiles, bemused at his own tale. "I was just a 22-year-old kid and I don't really know exactly why I didn't come back. President Kennedy was making a big push to improve high school science programs. He was offering draft deferments for science teachers at the time, so I went back to Oregon and started teaching math and coaching football. I know that had something to do with my decision. Then, too, as much as I enjoyed my time in Philadelphia, I missed the West Coast and living in a small town. All those things entered into my decision."

Wilcox supplied grit and speed to an outstanding "bomb squad." Most importantly, according to his peers, he embodied the unselfishness and hard work that bonded the '60 Eagles into a winner. There were no anonymous sideline hulks in the '60 bunch. Each member had a feeling of contributing and belonging. When their moment rolled around, they didn't mess it up.

"We all felt we were part of something bigger—more and more as the year went along," Wilcox says, racing down a field of memories. "The guys had tremendous mutual respect. Everybody felt that every other guy out there was contributing in every way he could. It was a pleasure to be in that kind of atmosphere."

So, when you're happy, you're 22, you're champion, and you're on top of the world, how do you walk, or ride, away from it all?

"I was young. Who knows what I was thinking back then?" Wilcox continues. "It was a wonderful year in 1960, and I can't say enough good things about the members of that team. Vince McNally sent me a contract for $7,500 for the '61 season. I sent it back to him, with a note saying I was sorry, but I wasn't going to return. A week later, he sent me a two-year contract—for $7,500 in 1961 and $8,500 in 1962. My salary had been $6,500 in 1960. That was more money than my parents had ever made! My teacher's salary in 1961 was only $3,500, but I was happy. I missed playing football. Even more, I missed the camaraderie. Still, when I look back, I've had a great life. I had that one year, that time as a champion. Most people never experience that. I have a wonderful wife that I wouldn't have met if I had gone back to the Eagles. We had three children, and we have five granddaughters. We're really blessed. I have no regrets."

The 1960 Eagles started breaking up almost before the last hurrah faded from Franklin Field. The three principle leaders, all driven by the same quest—winning one last championship—followed different paths once their dream became reality. Two days after the championship game, Buck Shaw officially retired. Buck sat politely and dutifully all day long at the Eagles' table for the NFL draft at Philadelphia's Warwick Hotel. Then he stole away from the town that had adopted him two years earlier. Timothy Lawrence "Buck" Shaw faded from Philly with the tranquility of a West Coast sunset.

Norm Van Brocklin retired immediately after the championship game. He anticipated filling the vacant Eagles' head coaching position. He was not offered the job, embittering him forevermore toward a club he felt had betrayed him. The Eagles offered Dutch the job of player-coach, but he wanted no part of it, growling, "That stuff went out with 'Blood McNally!'" The Birds' irascible quarterback stormed out of town and became the first coach of the expansion Minnesota Vikings.

Chuck Bednarik wanted one more crack at a championship. Chuck performed marvelously on the '61 Eagles, turning in his final All-Pro season.

CHUCK BEDNARIK: "That 1961 team, I think, for talent, may have been better than the '60 team. We had Irv Cross and we added Leo Sugar from the Cardinals. And Sonny Jurgensen was great. We just missed winning the Eastern Conference again. But I don't think anyone was going to stop Green Bay that year."

When an injury sidelined Chuck Weber, Bednarik's friend and neighbor in Abington (a suburb of Philadelphia), Bednarik slid over to middle linebacker, where he closed out his career in '62. Concrete Charley, football's last 60-minute man, was voted into the Hall of Fame in 1967, his first year of eligibility.

Jerry Reichow, Jerry Huth, and Bill Lapham followed the Dutchman to Minnesota in '61. Reichow became a Pro Bowler for the Vikings. Injuries ended Lapham's career that year. Huth's career ended in 1963. Bobby Jackson, who assisted in the championship game's final tackle, was dealt to the Bears in '61. He was out of pro football in '62.

The Eagles were a major power again in 1961 under coach Nick Skorich. Jerry Williams and Charley Gauer stayed on as his assistants. The '61 Eagles lost no momentum. They won all five of their exhibition games and whipped the College All-Stars, 28-14 (the Baron's title-day prediction was incorrect—the Eagles *were* favored over the All-Stars). They opened their regular season at home, once again against the Cleveland Browns. In front of 60,271 Franklin Field fans, Timmy Brown christened the 1961 season with a 105-yard kick-off return. This time, the Eagles topped Cleveland, 27-20.

The Birds cruised along in first place. They were 7-1 when they suffered an irrecoverable setback. Tom Brookshier was injured against the Chicago Bears at Franklin Field.

DON BURROUGHS: "Brookie was a tough character. I remember coming over to the sideline after he was hit in that Chicago game, and saying something smart-ass to him, like, 'Come on, Brookshier, quit lying around. Get up and play ball.' Maxie Baughan was there before me. He looked up at me, and said, 'Hey, Blade, I think it's bad. You can see the bone sticking out.' Maxie was right. You could see the bone. I knew Brookie was in trouble at that point. So were the Eagles."

Brookshier's career was snuffed out, and with it, the Eagles' candle started to flicker. They lost their next two games, first to the Giants, 38-21, and then to Cleveland, 45-24. Rebounding, they rolled through consecutive victories over the Cowboys and Steelers, before losing a heartbreaker to the Giants, 28-24. They closed the regular season by squeaking past Detroit, 27-24, before hustling into the locker room to listen to the conclusion of the Cleveland-New York game. The Giants entered the game with a 10-3 record. Had they lost, the Eagles and Giants would have ended the season tied for first. Unfortunately for Philadelphia, the Cleveland-New York affair ended in a tie. The Giants captured the title, finishing the campaign at 10-3-1, to edge the 10-4 Eagles by half a game.

Sonny Jurgensen blossomed into a Hall of Fame quarterback in 1961. He shattered practically every single-season NFL passing mark that year: most pass attempts (416), most completions (235), and most yards gained (3,723). He also equaled Johnny Unitas' 1959 standard of 32 touchdown passes. Sonny was selected to the All-Pro team, as was Bednarik and McDonald. The second-place Eagles again sent a large contingent (Jurgensen, McDonald, Retzlaff, J. D. Smith, Bobby Walston, Chuck Bednarik, and Maxie Baughan) to the Pro Bowl game. The 1961 campaign ended on a sour note when the Birds lost 38-10 to Detroit in the meaningless Runner Up Bowl, a short-lived travesty that pitted the second-place finishers from each NFL conference against one another. Tragically, the sour note from that game resounded for the rest of the decade.

The 1962 Eagles tried to put on a new face. They added new names, but in the process, cut out much of their heart and soul. Spirited leaders from their '60 championship squad, like Ed Khayat, Billy Ray Barnes, Bobby Freeman, and Bob Pellegrini, were shuffled to Washington. Rugged vets like Jesse Richardsen and Stan Campbell were waived. Big Jess wound up with the Patriots, while Stosh went to Oakland, finishing his career ignominiously with the 1-13 Raiders. The Swamp Fox and Chuck Weber retired. Leo Sugar, who had come over to the Birds in '61, called it a career.

In 1962, the Birds posted a 3-2 exhibition-season log before losing 27-21 to the Cards in the opener, despite an encore of Timmy Brown's opening-day magic. This time, he romped 99 yards against St. Louis on a blown field-goal attempt. The Birds lost to the Giants the following week, 29-13, before scoring a huge 35-7 victory over the Browns. The triumph was costly, however, as Retzlaff went down with a broken arm, and Ted Dean's foot, injured previously, had to be placed in a cast for ten weeks. The Eagles slid into last place the next week following a 13-7 loss to the Steelers. Things got even worse the next Sunday when Dallas beat Philadelphia for the first time in history, 41-19, on 100-yard and 101-yard touchdowns. The most notable losses of the '62 season, however, were two "payback" games. In the first, Norm Van Brocklin's Vikings knocked off the Eagles, 31-21. Jerry Huth, who was on the '62 Minnesota squad, recalls:

JERRY HUTH: "Dutch wanted that game. He wanted them all, of course, but he was real pleased with the win over the Eagles. He wasn't on very good terms with Philadelphia after he left."

The other payback game stung. Vince Lombardi's Packers paid their first visit to the Quaker City since the '60 championship game. They routed Philadelphia, 49-0. Unlike Philly's glory days, statistics *do* tell the story of this carnage. Green Bay gained 628 yards to Philadelphia's 54 yards. The first-down ledger read: Green Bay 37, Philadelphia 3.

In such a bleak season, a few bright lights shined. Timmy Brown led the Eagles in total yards, rushing, and points scored. He was second in pass-receiving yards, behind Tommy McDonald, who had a stellar season, breaking his own club record for receiving yards in a season. The future Hall of Famer led the NFL in average yards gained per reception and was second in touchdown passes caught.

Chuck Bednarik and Bobby Walston both bowed out after the '62 season. Their departure, for all practical purposes, crumbled the foundation of the '60 championship group. Whereas 78% of the 1961 Eagle roster had played for the championship team, only 47% of the 1962 edition could make the claim. The 1962 Eagles kerplunked into last place.

The rise and fall of the 1960 Eagles shows perfect symmetry. Their rise: last place ('58), second place ('59), first place ('60) mirrored their fall: first place ('60), second place ('61), last place ('62).

The next year, 1963, was worse. They won only two games. Their season started OK. They were 2-2 after four games. Then they came undone. They went winless the rest of the season. Their biggest stars were the few remaining 1960 alumni. Three of them: Maxie Baughan, Pete Retzlaff, and Timmy Brown were selected All-Pro. Timmy had an awesome season despite the fact that for the first time in three years he failed to return a kick for a touchdown on opening day. He just postponed the feat till week two, when he scampered 100 yards for a score. Timmy finished third in the NFL in rushing. He also set the all-time NFL mark for most total offensive yards (2,428).

~ April Fool's Day ~

"I found out I was traded to the Redskins at Dave's Delicatessen. I think it was at 18th and Spruce in Philadelphia," Sonny Jurgensen laughs. "I went there to get a sandwich or paper or something, and they told me they heard on the radio that I had been traded. It was April Fool's Day, so I didn't believe them. I told them, 'That can't be right. I was just in (Eagle head coach) Kuharich's office with him. I don't know where that story came from.'"

Sonny went right back to Kuharich's office. Sure enough, he had been traded, and the hometown fans weren't too happy about it. Sonny had some great days in Philadelphia. He was there for the highs of '59, '60 and '61. He was also there for the lows before and after. Sonny was the quarterback as the championship team was dismantled.

"Philly was a great place to play. But the fans could be tough when things didn't go right," the Hall of Famer chuckles, shaking his head. "Remember when they'd introduce the offensive or defensive unit before the game, and each guy would run out, one by one, to mid-field. After the whole unit was introduced, they'd huddle, and then run through a play. Well, I remember one game when they introduced the offensive unit at Franklin Field. As the quarterback, I was introduced last. As they were announcing the other guys before me, there were mostly cheers. We were losing a lot of games at that point, and I was getting booed all the time. So, when my name was announced, the whole stadium booed me the whole way out to mid-field. When I joined the rest of the offensive unit, we went into a huddle, and the whole offensive unit started booing me in the huddle!"

"The story doesn't stop there, though. It was an amazing day," Jurgensen continues. "My first two passes were intercepted. Now they could probably hear the boos all the way over in Jersey! But by the fourth quarter I had thrown five touchdown passes, and now they're cheering for me just as loud. Meanwhile, Moose Deddy, our trainer, had gotten into a fight with some fans. I had a friend in the stands who was watching the game. He told me later, 'People around me were looking at me funny 'cause I was the only one in the place that wasn't booing you. So I started to boo you too.'"

> Christian Adolph "Sonny" Jurgensen III left Philadelphia en route to becoming one of the finest quarterbacks in NFL history. His '60 teammates, unanimously, marvel at his arm and his ability. As Billy Ray Barnes put it, "I think Sonny had the finest arm there ever was in football. No one threw the ball like him."

In 1963, the Eagles got a new owner, Jerry Wolman, who purchased the franchise for $5.5 million. Wolman axed coach Nick Skorich and brought in Joe Kuharich to replace him. After Kuharich's arrival, practically every shred of the '60 squad disappeared. Kuharich dealt Tommy McDonald to Dallas for kicker Sam Baker. Sonny Jurgensen and Jimmy Carr went to Washington for Norman Snead (one of Philadelphia's most infamous trades). Ted Dean went to the Vikings for Ray Poage, Don Hultze, Chuck Lawson, and Terry Kosens. Clarence Peaks went to the Steelers for Red Mack; and J. D. Smith and others went to Detroit for Ollie Matson. Amid this flurry, the familiar face of Ed Khayat returned. However, by 1964, only six championship vets: Baughan, Brown, Burroughs, Gunnels, Khayat, and Retzlaff were still Eagles. Kuharich's new-look Birds climbed up to a third-place tie with a 6 - 8 record in '64, before slipping back to 5-9 in '65. In 1966, the Eagles gave their faithful false hopes of resurrection. They finished with a 9-5 mark, good for a second-place tie with Cleveland. The fact that they scored only 326 points to their opponents' 340 was overlooked in the euphoria. The year proved an aberration, as the Birds tumbled to 6-7-1 in 1967. The Eagles closed out the decade—one that had started with such promise—with two consecutive years in the cellar.

Pete Retzlaff retired in 1966, leaving Timmy Brown as the '60 championship team's sole survivor. Timmy left Philadelphia for Baltimore the following season, where he closed out his brilliant career.

The '60 team moved on, just like time, itself. Professional football, moved on too, into a glitzy, glamorous, modern era of high-stakes mega-spectaculars. By the mid-Sixties, the AFL and NFL partnered in the Super Bowl, a contest conceived 20 years earlier by the defunct All-American Football Conference. Shortly thereafter, when the NFL and the AFL merged, football climbed to the highest pinnacle of the American sport scene. More importantly, football migrated to the dead center of the nation's consciousness. Like all trips to glory however, football suffered casualties along the way. The game is not the same game it was when an Eagle team that had much more than a title cavorted for glory around a muddy collegiate field. Football is neither better nor worse now than it was then. It's just different. The game's coverage is astounding today. The sport's subtleties are more fully explored, more exhaustively explained. Many aspects of the business that needed improvement have been improved. Provisions for pensions and care for the injured are now in place for athletes who risk life and limb to entertain us. But, some innocence died too back when Buck Shaw caught his last train for the coast.

As the dollars in football have escalated, so has the distance between fan and player. Gone are the days when fan and footballer walked off the field together. The players seemed real, touchable, and approachable back then. They lived in our neighborhoods, shopped in our stores, talked to us on subway trains, and willingly gave us autographs. Some, like Chuck Bednarik, would jog across a street, unbeckoned, to give a kid an autograph. The sport's scale was less grandiose, more human. The game's gladiators seemed more humble and gracious, if for no other reason than society allowed them to be.

In 1960, football was still a seasonal business, like the neighborhood ice-cream store that shut down when September's evening cool doused out summer's flame. Competition for the game's huge purses would snuff out football's seasonality forever. The pro footballer's former role of fall warrior morphed into that of year-round entertainer—an entertainer who was more removed and aloof from the public. High salaries eventually plucked professional football players not only out of our neighborhoods, but out of our worlds, and, eventually, out of our reality.

Football's images were black and white in 1960. The images crackled, faded, and rolled across grainy television screens. Footballs were clunky. Uniforms were clutzy. Aside from a few innovators like Paul Brown, the sport operated in a universe parallel to the technical world that sprang up in the post-war period. In the '50s, football's original group of owners, a group that remained remarkably intact over football's first three decades, still ruled the game. In many senses, the original owners ruled from the perspective of a bygone era. The '60s brought change to football in every aspect—organizational, financial, and social. Pete Rozelle, the new Commissioner, along with a new breed of owners, spirited in a more calculating, businesslike approach to the sport. What used to be a college boys' game was transformed inexorably into a big business, and then into a big industry. Football franchises took on the look and style of the big corporation. The skimpy scouting anecdotes and matchbox notes of the past gave way to comprehensive stat sheets—reams of stat sheets—measuring everything but REM cycles on thousands of prospects nationwide. New training techniques—unfortunately, not all of them salubrious, pumped players up to behemoth size and prodigious strength. A game bounded by the budgets and conservatism of athletic organizations in small-town America now was unbounded.

By the end of the '60s, players relied increasingly less on off-season incomes. Over the decades, their football salaries shot up from insufficient to moderate to exorbitant. Their off-seasons withered away, owing to the demands of mini-camps, public appearances, off-season training regimens, and other obligations to the club. Fewer players retreated to the farm or the small town or the simple life. Youngsters came into the league richer, higher paid, and more savvy to the ways of the big city. They sought less mentoring. Society's forces changed the clubhouse drastically.

John Wittenborn's career took him through football's period of rapid change. He started his career in San Francisco in 1958, played in Philly from '60 through '62, and finished in '68 with Houston in the AFL.

JOHN WITTENBORN: "There were a lot of changes in the '60s, in our country, and, certainly in football as well. Big money changed things a lot. So did drugs. I first started seeing drugs come into football in the mid-'60s. That made the clubhouse so different from the way it used to be. When I first came up, guys used to play cards, drink beer, and read the sport pages—stuff like that. When drugs started to appear, and the big money came in, that all changed. Guys drifted apart. The guys on teams seemed closer in the old days. Once the big money came in, the big money guys would sit around by themselves and read the stock pages. They weren't playing cards any more! They were tracking their investments and were wrapped up in their contract negotiations. Guys wanted to protect themselves like they were protecting an investment. They didn't want to get hurt. They cared a lot more about themselves than their teams. There was a star lineman at the end of my career—I won't tell you his name—but he refused to play a couple of games 'cause he was afraid of getting hurt. That was unheard of when I started. You didn't tell the coaches what to do. They told you. A lot of dissension started to creep into the clubhouse when the big money came in. We didn't have that kind of clubhouse dissension when I first came into the league."

~ John Wittenborn ~

"I was the first guy from my high school who ever got a football scholarship, and then, I was the first guy from my college who went to the pros," John Wittenborn details, emphasizing the fact that he never seriously considered pro football as a career when he was growing up. John overcame a lot of obstacles on his way to the NFL, coming from a small Indiana town, and attending a small college, Southeast Missouri State. But John Wittenborn had much more to overcome than his resume.

"It happened when I was in college," John begins. "I felt terrible. I ached. I had headaches—just huge, bad, painful headaches. Then I passed out one day, and I thought I had food poisoning or something. It turned out I had polio. The doctors put me in the hospital right away, and called my parents. They told my folks that there were only two ways that I'd get out of that hospital—either crippled or dead. I weighed 235 pounds, and in no time at all, I dropped down to 150 pounds. I was 19 years old at the time. That was back in 1955. They put me in bed, and put my feet in stirrups so I wouldn't curl up in the fetal position. I was scared to death. But I didn't give up. When I started to get better, I went back home to the farm. I didn't even drop my college classes. I did them from home. The doctors took good care of me, and I recovered pretty well, but they also told me I'd never weigh 200 pounds again, and I wouldn't be able to play football again. I went out to prove them wrong. I set up my own program to build myself back up. I worked on the farm till I dropped. I ate six meals a day—yeah, six! I went back and played football the next fall at 215 pounds."

The rest, in John Wittenborn's case, is not history. The disease did not leave definitively or graciously.

"I still have to battle what they call 'Post-Polio Syndrome,'" the ex-Eagle explains painfully. "I get achy, with severe headaches—really bad headaches. In the first ten years after the disease, I used to get them more frequently, maybe five or ten times a year. They've tailed off over the years. I haven't had one now for about eight months. But I just dread them coming on. Back in '60, I got attacks during the games, on occasion. My head hurt so bad, I had to squint my eyes shut to handle the pain. But I didn't complain. I just tried to play the best I could."

Wittenborn handled the pain admirably. The college kid they said would never weigh 200 pounds again, went on to play over ten years in the NFL and AFL.

Yes, football has logged a lot of miles since Dutch and Concrete Charley and the rest of the Philly crew shook up the football establishment with their 1960 monument to the power of intangibles. Forty years after that championship season, the '60 Eagles remain Philadelphia's most recent NFL football champion. No, they didn't have the machine-like precision or intimidating talent of Lombardi's Packer dynasty, or Pittsburgh's Steel Curtain, or the 49ers of Montana and Young. They had a straightforward sincerity, a knack for miracles, and a squad that believed. And, if Philadelphia has but one NFL champion to look back on in 40 years, they can look back with pride at this group. They had so much more than a title.

SixteenSixteen**Sixteen**Sixteen

Where Are They Now?

BILLY RAY BARNES
Born: Billy Ray Barnes; 5/14/35; Landis, NC
High School: Landis, NC
College: Wake Forest
Drafted: 1957, Round 2, Philadelphia Eagles
AS A PLAYER:
Playing Weight: 5'-11", 201
Position(s): Running Back
FOOTBALL CAREER AFTER 1960:
Billy was with the Eagles in 1961, gaining 309 yards as a running back. In 1962, he was dealt to the Washington Redskins, where he stayed till 1963. In 1965 and 1966, Billy Ray played for Norm Van Brocklin in Minnesota. He retired in 1966.
SINCE HIS PLAYING CAREER:
Billy coached seven years, with the Falcons and Saints. He was in the construction business ("I built 350 houses.") in Norcross, Georgia. These days, he is retired back in Landis NC, and playing as much golf as possible (he's also playing at a much higher level than he did in his duffer days with the Eagles). He and former Eagle quarterback, Roman Gabriel, have remained close friends. Billy's Wake Forest jersey number 33, the same number he wore as an Eagle, is retired.

MAXIE BAUGHAN
Born: Maxie Calloway Baughan; 8/3/38; Forkland, AL
High School: Bessemer, AL
College: Georgia Tech
Drafted: 1960, Round 2, Philadelphia Eagles
AS A PLAYER:
Playing Weight: 6'-1", 230
Position(s): Linebacker

FOOTBALL CAREER AFTER 1960:
Maxie stayed with the Eagles till 1965, when he asked Joe Kuharick if he could be traded to either New York or Atlanta (to be close to home). He was dealt, instead, to LA, where he played till 1970. Maxie then went to Georgia Tech, where he coached in '72 and '73 before returning as a player-coach for the Washington Redskins in '74.

Maxie is picked as one of *Total Football's* "Top 300 Greatest Players" (In fact, the Baughan listing is followed alphabetically by Chuck Bednarik, Bobby Bell, and Bill Bergey—Bell being the only one in the foursome who was not an Eagle linebacker). In the late '60s, George Allen picked Maxie to captain the Los Angeles Rams' defense. Maxie was named to nine Pro Bowl teams, thus giving him bona fide Hall of Fame credentials.

SINCE HIS PLAYING CARRER:
After stints with Georgia Tech in '72 and '73, and the Washington Redskins in '74, Maxie coached at Baltimore and Detroit, followed by a six-year tenure as head coach at Cornell University. Maxie is now retired in Finksburg, Maryland. He has been a business partner with Pete Retzlaff for years. A few years ago, Maxie, Pete, and Ray Berry coached an Ivy League All-Star team that played the Japanese All-Stars in Japan. Maxie is having a log cabin built in North Carolina, and will move there when it is completed.

CHUCK BEDNARIK
Born: Charles Philip Bednarik
High School: Liberty, PA
College: University of Pennsylvania
Drafted: 1949, Round 1, Philadelphia Eagles
AS A PLAYER:
Playing Weight: 6'-3", 233
Position(s): Center - Linebacker
FOOTBALL CAREER AFTER 1960:
Chuck starred once again in 1961, moving over to play middle linebacker when Chuck Weber got hurt. Concrete Charley played one more campaign before retiring for good in 1962. In 1967, he was inducted into the Pro Football Hall of Fame to become the only Philadelphia Eagle ever inducted in his first year of eligibility.
SINCE HIS PLAYING CAREER:
When Concrete Charley retired, the jersey that he wore in his final game at Sportman's Park in St. Louis was placed in the Pro Football Hall of Fame. Chuck has also enjoyed a long, productive career off the gridiron in the business world. In his playing days, he spent several years working for Elmo Pio Wines of California. After leaving Pio, he worked for Warner Concrete, which permanently cast in concrete the name, Concrete Charley. In his last nine years before retirement,

Chuck worked for Regal Corrugated Box Company. He also worked the sidelines with Dick Vermeil when Vermeil was coaching the Eagles. Chuck now lives in Coopersburg, on the outskirts of Bethlehem. He's still in good shape and in good health, and he and his wife, Emma, keep an active and busy schedule.

TOM BROOKSHIER
Born: Thomas Jefferson Brookshier; 12/16/31 Roswell, NM
High School: Roswell, NM
College: University of Colorado
Drafted: 1953, Round 10, Philadelphia Eagles
AS A PLAYER:
Playing Weight: 6'-1", 198
Position(s): Defensive Halfback
FOOTBALL CAREER AFTER 1960:
Tom was in the midst of another All-Pro season when he was injured in the eighth game of the 1961 season. The injury ended his career.
SINCE HIS PLAYING CAREER:
Thanks to almost 25 years as a football analyst of CBS Sports, Tom is probably the 1960 Eagles' most recognizable face to fans outside the Philadelphia area. Beginning in 1962, Tom honed his broadcasting skills as Sports Director for WCAU radio in Philadelphia. In 1963, he assumed the same title for WCAU's sister TV station, a role he fulfilled till 1978. At the same time, Tom began receiving national exposure as a football analyst for CBS sports. Until 1987, Tom's perceptive and often humorous commentary added flavor to regular-season NFL games, college bowl games (the Cotton Bowl, Sun Bowl, and the Blue Gray Game), the NFL Pro Bowl and 13 Super Bowls (Super Bowls VI - XVIII). In 1988, Tom's wandering days with CBS came to an end, and he came back to his home on Philadelphia's Main Line and his radio roots—a morning talk show on WIP All Sports Radio. In 1992, he became joint owner of the station. This, along with various other business ventures, like real estate, and dozens of speaking engagements, keep him in high gear today.

TIM BROWN
Born: Thomas Allen Brown; 5/24/37; Knightstown, IN
High School: Indiana Soldiers and Sailors Children's Home, IN
College: Ball State Teacher's College
AS A PLAYER:
Playing Weight: 5'-11", 198
Position(s): Running Back

FOOTBALL CAREER AFTER 1960:

Timmy became one of the NFL's premier backs after 1960. He set the NFL record for total yards on offense in a single season in 1963 with 2,425 yards, by gaining 841 yards rushing, 487 yards receiving, 152 yards returning punts, and 945 yards returning kickoffs. He topped the NFL in kickoff return yardage, and was third in rushing behind Jim Brown and Jim Taylor. In 1965, Tim was third in the NFL in rushing once more, trailing Jim Brown and Gale Sayers. Tim made All Pro in '63, '64, and '66. He was the last member of the '60 champions to leave the Eagles when he went to the Baltimore Colts in 1968, his last year in the NFL. Tim still ranks in the top 20, all time, for number of kickoffs returned in a career and career kickoff return average, as well as career kickoff return yardage.

SINCE HIS PLAYING CAREER:

Tim spent a number of years as an actor, starring in "King Richard II," "Nashville," and other hits on the silver screen. He was in the TV series M*A*S*H. In recent years, Tim has switched careers again, and is currently living in Los Angeles as a correctional officer.

DON BURROUGHS

Born: Donald E. Burroughs; 8/19/31; Los Angeles, CA
High School: Fillmore, CA
College: Ventura College (Junior College), Pasadena College (Junior College), Colorado State
Drafted: not drafted

AS A PLAYER:

Playing Weight: 6'-4", 190
Position(s): Defensive Back

FOOTBALL CAREER AFTER 1960:

The Blade starred in the defensive backfield for Philly till he retired in 1964. He was one of the finest ever in his profession at shortstopping enemy passes. Twice he intercepted nine in a season. Three times he intercepted seven. He finished his impressive career with 50 interceptions, 14th on the all-time list.

SINCE HIS PLAYING CAREER:

The Blade was in the oil distribution business in Ventura, California, where he is now retired.

MARION CAMPBELL
Born: Francis Marion Campbell; 5/25/29; Chester, SC
High School: Chester, SC
College: Georgia
Drafted: 1952, Round 4, San Francisco 49ers
AS A PLAYER:
Playing Weight: 6'-3", 250
Position(s): Defensive Tackle, Defensive End, Offensive Tackle
FOOTBALL CAREER AFTER 1960:
The Swamp Fox again made the Pro Bowl in 1961 as an Eagle, but called it quits at the end of the '61 season.
SINCE HIS PLAYING CAREER:
Marion Campbell coached in the NFL for a number of years. He was the head coach for the Atlanta Falcons from 1974 - 1976, before coming back to the Eagles as head coach in 1984 and 1985. In 1987, the Swamp Fox went back to the Falcons, staying till 1989. Swampie is currently enjoying retirement in Alphatetta, GA.

STAN CAMPBELL
Born: Stanley Hugh Campbell; 8/26/30; Rochelle, IL
High School: Rochelle Township, IL
College: Iowa State
Drafted: 1952, Round 18, Detroit Lions
AS A PLAYER:
Playing Weight: 6'-0", 226
Position(s): Offensive Guard
FOOTBALL CAREER AFTER 1960:
Stan started again in 1961 for the Eagles, but was traded in 1962 to the Oakland Raiders in the AFL. He retired after one season at Oakland.
SINCE HIS PLAYING CAREER:
After his football career ended, Stan owned an industrial firm in Illinois that supplied pipes and fittings. He later owned a janitorial service and supply company. As the last century wound down, Stan was involved in a business that supplied maintenance services to shopping centers in Illinois. However, he plans to retire once and for all now that the new century has begun.

JIM CARR

Born: James Henry Carr; 3/25/33; Kayford, WV
High School: East Branch, WV
College: Morris Harvey, Charlestown, WV
Drafted: not drafted
AS A PLAYER:
Playing Weight: 6'-2", 210
Position(s): Defensive Halfback (he also played some Linebacker and Running Back earlier in his career)
FOOTBALL CAREER AFTER 1960:
Jimmy played for the Eagles through 1963, and then was traded to the Washington Redskins ("I was traded in the same deal as Sonny Jurgensen. Sonny was just a 'throw-in,' at least that's what I always tell him."). "Gummy" stayed with the Redskins till retirement in 1966.

Jimmy Carr

SINCE HIS PLAYING CAREER:
Jimmy enjoyed many more years in football, beginning in 1966 as an assistant coach for the Minnesota Vikings under head coach Norm Van Brocklin. He later moved to Atlanta where he continued coaching through 1994. Following that, he had the opportunity to enjoy the sights of Europe as a coach in the World Football League, first in Amsterdam (1995), then in London (1996), and finally in Scotland (1997). Today, Jimmy is retired, and reports that retired life is "Great!" He enjoys free time with his wife, Lila Lee, and his family. A little golf, some charity work, and good health makes for a happy life back home in Kayford, West Virginia.

TED DEAN

Born: Theodore Curtis Dean; 3/24/38; Radnor, PA
High School: Radnor, PA
College: Wichita State
Drafted: 1960, Round 4, Philadelphia Eagles
AS A PLAYER:
Playing Weight: 6'-2", 213
Position(s): Running Back
FOOTBALL CAREER AFTER 1960:
After 1960, injuries plagued Ted the rest of his career. In 1961, he averaged 4.9 yards per rush, to lead the Eagles in that department. He gained 321 rushing yards, as well as 335 receiving yards that year and was selected to the Pro Bowl. He played in only two games in 1962, and after the 1963 season, was traded to the Minnesota Vikings. After the second game of the 1964 season, while with the Vikings, Ted was in a near-fatal car crash that abruptly ended his career.

SINCE HIS PLAYING CAREER:
Once Ted was unable to play football, he returned to Radnor and started a long, fruitful career in the teaching profession. He has remained in the Philadelphia area for the entirety of that career, and is preparing now for a healthy, active retirement.

BOB FREEMAN
Born: Robert Clayton Freeman; 10/19/32; Birmingham, AL
High School: Decatur, AL
College: Auburn
Drafted: 1956, Round 5, Los Angeles Rams
AS A PLAYER:
Playing Weight: 6'-1", 202
Position(s): Defensive Back
FOOTBALL CAREER AFTER 1960:
Bobby played the 1961 season with the Eagles. It was the only year of his six-year career where he failed to grab at least one interception. He nabbed 15 interceptions in his career. Bob was traded to the Washington Redskins in 1962, which turned out to be his final year in the NFL. He intercepted three passes that year for the Redskins.
SINCE HIS PLAYING CAREER:
Bobby is currently in good health, living a happy life in his college town of Auburn, Alabama, where he has worked in real estate for a number of years.

GENE GOSSAGE
Born: Ezra Gene Gossage; 2/17/35; Columbia, TN
High School: Wadsworth, OH
College: Northwestern
Drafted: 1960, Round 1, Dallas Texans; 1958, Round 28, Philadelphia Eagles (Red Shirt)
AS A PLAYER:
Playing Weight: 6'-3", 240
Position(s): Defensive End, Defensive Tackle, Offensive Guard
FOOTBALL CAREER AFTER 1960:
Gene was a rookie in 1960. He played two more years (1961, 1962) for the Eagles before he was traded to the New York Giants. Gene played for the Hamilton Ontario Tigercats in 1963 and 1964 before retiring from pro football for good.
SINCE HIS PLAYING CAREER:
Gene is currently semi-retired from his position as Vice President of Sales for Stanley

Works in Connecticut. He worked for Stanley Tools for 20 years. He lives in Westbrook, Connecticut.

JOHN RILEY GUNNELS
Born: John Riley Gunnels; 9/24/37; Atlanta, GA
High School: Calhoun, GA
College: Georgia
Drafted: 1959, Round 10, Pittsburgh Steelers
AS A PLAYER:
Playing Weight: 6'-3", 253
Position(s): Defensive Tackle, Defensive End
FOOTBALL CAREER AFTER 1960:
Riley was a rookie with the Eagles in 1960. He played for the Eagles through 1964, and was voted the Eagles' defensive MVP by his teammates the year after the championship ("That's still my greatest honor. It means so much when your teammates choose you for something like that."). In 1965, Riley went to the Pittsburgh Steelers, where he stayed one more year, and retired in 1965.
SINCE HIS PLAYING CAREER:
Riley, like Bob Pellegrini, became a casino executive in Atlantic City. He's retired now, and living happily in Ocean City, New Jersey.

JERRY HUTH
Born: Gerald Bernard Huth; 7/23/33; Floyds Knobs, IN
High School: New Albany, IN
College: Wake Forest
Drafted: 1956, Round 24, New York Giants
AS A PLAYER:
Playing Weight: 6'-1", 232
Position(s): Offensive Guard
FOOTBALL CAREER AFTER 1960:
Jerry went to Minnesota in 1961, and played there for Norm Van Brocklin for three years till his retirement in 1963.
SINCE HIS PLAYING CAREER:
After retiring from football in 1963, Jerry moved his wife and children to California and worked for State Farm Insurance for 35 years as a Claims Adjuster. Jerry has three daughters and a son, as well as four granddaughters. He's now living in Las Vegas, with a second home at Big Bear Lake, California. Jerry's hobby is pho-

BOBBY JACKSON
Born: Bobby Gerald Jackson; 1/10/36; Geneva, AL
High School: S.S. Murphy, AL
College: Alabama
Drafted: 1959, Round 7, Green Bay
AS A PLAYER:
Playing Weight: 6'-1", 190
Position(s): Defensive Back
FOOTBALL CAREER AFTER 1960:
Bobby went to the Chicago Bears in 1961. He finished his pro career with the Bears that year.
SINCE HIS PLAYING CAREER:
After his playing career, Bobby went back to Alabama to get his degree. He worked with Shell Oil for awhile, ran his own business, sold real estate, coached three years of high school, and has now worked at Capitol Broadcast in Mobile, Alabama, where he lives, for 17 years.

SONNY JURGENSEN
Born: Christian Adolph Jurgensen; 8/23/34; Wilmington, NC
High School: New Hanover, NC
College: Duke
Drafted: 1957, Round 4, Philadelphia
AS A PLAYER:
Playing Weight: 5'-11"; 202
Positions: Quarterback
FOOTBALL CAREER AFTER 1960:
Sonny started for the Eagles at quarterback in 1961, replacing the retired Norm Van Brocklin. He remained with the Eagles till 1963, when he was traded to Washington. Sonny stayed with Washington the rest of his brilliant career. He retired in 1974, having amassed 32,224 yards passing. At retirement, he trailed only Johnny Unitas and Fran Tarkenton on the all-time list for yards gained

Sonny Jurgensen

passing. Sonny threw for more yards and more completions than any other quarterback in the decade of the Sixties.
SINCE HIS PLAYING CAREER:
Sonny is living in Mt. Vernon, Virginia, and has done the Washington Redskin game broadcasts with ex-Giant, Sam Huff, for a number of years. He also appears on the *George Michael Sport Machine*.

ED KHAYAT
Born: Edward Michael Khayat; 9/14/35; Moss Point, MS
High School: Moss Point, MS
College: Tulane
Drafted: not drafted
AS A PLAYER:
Playing Weight: 6'-3", 240
Positions: Defensive End, Defensive Tackle, Offensive Tackle
FOOTBALL CAREER AFTER 1960:
After one more year with the Eagles, Gentleman Ed was traded to the Washington Redskins where he played in 1962 and 1963, before coming back to the Eagles in 1964 and 1965. Ed spent his final season with the New England Patriots in 1966.
SINCE HIS PLAYING CAREER:
Once he left the playing field, Ed's football career continued in high gear as a coach for eight different NFL teams over 25 years (in order: the New Orleans Saints, Philadelphia Eagles, Detroit Lions, Atlanta Falcons, Baltimore Colts, Detroit Lions, New England Patriots, and Tampa Bay Buccaneers). In his stint at Philadelphia, in 1971 and 1972, Eddie was the head coach. Ed also found time to work for two-and-a-half years as a fund raiser for the Pennsylvania Special Olympics as the Central Development Director.

Ed lived in York, PA for many years, but has since relocated to Nashville, TN, where he is the General Manager of the Nashville Kats of the Arena Football League. He is in excellent health, and still finds time for golf and handball. Eddie named his youngest son William Palmer Khayat after Pete Retzlaff (Palmer is Retzlaff's given first name), who is also his godfather.

BILL LAPHAM
Born: William Gaius Lapham; 2/2/34; Des Moines, IA
High School: Lincoln, IA
College: Drake; Iowa
Drafted: 1958, Round 14, Philadelphia Eagles (Red Shirt)

AS A PLAYER:
Playing Weight: 6'-3", 238
Position(s): Center
FOOTBALL CAREER AFTER 1960:
Bill went to the Minnesota Vikings in 1961, which was the last season of his pro career, due to injuries.
SINCE HIS PLAYING CAREER:
Bill went to work with Wilson Sporting Goods in Iowa. He also worked as manager of a freight company in Des Moines, Iowa, where he and his wife are now retired.

DICK LUCAS
Born: Richard A. Lucas; 1/9/34; South Boston, MA
High School: South Boston, MA
College: Boston College
Drafted: 1956, Round 10, Chicago Bears
AS A PLAYER:
Playing Weight: 6'-2", 213
Position(s): Offensive End
FOOTBALL CAREER AFTER 1960:
In 1961, Dick caught eight passes for the Eagles, and five of them went for touchdowns. In 1962, he caught 19 passes for 236 yards and one touchdown. He played only three games in 1963, the year of his retirement from the NFL.

Dick Lucas

SINCE HIS PLAYING CAREER:
Dick remained in the Philadelphia area. He spent some years in the oil marketing business in West Chester, where he is now happily retired.

JIM MCCUSKER
Born: James Brian McCusker; 5/19/36; Jamestown, NY
High School: Jamestown, NY
College: Pittsburgh
Drafted: 1958, Round 2, Chicago Cardinals
AS A PLAYER:
Playing Weight: 6'-2", 246
Position(s): Offensive Tackle

FOOTBALL CAREER AFTER 1960:
Jim stayed in Philadelphia through the 1962 season. In 1963, he went to the Cleveland Browns. However, he spent the following season, which was his last, with the New York Jets.

SINCE HIS PLAYING CAREER:
Jim has been in the restaurant business for most of his post-football life. Currently, Jim is the proprietor of The Pub in Jamestown, New York, where he resides.

TOM MCDONALD
Born: Thomas Franklin McDonald; 7/26/34; Roy, NM
High School: Roy; Highland, NM
College: Oklahoma
Drafted: 1957, Round 3, Philadelphia Eagles
AS A PLAYER:
Playing Weight: 5'-9", 176
Position(s): Wide Receiver, Running Back
FOOTBALL CAREER AFTER 1960:
In 1961, Tommy caught 64 passes for 1,144 yards, which led all NFL receivers. In 1962, he came back with 58 catches for 1,146 yards, a personal high, and an Eagle record at the time. He left Philadelphia for Dallas in 1964, where he spent only one year before moving on to Los Angeles. In 1965, the ex-Oklahoma star registered his third and final 1,000-yard season. In 1967, Tommy spent one season with the Atlanta Falcons, before finishing his Hall of Fame career with Cleveland in 1968.

SINCE HIS PLAYING CAREER:
Tommy started a portrait business while still active in the NFL. He's kept it thriving all these years. He has several artists who paint portraits of numerous ball players and celebrities. Tommy is also kept hopping with speaking engagements, personal appearances, commercials, etc. He lives with his wife Patty in their home in suburban Philadelphia where they have lived for almost 40 years. They have four children and five grandchildren—all living a short distance from Tommy and Pat.

CLARENCE PEAKS
Born: Clarence Earl Peaks; 9/23/35; Greenville, MS
High School: Central (Flint, MI)
College: Michigan State

Drafted: 1957, Round 1, Philadelphia Eagles
AS A PLAYER:
Playing Weight: 6'-1", 218
Position(s): Running Back
FOOTBALL CAREER AFTER 1960:
Clarence carried the ball 135 times for the Birds in 1961 (and scored five touchdowns) and 137 times in 1962. In 1964, he was traded to the Pittsburgh Steelers, where his backfield mates were John Henry Johnson, and 1960 Eagle alumnus, Theron Sapp. With Pittsburgh, Clarence averaged 4.3 yards per carry in 1964, and 4.9 yards per carry in 1965, the year he called it quits.
SINCE HIS PLAYING CAREER:
Clarence long ago eschewed the spotlight, wishing to live his life outside the public eye. He has devoted himself to esoteric studies, saying simply to tell everyone that he "wanted to know."

BOB PELLEGRINI
Born: Robert Francis Pellegrini; 11/13/34; Williamsport, PA
High School: Hannock Valley (Rural Valley, PA)
College: Maryland
Drafted: 1956, Round 1, Philadelphia Eagles
AS A PLAYER:
Playing Weight: 6'-2", 233
Position(s): Linebacker, Offensive Guard
FOOTBALL CAREER AFTER 1960:
Pelly played with the Eagles in 1961, before being traded to the Washington Redskins in 1962. He spent four years with the Redskins, before retiring in 1965.
SINCE HIS PLAYING CAREER:
Bob coached with the Miami Dolphins for awhile in the NFL. He has worked in the Casino business since 1979, when he debuted with Bally's. For the past four years, he has been with Showboat Casino, where he currently holds the title of Director of Player Development. Bob lives in Ocean City, NJ.

JERRY REICHOW
Born: Garet Neal Reichow; 5/19/34; Decorah, IA
High School: Decorah, IA
College: Iowa
Drafted: 1956, Round 4, Detroit Lions

AS A PLAYER:
Playing Weight: 6'-2", 217
Position(s): Offensive End, Quarterback
FOOTBALL CAREER AFTER 1960:
In 1961, Jerry played for the Minnesota Vikings, caught 50 passes for 859 yards, and was picked to play in the Pro Bowl. He followed his 1961 season with 39 catches and 35 catches in 1962 and 1963 respectively. He retired after the 1964 season.
SINCE HIS PLAYING CAREER:
Jerry got into personnel work for the Vikings as soon as his playing days were done. He was "in the office for six or seven years," before getting involved with scouting operations. In the Eighties, he was the Director of Operations for the Vikings. At present, he's constantly on the move, traveling around the country as a scout for the Vikings. When he's not on the road scouting, he lives in Santa Fe, New Mexico.

PETE RETZLAFF
Born: Palmer Edward Retzlaff; 8/21/31, Ellendale, ND
High School: Ellendale, ND
College: Ellendale State ND (Junior College); South Dakota State
Drafted: 1953, round 22, by Detroit Lions
AS A PLAYER:
Playing Weight: 6'-1", 211
Position(s): Offensive End, Tight End (also played Fullback earlier in his career)
FOOTBALL CAREER AFTER 1960:
Pete Retzlaff, the "Baron," was the split end who led the 1960 team in receptions with 46 that championship year. He played his entire career (except for some exhibition games he played as a Detroit Lion), from 1956 to 1966, wearing Philly's kelly green. When he retired, Retzlaff was the all-time franchise leader in receptions (452), and receiving yards (7,412). As the new century begins, Retzlaff remains in second place on the all-time Eagle list, having been surpassed in both of these categories by Harold Carmichael. The Baron was a five-time Pro Bowler, who was inducted into the Eagles Honor Roll in 1987. He received the Bert Bell Award from the Philadelphia Maxwell Club as the NFL Player of the Year in 1965, when he caught 66 passes for 1,190 yards for the 5-9 Eagles.
SINCE HIS PLAYING CAREER:
During the late Sixties, and again through the mid-Seventies, he was a radio and television sports broadcaster for Philadlephia's WIP radio and CBS television. From 1969 to 1972, Pete was the Eagles' General Manager. The Baron is also in the ranching and grain business in Texas with three other former NFL players (1960

teammate, Maxie Baughan, Claude Crabb, and ex-Packer linebacker, Tommy Crutcher).

Since his playing days, Pete has made Montgomery County, Pennyslvania, his home. He serves on the Montgomery County Open Space Commission, and also serves on the Board of Directors of three companies: Teleflex, Harleysville National Bank, and Paris Business Products. On January 25, 1999, Pete Retzlaff received the Living Legend Award from the Philadelphia Sportswriters Association.

THERON SAPP
Born: Theron Coleman Sapp; 6/15/35; Macon, GA
High School: Lanier, GA
College: Georgia
Drafted: 1958, Round 10, Philadelphia Eagles
AS A PLAYER:
Playing Weight: 6'-1", 203
Position(s): Running Back
FOOTBALL CAREER AFTER 1960:
Theron stayed with the Eagles through the fourth game of the 1963 season, when he was traded to Pittsburgh. In ten games as a Steeler that season, he carried the ball 96 times, gaining 431 yards, averaging 4.5 yards per carry. He spent the next two seasons as a Steeler. In training camp in 1966, Clendon Thomas broke Theron's leg in a practice session, and Theron's career came to a halt.
SINCE HIS PLAYING CAREER:
Over the past several years, Theron owned four Maryland Fried Chicken stores. At present, he only runs one store, in Evans, Georgia, where he resides. Theron plans to retire in the next few years.

J.D. SMITH
Born: Jesse Daley Smith; 5/27/36; Richland Springs, TX
High School: Richland Springs, TX
College: Rice
Drafted: 1959, Round 2, Philadelphia Eagles
AS A PLAYER:
Playing Weight: 6'-5", 250
Position(s): Offensive Tackle
FOOTBALL CAREER AFTER 1960:
J. D. was picked for the Pro Bowl in 1961. He stayed with the Eagles through 1963, when he was traded to the Detroit Lions. J. D. remained with the Lions till his retirement in 1966.

SINCE HIS PLAYING CAREER:
J. D. sold harvest equipment and was a rancher in Richland Springs, Texas. He still lives on the ranch, but, he's also working for an energy services company in the briskly active energy market in Austin, Texas.

CHUCK WEBER
Born: Charles Fredrick Weber, Jr.; 3/25/30; Philadelphia, PA
High School: Abington, PA
College: West Chester
Drafted: Not Drafted
AS A PLAYER:
Playing Weight: 6'-1", 229
Position(s): Middle Linebacker
FOOTBALL CAREER AFTER 1960:
Chuck was the defensive captain for the Eagles in 1961, but injuries forced him to retire at the end of the campaign.
SINCE HIS PLAYING CAREER:
Chuck coached Abington High School in 1962 and 1963. He was the defensive coach for the Boston Patriots from 1964-67, the San Diego Chargers, in 1968-69, the Cincinnati Bengals, from 1970-75, the St. Louis Cardinals, in 1976-77, the Cleveland Browns in 1978-79, Baltimore Colts, in 1980-81, and the San Diego Chargers, from 1982-85. In 1977, he was voted the Greatest Athlete in the history of West Chester University. Chuck also served as the Mortgage Loan Officer of the Great American Bank in San Diego from 1986-92, when he retired once and for all. Chuck's health is good, and he stays active by golfing, bowling, and playing poker and softball. He even works as a golf ranger two days a week.

JOHN WILCOX
Born: John Dale Wilcox; 3/15/38; Vale, OR
High School: Vale Union, OR
College: Oregon
Drafted: 1960, Round 15, Philadelphia Eagles
AS A PLAYER:
Playing Weight: 6'-5", 230
Position(s): Defensive Tackle
FOOTBALL CAREER AFTER 1960:
John played only in 1960, rejecting Vince McNally's two-year contract offer of $8500 in 1961 and $9500 in 1962.

SINCE HIS PLAYING CAREER:

John taught and coached high school for six years, starting in 1961. Over the past 29 years, he has held various positions teaching and coaching at Whitman College in Walla Walla, Washington. He was, at various times, football coach, basketball coach, and Athletic Director. He was also the woman's basketball coach for 15 years. He and his wife, Remi, own and operate a small apple orchard in Milton-Freewater, Oregon. They have three children, and five granddaughters. NFL Films produced a short film, "Twist of Fate," about John and brother Dave. Dave, a Hall of Famer, played 11 years with the 49ers without ever playing on a championship team. John had a one-year career with the Eagles, and walked away with a championship ring.

JERRY WILSON

Born: Gerald Roscoe Wilson; 12/9/36; Birmingham, AL
High School: Phillips, AL
College: Auburn
Drafted: 1959, Round 2, Chicago Cardinals

AS A PLAYER:

Playing Weight: 6'-3", 238
Position(s): Defensive End

FOOTBALL CAREER AFTER 1960:

Jerry was traded to the San Francisco 49ers for John Wittenborn after the fourth game of the 1960 campaign. He finished out the season, which turned out to be his last in the NFL, with San Francisco. He was sent overseas when the Berlin Crisis was raging. When he returned, he went to Canada and played four years. He was forced to retire due to knee injuries.

SINCE HIS PLAYING CAREER:

Jerry says Philly was a long way from his home, but he loved the city and its people. He quickly adapted to (and fell in love with) Philly cuisine, particularly South Philly cuisine. He worked for 30 years after his playing days with Universal Atlas/Lehigh Cement. He is now retired in Birmingham, Alabama, and is very proud of his daughter, Jeannie Wilson, who was born with spinal bifada. Once Jeannie got past the critical stage of her illness, she started wheelchair sports. Jerry bought a weight-training machine for home usage. Jeannie took to weight training like a champ. His daughter has since won three World Championships and eleven National Championships.

JOHN WITTENBORN
Born: John Otis Wittenborn; 3/1/36; Sparta, IL
High School: Sparta, IL
College: Southeast Missouri State
Drafted: 1958, Round 17, San Francisco 49ers
AS A PLAYER:
Playing Weight: 6'-2", 238
Position(s): Offensive Guard, Kicker
FOOTBALL CAREER AFTER 1960:
John was with the Eagles in 1961 and 1962. He was out of football in 1963, but returned again in 1964 with the Houston Oilers in the AFL. He stayed with Houston till his retirement in 1968. John also kicked with the Oilers when George Blanda left in 1966. He scored 72 points in 1967 and 23 more in 1968. He ended his career a perfect 41 out of 41 in Points After Touchdowns.
SINCE HIS PLAYING CAREER:
John was an offensive line coach at Houston and Tulsa in the college ranks for several years. He moved back to Illinois and bought a house 12 miles from where he was raised. A few years ago, he went looking for a part-time position as a bus driver in his new school district. He didn't have the right forms, and, in talking with the administration people, he found out they needed a football coach. John took the job, and had a 30-9 record with a team of kids who had never before played football ("One of the kids came back to the sideline, and I told him to watch the clipping. The kid looked at me and said, 'What's clipping, coach?'"). John is retired now, and enjoying the beauty of nature in Cutler, Illinois.

DECEASED MEMBERS

GENE JOHNSON
Born: Gene Paul Johnson; 9/18/35; Clay, WV
High School: Charleston, WV
College: Cincinnati
Drafted: 1959, Round 9, Philadelphia Eagles
AS A PLAYER:
Playing Weight: 6'-0", 187
Position(s): Defensive Back
AFTER 1960:
In 1961, Gene went to the Minnesota Vikings. He played seven games for the Vikings, before going to the New York Giants, where he played three

Gene Johnson

games, before calling it a career. Gene was a photographic supply distributor in Cincinnati before he passed away in the Eighties.

HOWARD KEYS

Born: Howard Newton Keys; 1/24/35; Orlando, OK
High School: Stillwater, OK
College: Oklahoma State
Drafted: 1959, Round 12, Philadelphia Eagles
AS A PLAYER:
Playing Weight: 6'-3", 240
Position(s): Center, Offensive Tackle, Offensive Guard
AFTER 1960:
Howard played his entire professional career as a Philadelphia Eagle. He called it quits in 1963 after two games. Howard passed away in Cleveland in 1971 after surgery at Shaker Medical Center.

Howard Keys

JOHN NOCERA

Born: John Stanley Nocera; 5/4/34; Youngstown, OH
High School: Rayen, OH
College: Iowa
Drafted: 1957, Round 16, Philadelphia Eagles (Red Shirt)
AS A PLAYER:
Playing Weight: 6'-1", 220
Position(s): Linebacker
AFTER 1960:
John played for the Eagles in 1961 and 1962. He ended his career with the Denver Broncos of the AFL in 1963.
John succumbed to lung cancer in 1981 in Youngstown, Ohio.

DON OWENS

Born: James Donald Owens; 4/3/32; St. Louis, MO
High School: St. Marks, MO
College: Southern Mississippi

Drafted: 1957, Round 3, Pittsburgh
AS A PLAYER:
Playing Weight: 6'-5", 255
Position(s): Defensive Tackle, Offensive Tackle
AFTER 1960:
Don was traded to the St. Louis Cardinals after the third game of the 1960 season. "The Sarge" played the rest of his career with St. Louis, retiring after the 1963 season. Don was a labor official in Jefferson City, MO, before his death.

JESSE RICHARDSON
Born: Jesse William Richardson; 8/18/30; Philadelphia, PA
High School: Roxborough, PA
College: Alabama
Drafted: 1953, Round 8, Philadelphia Eagles
AS A PLAYER:
Playing Weight: 6'-2", 261
Position(s): Defensive Tackle
AFTER 1960:
Jesse started for the Eagles again in 1961, and was chosen by the *Sporting News* to the All-Pro team. In 1962, Jesse went to the Boston Patriots in the AFL, and finished his career with them in 1964. As one of only two native Philadelphians on the '60 squad (Chuck Weber was the other, and Ted Dean hailed from the nearby Philadelphia suburb of Radnor), Big Jess was extremely popular with the Franklin Field crowd. Born and raised in the East Falls section of the Quaker City, Jesse went off to college at Alabama, and was drafted in the eighth round by the Eagles in 1953. In the off-season, he sold printed circuit boards—a trade incongruous with his brawling on-the-field persona. Jesse was the last lineman in the NFL to play without a face mask. Jesse mellowed, according to Jesse, after he was selected to the 1959 All-Pro team (his first selection as an All-Pro) and socialized with his usual adversaries. "Now, I think three times before taking a cheap elbow shot on the blind side at someone."
Jesse died of kidney disease in Philadelphia in 1975.

JOE ROBB
Born: Alvis Joe Robb; 3/15/37; Lufkin, TX
High School: Lufkin, TX
College: Texas Christian
Drafted: 1959, Round 14, Chicago Bears

AS A PLAYER:
Playing Weight: 6'-3", 238
Position(s): Defensive End, Linebacker
AFTER 1960:
Joe did not play for the Eagles in 1961. He was traded to the St. Louis Cardinals, where he remained until 1967. In 1968, he left for the Detroit Lions, where he performed till his retirement in 1971.
Joe was a sales representative in Houston, Texas, before he passed away in 1987.

Joe Robb

NORM VAN BROCKLIN
Born: Norman Mack Van Brocklin; 3/15/26; Eagle Butte, SD
High School: Acalenes, CA
College: Oregon
Drafted: 1949, Round 4, Los Angeles Rams
AS A PLAYER:
Playing Weight: 6'-1", 190
Position(s): Quarterback
AFTER 1960:
Dutch retired as a player after the championship season in 1960. In 1961, he became the first coach for the Minnesota Vikings. He stayed in Minnesota till 1966. After a hiatus from coaching for a year, during which he worked as a broadcaster, Dutch returned to the sidelines as head coach of the Atlanta Falcons. He remained in Atlanta till 1974, when he retired from professional coaching for good. Dutch also spent a short time as assistant quarterback coach for Georgia Tech.

Norm Van Brocklin died in Social Circle, Georgia in 1983. The funeral service was held on Dutch's pecan farm, where he and his family lived. His daughter, Kirby, describes her father's funeral: "The ceremony was concluded with songs sung by Josh Powell. His deep baritone voice that we had first heard boom out over a stadium audience, now rang out into the orchard of our farm. He sang dad's favorite songs, including "Ole Man River," and he concluded with "God Bless America." We received friends into our house, and then filtered out onto the deck. A Dixieland band was playing, and food and drink awaited all in the log cabin behind the house. Many people walked around in disbelief, hearing the jazz music, no doubt feeling sacrilegious! Others, who knew dad best, walked around with knowing smiles on their faces. This was a day to pay respect and love for dad's life, not a day to mourn, second guess, or regret what had been. Dad would never have tolerated it. He led his life looking forward, never backward. Now it was our turn, the challenge to look forward, and keep on moving."

BOBBY WALSTON
Born: Robert Harold Walston; 10/17/28; Columbus, OH
High School: Linden-McKinley, GA
College: Georgia
Drafted: 1951, Round 14, Philadelphia Eagles
AS A PLAYER:
Playing Weight: 6'-0", 190
Position(s): Offensive End
AFTER 1960:
Bobby played two more seasons in the NFL, ending his 12-year career, spent entirely as an Eagle, in 1962.

Bobby Walston was a sheriff in Georgia. In the Eighties, he was a United States Football League scout in Schaumburg, Illinois. Bobby died in 1987 in Roselle, Illinois.

PRE-1960 EAGLES

DICK BIELSKI
Born: Richard Adam Bielski; 9/17/32; Baltimore, MD
High School: Patterson, MD
College: Maryland
Drafted: 1955, Round 1, Philadelphia Eagles
AS A PLAYER:
Playing Weight: 6'-1", 224
Position(s): Offensive End, Fullback
AFTER 1960:
Dick left Philadelphia in the expansion draft of 1960, and became a charter member of the Dallas Cowboys. He stayed with Dallas in 1960 and 1961, before going to the Baltimore Colts in 1962, where he remained till he retired as a player in 1963. Dick went on to coach for 21 years. He coached with Baltimore from 1963 to 1972, with the Washington Redskins from 1972 to 1977, and then with the Colts again from 1977 to 1982. Dick says, "I'm the only coach in the NFL who graduated four kids from the same high school!"

Dick owns the Charles Village Pub in Towson, and operates two other establishments, also called the Charles Village Pub. One is near Johns Hopkins and the other is in West Baltimore. In the winter, Dick and his wife go to Florida, where Dick does a lot of bicycling ("I got the first bike I ever had in my life in 1967.").

VIC SEARS
Born: Victor Wilson Sears, 3/4/18; Ashwood, OR
High School: Eugene, OR
College: Oregon State
Drafted: 1941, Round 4, Pittsburgh Steelers
AS A PLAYER:
Playing Weight: 6'-3", 223
Position(s): Defensive Tackle, Offensive Tackle
AFTER RETIREMENT:
Vic starred on both Eagle championship teams of the late Forties. He played through the 1953 season. After retirement, he was an Assistant Coach at Episcopal Academy in Philadelphia, and a manufacturer's representative, which he did till 1980, when he retired. At retirement, Vic moved back to Eugene, Oregon, where he purchased and operated a small berry farm. He returned to the east coast in the Nineties to be closer to his children and grandchildren. "Tarz," as he was known, used to do trick riding at full gallop on the horses on his parents' farm, as a youth growing up. These days, Vic stays active gardening, woodworking, and reading.

JIMMY GALLAGHER
Jimmy Gallagher never toted a pigskin on Connie Mack Stadium or Franklin Field sod, but he bleeds Eagle green. Jimmy was the do-it-all guy in the Eagle front office, as well as the guy who set up the Eagles' first scouting operation with Bucko Kilroy in 1956. Spry, sprightly, and optimistic after a half-century of dealing with Eagle matters, Jimmy lives just outside Philadelphia in Plymouth Meeting. He still spends endless hours assisting Eagles and ex-Eagles, as well as guiding authors in search of their characters.